I0192602

A New Leaf:
12 Spiritual Truths
for Starting Over

Karen M. Croley

All rights reserved. This book or any portion thereof
may not be reproduced or used in any manner whatsoever
without the express written permission of the publisher
except for the use of brief quotations in a book review. Sale of this book
without a front cover may be unauthorized. If this book is coverless, it may
have been reported to the publisher as "unsold or destroyed" and neither the
author nor the publisher may have received payment for it.

The scanning, uploading and distribution of this book via the Internet or via
any other means without the permission of the publisher is illegal and
punishable by law. Please purchase only authorized electronic editions, and do
not participate in or encourage electronic piracy of copyrighted materials. Your
support of the author's rights is appreciated.

Copyright © 2014 Karen M. Croley
All Rights Reserved

ISBN-13: 978-0-692-21653-8
ISBN-10: 0692216537

Cover photo by Karen M. Croley

Printed in the United States of America
First addition, 2014
A New leaf; personal life coaching press
http://anewleaf4you.com

This book is dedicated to the journey to your heart.

"Let your mind start a journey through a strange new world. Leave all thoughts of the world you knew before. Let your soul take you where you long to be . . . Close your eyes, let your spirit start to soar, and you'll live as you've never lived before."

~Erich Fromm

Contents

Acknowledgments

I am extremely grateful to the following people: thank you to my parents whose love and support gave me the courage to see this book through; to my coach Anthony Taylor who helped me to stay inspired and who helped to shape the book; to Julie Stahl who rescued me with her gifts in editing. To Caroline Donahue, for coming to my rescue in fixing formatting issues; to Leigh Binder for his unwavering support; I will see you in the next lifetime, my friend! Thanks to my dear friends Ann and RoseMarie in giving their time and energy to read through drafts; and to Rosemary Sneeringer for holding my hand during the process of getting this book to the publisher.

Most importantly, I am eternally grateful to the special group of women who worked through this book inside the support group I facilitate, *Women Starting Over*. Without their participation and feedback, this book's content would not have been as prudent or complete. I am continually inspired by their blooming hearts.

And most lovingly, to my three sons. You share the heart of this book in our desire to make our lives meaningful for the greater good of others. Thank you for sharing your bright light to help make this book shine.

I had begun this book in 2010, and then put it aside until I picked it back up again with Spirit, in December of 2012. While I had the motivation and the open heart to receive, it was Spirit who came forth and effortlessly partnered with me to produce most of the content within 90 days.

Clients and friends whose stories are described in this book gave me their full permission to use their material. Clients' names and minor modifications to their backgrounds have been changed to protect their identities.

Introduction

"In ancient Roman religion and mythology, *Janus* is the god of beginnings and transitions, thence also of gates, doors, doorways, endings and time. He is usually a two-faced god since he looks to the future and the past. The month of January was named in honor of Janus by the Romans."[1] My middle son Keedon, came home from school one day sharing this information. He said, "You can use this for your book!" Indeed I will, son, thank you, as it fits perfectly into the topic of this book: starting over.

It's my own story that propelled me to write this book because I knew at a deep level that my experience would resonate with others. Starting over felt completely overwhelming and I had no sense of stability about this task. However, with three small children to care for, I desperately wanted to get myself together, so I could be there for them. I knew my divorce was a huge turning point, *but how and what would I turn into?* The anxiety I felt was enormous. I needed some answers to help me get my sense of stability back. That's when I began my journey of personal transformation. I drew on 12 spiritual truths to help me. The first spiritual truth, "Your Heart is Your Source of Connection" is where I began.

I found that when I stopped and took time to listen to my heart, I found a sense of inner peace. It felt sacred and special, my own personal sanctuary. The connection to my heart became a way to re-unite with my soul and a greater power. I tuned into my heart during the day to ask, "What am I feeling and what do I want?" In doing so, I built a relationship with myself that solidified my position in life. I was able to form a greater sense of self and capability to master my own life without relying on others for answers. I could find the answers to what I needed within my own heart. Seven years later, I continue to benefit from these truths. I feel a deep sense of inner peace and I feel content. Now, I'd like to help others do the same.

I believe all major events that force our lives to go through a transition are points of contention: do we wake up and make the change or do we fall back and repeat the same story? For me, it was a matter of feeling tired and wanting to feel good again. Sometimes it's as simple as that. You just want to feel good again.

How many times have you imagined yourself having a bright future only to feel deflated by the reality of where you are now? The path to get from here to that bright future may seem daunting, if not downright impossible. And yet, you are full of potential! You only have to be willing to open your heart to it.

As a life coach, I have seen both clients and friends decide to open their hearts to the possibility that transitions can offer an exciting future. I myself embrace this belief. Once the decision is made, possibility becomes potential. We begin to experience the hope that potential brings. Hope then fuels our inspiration to act in new ways that foster the changes we need to make. Adopting and living out certain spiritual truths can lead us back to the place where everything begins: ourselves and specifically our hearts. Soon we are far from despair and lack of motivation. We begin the path toward more soulful living that provides us with many joyful and passionate moments.

The ideas in this book will help with all different types of transition. Maybe you have just received a diagnosis for an illness. Or perhaps you have just lost your job/career that was built upon years of devotion. Maybe you have ended a relationship or are going through a divorce. I've had clients appreciate these ideas after getting sober/clean. Women in the support group I facilitate, *Women Starting Over,* who've lost a loved one have also benefited from this information. Each transition is unique in individual experience, and yet these spiritual truths resonate regardless of our differences. We all experience the same emotions: feeling overwhelmed, stress, fear, anxiety, anger, sadness, love, joy, hope... Starting over is starting over, no matter what your circumstance.

I believe these 12 spiritual truths can apply to everyone. They offer wisdom of the ages dating back in time. Some part of you will recognize them at a deep level. Once you have re-connected with them they will help you learn from your transition, gently move you forward and offer you fresh perspectives. These truths will aid your personal transformation, so you can feel good again!

Why these twelve in particular? They are the ones that have helped my clients and me the most. Clients have learned that once they re-connect to their hearts (1st Spiritual Truth), they feel empowered to make better decisions, direct their thoughts and manage their feelings. Once I began living in the present moment (2nd Spiritual Truth), my anxiety went away, and I could capture the fun in each moment with my children. Women in the support group I facilitate have found forgiveness is liberating (7th Spiritual Truth), and that letting go allows them to find acceptance (6th Spiritual Truth). Experiencing these truths has led to major breakthroughs allowing us to feel good again.

For those of you who may be feeling overwhelmed by the idea of moving forward, you too will find relief. I understand that until you have a clear head and heart, you cannot truly digest new information, let alone move forward. For you, I am planting a seed for what is possible. This is why I invite you to look at the present first (Part One). Now is not the time to deal with the past because for you the hardest part may be just getting out of bed in the morning.

Until you can address what is going on for you right now, the mass of confusion and feelings of being overwhelmed will continue to hang around. This is especially true for those of you who are coming off of addiction, suffering the loss of a loved one, or experiencing a relationship break-up. It's why I decided to sequence the book beginning with the present. Big changes can throw us off, therefore, it's important to make ourselves our first priority, so we can feel stable again.

We use time as a framework to experience life because that is what we relate to the most. So I have divided the content into three parts: present, past and future. The sequencing is deliberate so that you can address each part of your journey. This order has been tested and proven beneficial with my women's groups.

We begin with your present moment, helping you to achieve a strong sense of stability from within. In Part One, you will learn the foundation to master your body, heart and mind using the first four spiritual truths. Here you will learn about your heart, and the connection you have available to you there, and how to live from that space as the co-creator that you are. Do we have complete control over everything that happens in our lives? No, but we can learn to Co-Create our reality with our spiritual beliefs. Living from your heart will give you greater ability to direct your thoughts and be in the present moment. It will become easier to function and feel alive. Loving yourself will take first priority, helping you to experience greater inner strength. Wouldn't it be great to feel like you have a strong inner core, something you can feel secure about? From your conscious self, you will learn how to experience your emotions by staying connected to your heart. You will realize that this process isn't as frightening as it may seem at first. Here are the first four spiritual truths we explore:

- Your Heart
- The Present Moment
- I AM Love
- Managing Emotions

By the end of this section, you will feel victorious about your present and ready to meet any challenge or bit of drama that comes your way.

In Part Two, we will delve into the past for the purpose of learning how to return your heart back to love and transform wounds into wonderful lessons learned. Within these four spiritual truths, you will relieve any suffering you may be feeling from your past. You will also be provided with exercises to resolve any issues that need closure. It can be difficult to move forward with clarity if you still have emotional baggage. Unknowingly, we can keep ourselves in the past by having a victim-like consciousness. For example, asking yourself "Why?" feeds never-ending thoughts and contributes to your feeling like a victim, whereas using a new perspective will help you to feel victorious over your past. You will also learn how to let go and find forgiveness to empower yourself. The appreciation for your past experience (believe it or not), will happen naturally after this process has begun and provide the perfect springboard from which to jump into building your future.

INTRODUCTION

The four spiritual truths presented and explained in Part Two deal with:

- Perspective
- Letting Go
- Forgiveness
- Appreciation

When you have finished Part Two you will feel lighter, freer and more capable of moving forward with your future.

Lastly, we conclude with four spiritual truths to help manifest your new future. In Part Three (Building a Bright Future), you will be ready to use the clarity you achieved from Part Two and put it to good use! Having a clear head and heart are important, and just like using emotion to fuel our actions, we can use clarity to set forth action as well. Here you will use your heart to turn the wheels of creation using *energy;* direct your experience with the *Law of Attraction;* and set *intentions* using certain methods to create wonderful things for yourself and loved ones. The final chapter, introducing a state of *grace* as an outcome, will help you to recognize when your experiences in life flow with ease and synchronicity. By the end of Part Three, all 12 spiritual truths will have become a part of your daily living, allowing you to feel completely capable of creating the life you want to live. The spiritual truths revealed in Part Three are:

- Energy
- The Law of Attraction
- Intentions
- Grace

The book is designed so that you can move around between present, past and future. You can skip ahead to the future (Part Three), or repeat Part One (focusing on the present moment). Whatever you feel that you need to learn that day, simply choose which section you think fits best.

The language I used to describe some of these spiritual truths became a quandary because not everyone relates to or likes certain words. Words such as; God, Universe, Creator, Great Spirit, Source, and Higher self, could all have been used, but they may have been confusing at the least and maybe offensive to some. It's true; I didn't want to repel readers who are of any particular religious affiliation or those who are of none. So for simplicity's sake, I chose to use "Spirit" with the highest intention to represent all of those words, in the most sacred way. However, there were times I used God, Mother Nature, the Divine and Co-Creator due to the context of the content. I felt they best fit at the time. I invite you to substitute your own word if you see fit. My own belief that we Co-Create our reality with Spirit is inherent throughout the book. I leave the concept of Spirit undefined so that you can own it as your own. I do not agree that there is "one true God" but rather a universal all loving energy that not only resides externally but within our hearts as well. Later I state that we are a "sparkle of the Divine," to share my belief that we are a part of this loving energy that connects us all together in a matrix where literally our cells originate from the same existence: "star dust" from the cosmos.

Each chapter of the book will provide at least one exercise for you to complete. I teach psychology classes for the University of Phoenix and my style of teaching is hands-on: *introduce the material that is helpful to you… then apply it to your life.* My students are always appreciative of this approach because it has proven helpful to integrate and process new information. Without this kind of application, the content stays purely mental and does not travel to your heart space. *I invite you to regard your heart space as the command center for experiencing your soul.*

The more you can interact with the 12 spiritual truths by way of the exercises, the better able you'll be to incorporate them into your daily living. This process will teach you how to develop deep and lasting transformation at a soul level.

I'd like you to know that I have walked this path—I "walk the talk." As you will learn, I have been in that hopeless place and thought I would never feel good again. However, learning to live these 12 spiritual truths has made my transition something for me to feel grateful for. No doubt, my work experience counseling others for the past twenty years after finishing my education has helped. During that time, I also devoted much of my time and energy to my own personal growth. It's been an amazing journey I wouldn't trade for anything.

INTRODUCTION

I share my own personal story of a difficult divorce, only to show you how I moved out of confusion and through my transition using these spiritual truths. My intention is that you can learn from my examples. I had a deep sense that I would someday draw on the changes that happened that seemed so traumatic at the time. I remember journaling those very words: "Going through this will help me to help others." I'd get signs and feedback from others with this message: "You are here to teach your greatest wound." So I have learned that this is the crux of my purpose for being here. It is these very lessons that will be most helpful for others.

Turn Over a New Leaf and Move Forward

So what exactly is transition and what does it include? I looked up the meaning in the dictionary, and it stated:

1a : passage from one state, stage, subject, or place to another: change
1b: a movement, development, or evolution from one form, stage, or style to another
2a : a musical passage leading from one section of a piece to another
2b : an abrupt change in energy state

Who would have thought that music would be involved in the definition of transition? I sure didn't, but logically speaking it fits into music writing and theory. That's an inspiring way to think about transition, is it not? Words such as "divorce" connote gloom and doom, so we automatically feel bad when we hear them. Rather, we can think of divorce as a musical passage leading us from one time in our life to another. Oh, now that feels so much better, doesn't it? It fits in so nicely with my own belief that everything we go through can be considered a learning experience. We are all learning in this journey of life, so there is no right or wrong way to do it. Each experience and choice leads us to the next. We are *builders* really. With each choice and decision we make, we build our lives. Why not hum a little tune to make it musical, fun, interesting, even exciting, as we make our transition from one stage in life to the next?

Introducing Your Heart

"To bow to the fact of our life's sorrows and betrayals is to accept them; and from this deep gesture we discover that all life is workable. As we learn to bow, we discover that the heart holds more freedom and compassion than we could imagine.²"
~ Jack Kornfield

We cannot move forward through any transition in life until we have clarity. Consider that your path in this journey begins with your heart, and all clarity from here forward manifests there.

Hand over heart. Breathe. I invite you to place your hand over your heart right now and take a deep breath. You are home now… Take another breath, but this time direct your breath to your heart. Bring all attention and focus there. Inhale with the intention to connect to your heart. Exhale with the intention to ground into your heart. Notice how your body feels now. Does it feel centered? Exactly right. I'll be inviting you to stop and practice this throughout the book. It's intended to provide you with the opportunity to connect to your heart, and with more practice, establish an ongoing place for you to find peace.

Now, I am going to ask you: Can you achieve clarity by way of the heart? The answer is yes. I know you are thinking, *what?* I know and understand, it's probably a foreign concept. We simply don't live this way, right? We think about our hearts all the time but not in a spiritual sense. Most of the time we consider our hearts to be biological organs we have to pay attention to for health reasons.

Your heart is a space that is sacred and special: it is uniquely yours. And just imagine, your heart is there for you all the time! It's simply a matter of tuning in to it. This is your place of true knowingness… of clarity. For those of you who love to think, you are more than likely disconnected from your body. The best way to get back into your body and establish that mind-body connection is through your heart.

It's my intention that by the end of reading this book, you will feel like your heart is home base. Your connection between heart and mind will be firmly established. This is usually "the missing piece" for people who want to change but haven't been able to do so yet. It's due to the fact that all learning was centered in the mind or head space. Bringing down changes into your heart will anchor them and make them permanent.

It will also help you to build a relationship with your heart where you can feel connected and centered. After practicing often, you will have a solid sense of your heart center—your place of power, connection and inner strength. Will you take the time to slow down and listen to your heart?

Emotions are our heart's way of speaking to us. Recall a time when you felt out of control and your heart skipped and clenched. Were you experiencing fear? If so, what do you do when you experience fear? Do you go up into your head and rationalize the fear away? Do you dismiss it altogether? Or do you listen to the fear and let yourself feel it and wait to see what feeling comes next? Most people use their heads to figure out why they are afraid, because that's what we have been taught in this culture.

This process of listening to our hearts will lead to achieving clarity. When you're tuned in, listening to your body, feeling your emotions, you become clear. There is no garbage in your way. No thoughts of fear and doubt to bog you down that leave you feeling confused and cause you to cry out in uncertainty, *"I don't know why I am so stuck in life!"*

I really love the concept of clarity! *Achieving clarity* is a universal need. You cannot make progress or move forward without it. Teachers and spiritual gurus alike talk about it. But do we truly *know* what it means? Furthermore, how do we *live it*? The motivation is that once we achieve clarity, brilliant things will happen!

Clarity

Clarity is really a passage way for our transition.

Do you know that feeling when you wake up and look out the window and there is no sunshine but lots and lots of fog? It's a lot tougher to get your day going. When I don't see sunshine, I feel it in my body as sluggishness, as if I have fog in my brain. It's harder to feel energized, motivated, and it's difficult to think.

However, when the clouds part, the sun shines down and fills up the sky with light. My mood lifts, and I feel energized again. I can think!

When I have a decision to make, I don't make a move until I am clear. This means that only after I feel it in my heart do I feel clear about a *yes, no,* or *maybe.* The reason I won't make a decision to act until I am clear is because I have learned from past experience — that without clarity, I create thoughts open to doubt and fear, and this in turn creates anxiety.

To be clear is to know.

To be in your own truth without a doubt is a place of empowerment.

Clarity is a place where we are honoring and steadfast. Everything that comes out of that place of clarity, that place of *being* will include our highest interest for us and for our loved ones. Having clarity is the beginning of having faith that everything will work out magically fine.

Can you think your way into clarity?

We have all been taught to think our way to clarity by trying to figure things out. We were taught that our emotions would lead us astray. We were asked, "What are the pros and the cons?" We were told, "Figure it out!" "Analyze which solution is best." "Think on it." These are only some of the common statements that reinforce the false belief that thinking our way to clarity is best. To say that you'll arrive at a clear answer by thinking about it is terribly misleading. We need to include our hearts in our decision-making.

When we think, we are using our minds/brains—we are in our head space. *That's when it feels like we are making "head-way."* We believe we are figuring things out intellectually, but only because that's what we've been taught. Parents exclaim, "Use your brain!" when they catch their children misbehaving. What they really mean is, "Be present!" "Be aware of what's going on!"

We have been taught to overrule our hearts with our intellect, but it's an unhealthy practice. This is what happens when we intellectually process our feelings:

- Intellectualizing leads you away from your heart
- Intellectualizing makes you *not present*
- Intellectualizing fools you into thinking you are right—and that right or wrong is important to you
- Intellectualizing doesn't allow for feeling, which is vital for listening to your heart and your "gut"

John Mackey, founder of Whole Foods Market, said he started the company with his intellect. However, there came a point when he said he knew that he needed to engage his heart, his love, in order for his company to be successful[3].

Still not convinced that "figuring things out" in your head will not get you to clarity? Recall a time when you took time to figure something out... Did you put a time frame on it? Most likely you didn't and are still thinking about it. The problem with thinking about it is just that—it can go on forever! Our mind loves it! It's like feeding it, only there is never enough, so it's a never-ending feed. When you think about feeds, they are constant, running all the time . . . those are your thoughts! When you try to figure things out it's like hopping onto a wheel that spins around and around and never goes anywhere. You don't get to clarity by way of your thinking. All that is truly going on is a feed/loop of thoughts on a track that your brain replays over and over again.

Sure, we need our rational, logical thought processes. Our left brain contains these capabilities and we were given them for good reason! I am making a case for not getting stuck there, to include our hearts. To open up and expand your heart by way of feeling and intuiting.

When we tune into how our heart is feeling, we are listening to our soul. Our soul wants so badly to be present and help us master ourselves to reach our highest potential.

Confusion Versus Clarity: Using My Story

Now consider the polar opposite of clarity—confusion. Confusion can be such a trap that takes hold of us and keeps us stuck. Confusion prevents us from moving forward and making decisions. It's also an easy out. Think about how many times you have answered someone with, *"I don't know . . ."* In my own life, confusion has been a place of stagnation, where I could stay and muddle in my confusion with the perfect alibi: *"I don't know yet!"* On the other hand, with clarity comes understanding and compassion for your next step. It's the light-bulb response you get.

I worked as an L.P.C. (Licensed Professional Counselor) in Denver, Colorado and prior to that I worked with children in transition through child protective services. I've helped women in crisis at a women's shelter for domestic violence, and aided homeless families via transitional housing programs. I've also helped people working through grief counseling at hospice. The people I worked with, whether in case work or counseling, were all in transition. However I kept ignoring my *own* need to change. It wasn't until I dealt with my own state of confusion that I began to achieve clarity and the spiritual understanding I needed.

Looking back there were certain times I was forced to look at the role confusion played in my life. I began to see that confusion was constant, almost like a best friend. Feeling confused was definitely my comfort zone. I'd use my head and analyzing tendency to ask "Why?" all the time, never knowing the answer, and pining away because I couldn't figure it out was a way of life for me. It also set up a conundrum for taking action because I was damned if I did and damned if I didn't. The benefit was that it kept me safe and away from big changes.

I was in a relationship with the father of my three sons for sixteen years, married for twelve. The entire time I was confused about my feelings for him. It was really tough going back and forth with doubt, worry, fear . . . and then to the other side of love, compassion, and commitment.

I experienced such agony in always feeling confused, with only brief glimpses of clarity, that there was no sense of emotional stability. Each time I'd consider the alternative lifestyle (divorce/single motherhood), I was filled with doubt and fear. I couldn't trust my own feelings. The roller coaster ride of highs and lows inside the relationship, coupled with feelings of insecurity—that place of feeling stuck—had been my life for a very long time.

There was a saving grace, however I didn't have to make any decisions that would change our lives, rather, I could just stay confused. To live with, "I don't know," allowed me to stay put and avoid change, which I thought was easier than the alternative. The safest place to be seemed to be in a state of confusion.

I was out of touch with my heart's desire. I tried to use my mind, to no avail. I was always in my head or trying to use the power of my mind to achieve clarity. Well, it didn't work! Has it worked for you? Going around and around with your thoughts in your head can *feel* productive, but in actuality it's not. You'd be better off going to a spin class at your local gym. You might as well be spending your life on an exercise bike at the gym if you want to spin your wheels all the time.

Going back to my story, I was in such a state of disarray and disconnect with my own truth that I ignored all signs of dishonesty in my husband, and I had another (third) child with him. Six months into my pregnancy, I was in such a state of confusion that I put all my faith and hopes into our marriage counselor to repair the damage and start out fresh again. I was in such a state of confusion that it took my best friend to nudge me to check out his actual whereabouts while on a business trip.

Do you see how being in a state of confusion is denial when the facts are ignored? When we can't see clearly what is before our eyes, we are in illusion. The veil of protection is torn off when we finally get some clarity. Only then can we move forward.

Hand over heart. Breathe. Place all of your focus and attention on your heart. This is your "home base." Can you feel a deeper connection to yourself now? Does this make you feel more connected to what is going on inside yourself? If the answer is yes, it's because it's a quick and easy way to calm anxiety and prevent shallow breathing. This practice will help bring your focus and attention to your heart and breath for immediate connection.

You're now ready to learn how to get immediate relief. Part One is designed to learn self-mastery, including life skills that can be incorporated into your daily living right now! I'm excited to begin this journey with you because I feel sure you will benefit from integrating these truths into your life!

Part I:
Learn How to Master Your Body, Heart and Mind

Chapter 1
Your Heart is Your Source of Connection

"Nobody has ever measured, not even poets, how much the heart can hold."
~ Zelda Fitzgerald

The first spiritual truth you will begin to learn and practice is that *your heart is your point of connection—your epicenter for all things true that resonates from your essence within.* The objective here is to use your heart as a center for navigating your daily life. It's your opportunity to begin living your life from your heart.

First, I will provide information about this special space otherwise known as your heart, to help you become acquainted with it. Then you will begin practicing how to live your life using this point of focus. To help you do this, I introduce the following concepts: how to connect to your heart; communicating with your heart; listening to your body; de-cluttering your heart; surrendering and having self-compassion; and finally, using your empowered heart. These concepts will help make your transition into a new life much easier because it will become your core—that part of you that remains steadfast no matter what is going on outside of yourself.

I have come to realize there is great power and wisdom found in one single place—our hearts. It functions just like your brain in that it has the ability to send messages to your bodily organs and mind. It has so much capacity to hold our emotions, it's unbelievable!

In recent years (thanks to some very good teachers), I have realized and practiced living from my heart space. It's been very rewarding. What are some of the benefits? Peace! Authenticity! Love! Integrity! Knowing! Intuition! Inner peace!

Remember, your heart is a space that is sacred and special—it is uniquely yours. It's simply a matter of tuning in there. This is your place of true knowingness… of clarity. For those of you who are suffering, this is where you will find some relief.

Broken Hearts

Maybe this is where you are now. You may be feeling like you don't want to tune into your heart because it's too painful there. You're heartbroken to the point where it literally feels like your heart has been shattered into a million pieces. As difficult as this may seem, this *is* the place to start. If you don't heal your heart, what do you have left? You may rationalize that you still have your mental capacity because after all your brain is working pretty well. Okay, but wouldn't you rather get to a point where you can enjoy life again—when getting up in the morning isn't a chore, but rather a new day to look forward to?

By giving your heart some of your loving attention, you can begin to heal and feel better. Whatever has happened, you will reach a point where you want to pick up the pieces and start over again. I know it can seem unbearable… believe me when I say I do. After my divorce, my life was torn in half. My situation included caring for a newborn and two young sons with a newly broken heart and no family in the area to help me out. But I learned, and so will you, that it takes baby steps. It's a process of orienting your life towards feeling good again inside your heart.

First, be gentle with yourself and treat yourself with loving kindness. Act as if you would to your own children or precious pet. Give yourself compassion and take care of your needs during those times when you can. I remember there were days when the minute my kids hit the school grounds, I couldn't wait to get back to bed and hold myself for a while.

Get some breathing space by using perspective. I found I could feel a little better if I reminded myself that I was not alone, that there were other people going through this too. And I could feel a little better if I could imagine a brighter future, whether that be a few days from now or a year from now. In the middle of the night, there were times when I looked to the night sky; focusing my attention on the moon and the stars, helped me to remember my place in the world. Most importantly when you have a broken heart, *choosing* to put it back together will begin the healing process so that you can feel good again.

The emotional support I received from family and friends helped, but ultimately it was me and the choices I made to give myself love that turned things around. To help you incorporate this concept, Chapter Three will go deeper to help you to build your heart back together again. You will realize the benefits of having a loving relationship with yourself. For now, simply build your awareness.

The following exercise will bring some relief for those of you who are suffering from a broken heart. However, you definitely don't need a broken heart to feel the benefit! This exercise helps everyone to feel centered and whole inside. *When we stop and tune into our heart, we are coming back "home" to re-connect with our spirit.* It may feel very awkward at first—after all, your heart has been hurting for a while. You will need to place some faith in your imagination. It could take several times of doing this exercise in order for you to really feel it.

Hand Over Heart. Breathe. Listen to Your Heart Exercise:

Close your eyes and give yourself five minutes. Tune into your breathing by paying attention as you inhale and exhale. Begin to count the inhale and hold for a brief moment prior to exhaling. See if you can make your exhale last longer than your inhale. And again pause for a *brief* moment without straining, prior to inhaling and exhaling again. The pauses between the breaths are sacred moments—pay attention to the stillness and the peaceful feeling it brings you. Now you have established what is called *"circular breathing."* It's beneficial, because it causes your brain/body to interact and create a rhythm.

Now bring your attention to the space around your heart in the center of your chest. Keep breathing slow and steady circular breaths. With each inhale you are connecting to your heart. With each exhale you are grounding this connection. Begin to get a sense for what this space feels like. See if you can engage your senses. What does it look like there? Do you see colors or light emanating within the space? Maybe you get a sense that it's stuffy or clogged up in there … Stay with it and simply observe without any judgment. You are building self-awareness. Keep breathing slow and steady breaths. Feel the corners of your mouth lift to give your heart a smile and send your heart some love. Feel your warmth and lightness of being. Be still. Continue breathing, listening to your heart. Just *be*. There is nothing you need to do other than send it your loving attention.

Notice any feelings that come up as you do this. If you find yourself feeling emotional, let it happen. Now that your heart has your attention, it's trying to tell you something. Keep listening and breathing with gentle loving kindness. Maybe your heart was clogged up with emotion so it's thanking you for this release. Let the tears come and wash away any pent up grief, sadness or despair. Be here as long as you need to be. Then thank your heart for communicating with you. Thank yourself for establishing this connection. This is the beginning of a beautiful relationship.

Giving to yourself this way helps to heal your heart and provide some relief in realizing that *you hold the power of connection within yourself*. You will begin to see that placing your attention there will make you stronger and more capable. I recommend that you use this practice on a regular basis to strengthen your connection. Your heart will thank you for it!

For those of you who avoid being alone, this exercise will begin to make it more comfortable. You will learn that by tuning inward, you will never feel alone. Making time for this connection will soothe your soul.

That was pretty powerful, now where do we go from here?

Your Heart Communicates

First of all, let's get the location of the heart right! We in The United States are taught to say the pledge of allegiance (an American practice of showing national pride) with our right hand on our heart over our upper left side. I don't know about you, but this act led me to believe that my heart was located on the upper left side. However, your heart is actually located in between your breasts and lungs, in the center of your chest. It makes sense if your heart is truly your center, your sacred space.

Your heart interacts with you. Recall a time when you felt joy. .

. It may be a stretch for you right now, so consider the following: maybe it was opening up a gift to find a beautiful piece of jewelry, maybe it was watching your child's eyes sparkle with love for you . . . maybe it was winning a game. That feeling of joy is your heart singing! It gives us a high like nothing else. I'd be remiss if I didn't mention love here, too. Your heart hums when you feel love. In the science publication, *Science of the Heart (HeartMath)* they measured feelings of love and detected a certain frequency or vibration that has been known to increase hormones like oxytocin, the likes of which are just as high in concentration as in the brain.[4] The heart also has its own electromagnetic field. "The electromagnetic field is 100 times greater in strength than the field generated by the brain and can be detected a number of feet away from the body in all directions. This suggests that the heart's field is the most important carrier of information.[5]" Your heart has this kind of brain-like capacity, so let's use it!

Communication between your brain and your heart is an ongoing two-way dialogue. Biofeedback has shown us that when we hook ourselves up to a computer, our heartbeat registers every single feeling in present time—*live*. It's an interesting concept, to be hooked up and watch your heartbeat change with each and every thought that registers in your head . . . It's a powerful reminder that our thoughts create our reality, isn't it? The second you remember a stressful event, your heartbeat changes. And it actually takes some effort and time to get your heartbeat back down to "resting/normal" state. Biofeedback is a wonderful way to learn how to sync your mind/thoughts with your body/heart. The benefits of doing so are huge and have been scientifically proven. Our health improves when we can be in sync with our hearts and mind, thoughts and body. We can change how we manage stress. And we are more balanced and capable[6].

Your heart also operates in a similar fashion to your brain. It's a message center where all incoming messages are received and outgoing messages are delivered. Just like the brain communicates with your body parts, so too does your heart. For instance, emotions are sent to your liver to be digested and then to your kidneys to be flushed out. So if you find yourself angry a lot, for example, your liver will be feeling it like a toxin and the anger will get stuck in there, unable to be digested properly. It's my feeling that we feel empowered when we are angry but our liver can't take it very well; it gets beat up. Why doesn't anger stay in the heart you may wonder? I believe it's because love and anger cannot co-exist. And love reigns in the heart space. So you could say anger is rejected by the heart.

In the science publication, *The Power of Emotion, (HeartMath)*, it's explained that "The heart actually has its own nervous system which gives it the ability to sense, learn, remember and make functional decisions independent of the brain. In fact the heart sends powerful messages to the brain and the rest of the body in four different ways—neurologically, bio-physically, hormonally and energetically.[7]"

The heart affects our ability to have mental clarity, to be creative, to have emotional balance and to be personally effective. But for reasons I don't understand, the heart has been ignored in our society. We grew up learning that our hearts have only to do with love relationships, heart attacks or Valentine's Day. We hear "listen to your gut" more times than we hear "listen to your heart." We are taught to hold our hand over our heart when we say the pledge of allegiance ... but why? Did anyone ever tell you why? We hear stories of people having triple bypass heart surgery, but do we know what that really means? How about this saying: "Cross my heart, hope to die"—who started that awful saying? When in love, "I give you my heart" is thought to be such a nice gesture but knowing what that really means, I don't think that's a good idea—never give anyone your heart! Would you want to give someone your brain? (grin)

Your heart is:

- Your power center for truth
- The seat of your true emotions
- The epicenter for knowing and intuition
- *Love* in the purest shape and form—it is universal energy

Our hearts hold our strongest magnetic field... so feeling there inside our heart is very powerful. *Our outer world mirrors what is true for us in our hearts.* Later, in Part Three, you will reach a better understanding from chapter ten about the Law of Attraction. This will help to explain how the outside world reflects what is true inside your heart.

Your heart holds the wisdom of your emotion because it's

where your true essence emanates—the essence of your soul. So then it's a good idea for you to make your heart your home, right? Your heart is your source for feeling good. Therefore we should visit more often!

How many times have you ignored your heart? Many times, if you are like most people. Or maybe it's some of the time if you already feel connected there. Not all matters of the heart involve a love story either. To make a good decision is to use your heart and trust yourself. Here is a story of what can happen when you ignore your heart. Carrie was thirty-seven and had led a very successful life. She had a job where she felt acknowledged and rewarded, traveled on her vacations, and had a close circle of friends. But as time passed, she began to feel guilty and ashamed for not marrying or finding a man to settle down with. Her critical thinking took over, making her feel inadequate and insecure. So when a man she began dating did ask her to marry him, she agreed. She was doing the right thing according to her mind.

Carrie wasn't tuning into her heart during that time. Therefore, she didn't catch the red flags about this man. Her heart would tug and tighten but she never *felt* it. She was caught up in her thinking that she needed this man to feel that her life was complete. Soon after, the emotional abuse began; she was caught in the cycle in which her thoughts continued to lead her astray, and her heart yearned for freedom. Years went by disconnected from her heart's longing and desire. She overruled her heart to place all importance on her thinking. Twenty years in an abusive marriage passed until she was forced to listen to her heart again. During her divorce, she nearly died from a bleeding ulcer. Now, after "rock bottom" she is listening to her heart again. She left her husband and found a new home and is filling it with tender loving care. She is making new friends. Tuning into her heart now, she realizes how so much of herself was lost in that relationship. She vows never to stray from her heart again.

De-clutter Your Heart

Maybe you are having trouble connecting to your heart, so it's not a place that feels good yet. Starting over can feel pretty overwhelming, making it difficult to tune into your heart. When we interpret that there is too much going on and we think we can't handle it, we feel overwhelmed. We might not feel safe or secure.

Emotional pain can make us feel this way. When you connect to your heart, let yourself feel the emotions there. Just like we can have emotional baggage in our heads, so too can we feel it inside our hearts. Once you feel the emotions that are clogging up your heart space, your heart will begin to breathe more easily. The connection you are establishing with your heart will then feel easier to get to. The space around your heart will feel more pleasant when you feel in to it. You want this connection to feel good so that each time you go there it brings you a sense of peace.

You can also de-clutter your heart by physically de-cluttering your physical space. Consider the fact that when we want something new to enter into our lives, it won't fit if there is no room for it! For instance, if you desire a new romantic partner but don't have space in your closet because it's overflowing with your stuff—there is no potential space to have their things there someday. Maybe it's time to get rid of the bed you shared with your ex-husband and get a new one. Are your closets full of stuff that you don't use anymore? We subconsciously stuff our grief by holding onto things from our previous life. These things create clutter in our hearts, burdening our desire to move forward with starting over. Get rid of all the stuff and you will feel clear, free and capable!

Spending holidays alone can be challenging, would you agree? Maybe you lost a loved one or you are divorced and don't have your children with you because of the custody arrangement. (In my case, we split up the holidays so there are times when I won't see my children on Christmas or the Fourth of July, etc.) One way to de-clutter your heart and feel better on these days is to involve yourself in a meaningful project. This past Easter I decided to do some heavy duty spring cleaning in my garage. I got rid of so much stuff I had enough for two yard sales *and* the Goodwill. As a result I felt better; I accomplished a task, I involved myself in something meaningful, and it distracted me from feeling lonely for my children. It also freed up some emotional space in my heart. I no longer felt sorrow for what I *didn't have*, because in the act of cleaning out what I didn't need I gained a sense of appreciation for what I *do* have.

The most important part of cleaning out your clutter is that it forces you to deal with those things that bring back memories. Finding old things that you shared with a loved one who is no longer around will lead you to feel emotions that haven't been resolved yet. This process will help your heart shed another layer of grief, get clearer about your next step, or just plain let go. Do you know what I found while clearing out the recesses of the space underneath the stairs in my garage? My ex-husband's vest that he wore in our wedding! I must have thrown it back there and forgotten about it. Funny, right? That was my way of not wanting to deal with it. But this time around, instead of throwing it back in there, I was able to throw it away into the garbage can without any emotional attachment.

Our hearts feel cluttered because we aren't allowing feelings to enter into our consciousness. Listening to your body and allowing those emotions to rise to the surface will help. Once you clear your heart space, you will take pleasure in connecting to your heart. Well-known anthropologist, author and teacher, Margaret Mead, had her own practice releasing the clutter from her heart. Each night, she chose to release everything that was weighing her down before she went to sleep at night. This allowed her to begin each day feeling fresh and full of energy, providing herself with a clean slate.[8]

Realize too, that this can be a challenging task—there is no shame in calling a professional to help you. You may also want to skip ahead to Chapter Four for a more in-depth look at how to manage your emotions.

Surrender and Have Self-compassion

Living from your heart space will let you know when it's time to surrender and have self-compassion. When you feel strongly about something it impacts the reality of the situation. So *be careful how you choose to feel* when drama shows up. What I mean is maintain that sense of connection with your heart space, and decide how you want to feel. Choose wisely. You can respond to the drama using your conscious awareness. *Direct your experience by focusing your attention on the solution or a positive outcome.*

At times, our hearts will feel full and we might find ourselves in a bit of a pity party. How is a pity party different from having depression? Good question, as they can look very similar! A pity party is when you are attached to sadness or depressing thoughts, otherwise known as "having the blues." They are temporary

A NEW LEAF: 12 SPIRITUAL TRUTHS FOR STARTING OVER

feelings that are super negative but have grabbed hold of you, making you feel as if there is no way out, whereas depression is a chronic condition that lasts for at least two weeks.[9] It comes with an array of symptoms including lack of motivation and inability to concentrate.

Forcing good moods will never work. Force entails lots of effort and it's disheartening. Too much effort is never a good thing. I know . . . we have been taught the opposite, right? We are told via advertisements, "Work hard, play hard" "Give it your ALL" "Give it 150%!" "Charge!" Sure, that all sounds good and motivating, but is your heart engaged? Is your body on board with that? The same holds true for when things aren't working out the way you had planned, or there simply is just too much drama.

Find relief from strong emotions such as anger and grief by re-connecting with your heart and use self-compassion. This will help you to remember that you always have your best interest at heart. It's good to let go of the grip of emotional vices every once in a while to pat yourself on the back. You won't dissolve into a million pieces for doing so. Give yourself a moment to feed yourself a break.

How do we give compassion to ourselves? It can come in many forms—simply being gentle with ourselves rather than forcing another activity or errand to take place; saying "no" to pleas for help when you don't want to; taking a nap or a bath; softening the muscles on your face until you feel a smile rise up the corners of your mouth, giving yourself a smile. Call a friend or purchase your favorite drink/beverage—maybe it's a mocha or a caramel latte. These are small acts of kindness that are directed toward ourselves. See what happens after you do so. Notice your body and mind lighten up and feel tender again. Sometimes we get into a mode of being where we harden up, clench our jaw and force through the day—especially if it's busy. Pretty soon all that effort has us feeling worn out and resentful. Give yourself compassion and soften. You will feel better.

Yoga is a wonderful way to get in touch and listen to your body using a simple concept: movement in alignment with your breath. Not only does it help to solidify the mind-body connection, yoga helps us to rectify any self-estrangement.[10]

Yoga was my first conscious introduction to body awareness. Prior to that, I had been living life in my head which means I was

26

disconnected from the rest of my body. I was a big thinker—not a big feeler. I can still remember my first yoga class even though it was fifteen years ago because I didn't like it at first! I thought, "I don't get it!" "Why do people say this is so great?" (Notice the intellectual "Why?" and the trying to figure it out mentality? Yes, I was very good at that mind stuff.) Well, something in me said to stick it out. I decided/willed myself to commit to going to my yoga class once a week, and finally after about three months I got it. It was like an epiphany (I know how corny) but it was! Everything came together for me when I observed with sheer wonder how my body began to listen to my directed thoughts.

The simple act of calling my attention and focus to a specific part of my body (during a stretch for my hips, for example,) was entirely new to me. I was skeptical, but I tried it. I sent my thoughts to that hip joint telling it to release. I didn't let any other thought come into play. And sure enough, I could feel the change and see the change at the same time. That place in my hips began to relax, stretch, and release more and more . . . It was all the proof I needed. My mind and body connection was born! I've been practicing yoga every week ever since for 15 years. I also appreciate that each class begins with a direction from the teacher to "set an intention for your practice." I benefit from the instruction during poses to "listen to your body; what is it telling you?"

When we identify too much with our minds and lose our connection to heart and body, we fall into negativity. Anxiety is a result of thinking too much. We worry over the future about things that haven't even happened yet. It's a space we occupy in our heads, not our hearts. It's our attempt to gain control. But our control center is inside our hearts. Feeling anxious is an immediate clue for us to notice we are not in our bodies, rather we're spending too much time in our heads. These feelings initiated by thought and mind aren't in alignment with the present moment. Anxiety means there is too much thinking going on and not enough feeling in the moment.

I had begun to notice on those days of skipping yoga that my body would feel different. My body would feel different because I had disconnected from my heart without knowing it. But once we have a solid sense that we are more than our bodies—that we are spirit/soul inhabiting a body, our body becomes a messenger. If we stay connected then we can benefit from the messages and in turn give the body what it needs to remain healthy. It's a relationship where there is give and take, but when anxiety takes over, we lose sight of this. I realized that when I didn't practice yoga, I'd have an underlying thread of nervousness running through me and my breathing was shallow. This is another clue that you're anxious—when your breathing is irregular.

Hand Over Heart. Breathe. Belly Breathing Exercise:

Try it right now and see what a difference it makes when you tune into your breathing. Your breath is the quickest way to get "reconnected" to your body. How is your breathing—shallow, regular, or holding? It's also a clue to revealing where you are emotionally. Remember, emotion is energy (more about that in Chapter Four) so your breath will be an indicator of how you are feeling. If your breathing is shallow, you are feeling anxious or bothered. If your breathing is even and steady, then you are focused and paying attention. Now that you're tuned in, you can do something about it. Isn't this great information? See how empowered you can be just by listening to your body.

Take some time to use diaphragmatic breathing. This type of breathing involves your belly rather than your chest. You want to inhale and exhale using your stomach. When you take a breath, inhale into this area as much as you can. You can place your hand there to see if you can make it rise and fall. If you can do this, then you know you are diaphragmatically breathing[11].

To perform this exercise while sitting in a chair:

1. Sit comfortably, with your knees bent and your shoulders, head and neck relaxed.
2. Place one hand on your upper chest and the other just below your rib cage. This will allow you to feel your diaphragm move as you breathe.
3. Breathe in slowly through your nose so that your stomach moves out against your hand. Tighten your stomach muscles, letting them fall inward as you exhale. The hand on your upper chest must remain as still as possible.[12]

I invite you to remember to check in with yourself during your day to stop and breathe. Pay particular attention to the lapse in time between your exhale and inhale. Notice how there is a slight pause? Bring your attention to that pause in between breaths. Continue breathing as you have just learned, but let yourself experience that point of stillness. Even if for only a few minutes, deep breathing such as this will reconnect you back to your body and heart.

Besides remembering to breathe, one of the most valuable practices I incorporated into my life during my divorce was working out at the gym to get a stronger body. I noticed that my body felt better after each workout, and as a result, so did my mind. And if my mind is strong, then my heart is strong, as this interconnection is what makes me whole and complete. *Strong Body = Strong Mind.* Having this connection between my mind and body provided a strong foundation from which I could learn to trust my heart. At this point, my body was as much of a friend to me as my mind. I could see and feel the connection.

Listen To Your Body

So then how *do* we listen to our hearts? How do we know what it's trying to tell us? This part of the process of learning to live from your heart will feel awkward at first, especially if you are like most people and are in the habit of using your mind. We'd like to use our hearts to make decisions and we'd like to give our hearts due importance, but we don't know how. Once you begin to tune into your heart on a regular basis it will become a new habit. Just like anything new—if you practice consistently it will become a part of who you are. Gradually you will learn to trust feeling with your heart just as much as you trust thinking with your mind. First you need to become more aware of the connection you already have between your mind and body.

Living from your heart space means listening to your body and all of the signs it gives us. *Our body speaks to us in nothing but the truth. It is our one true source of information.* So many times we can't bear to listen. We minimize those bodily feelings by blaming something we ate, or dismiss them all together. But, we can learn to befriend our bodies by tuning in more. And with practice we get better and better at reading the signposts. For example, a sudden headache could tell you you're putting too much effort into your task and thus it's literally stressing your brain out. A canker sore in your mouth could tell you those angry words you held back from expressing need to get out! And that place in your stomach so many people call your "gut" is where your "solar plexus" registers emotion — about yourself and others; it's also your intuition to guide you in making decisions.

"Feeling is a language that speaks to us through our bodies."
~ Greg Braden

When you live from your heart space you know that your body speaks. A previous client was having a tough time trusting herself and her decisions. In other words, she was disconnected from her heart. She had just graduated from college and was living with her boyfriend. They had been together for a couple of years and she loved him very much. She described to me an occasion during which she was listening to her boyfriend talk about a night out he had had with his friends. While listening, she was struck with the notion that he had met another girl. And as he spoke, she felt a sinking feeling in her stomach. She read the signal her body was giving to her and listened more closely to try and determine if he could be lying to her. But he looked right at her as he spoke and his eye contact made him seem sincere. She wanted to believe him; she loved him. She believed he knew how much it would hurt her to lie to her face and she didn't think he would want that. So she decided to question him to see if he faltered and he didn't. She accepted his story. And yet that night, she had trouble falling asleep. She rewound the conversation in her mind searching for any stray words that could give him away.

However, that was the missed opportunity—her focus was on trying to figure *him* out rather than on staying with how *she* felt inside her heart. What would have happened if she stayed with those bodily sensations, "that sinking feeling" in her stomach? What would it have told her? In working with this client, I was able to coach her how to stay in the present moment with what her heart was trying to tell her. Gradually she learned to trust and use her heart's infinite wisdom. She realized that she could depend on herself for answers rather than drill her boyfriend in an attempt to detect a lie.

As 14-year-old Lilly says in the book/movie, *The Secret Life of Bees*, *"The body knows things . . . before the mind catches up to them."*

Larry Dossey teaches that *"Physical sensations can alert us that something important is about to happen—an early-warning premonition system."*[13]

If you listened to that sinking feeling—more often than others tell you to—you'd feel empowered rather than at their mercy as to whether or not they are telling you the truth. This holds true especially with people who lie because they are so good at convincing and manipulating others. *Their words won't ever be the red flag that you are looking for. The more you can rely on your own truth, the better you will be able to call a liar a liar or a manipulator a manipulator.*

Growing up, we aren't taught this skill of listening to our bodies. In fact we are taught just the opposite; we are told to pop some ibuprofen for a headache or sleeping pills for a good night's rest. It seems a lot quicker and easier—definitely a short term fix. But what happens is we become more dependent on sources *outside of ourselves* to tell us if we feel good or not. Or we get so caught up in our heads trying to figure things out that we lose sight of what our heart is saying. Analysis or analyzing others takes us in only one direction—a loop. We can visit each branch of that twisted tree we don't understand until we've got ourselves so wound up we can't find our way back to the root of the problem—the root of *who we are.* How does it feel in your heart? This is all you need to know.

Hand Over Heart. Breathe. Connect With Your Heart Exercise:

Place your hand over your heart in the center of your chest. Bring your attention and focus there. Ask yourself, "Am I in my head or in my heart?" How will you know? Your depth of feeling is felt in your heart. When you speak you will hear your heart resonate in your voice. Try it by saying aloud, "All is well in my heart." Listen to your voice to see if it's a higher sounding pitch as opposed to a guttural grounded voice. If your voice isn't resonating with your emotion, then you're still up inside your head responding from a mind space versus a heart space. Now repeat, "All is well in my heart" until your voice resonates with that feeling that all really is well. Observe how it shifts and places you into a more grounded, more centered space.

Here are some suggestions if you are having trouble feeling into your heart space.

Use your breath: Inhale with your desire for connection. Exhale to ground the connection. It may take 11-20 conscious breaths to feel the difference. After practicing for some time, it won't take as long.

- *Be* with yourself: be present in a loving-kindness way, offering support, friendliness and your deep sense of caring.
- Use prompts: Tell yourself, "Drop down." "I am here."
- Use imagination: See yourself inside your heart, see light or colors, visualize a power place.
- Ask Spirit for guidance. Be still. Be patient. Wait, without attachment to the outcome.

Benefits: Inner peace, knowing, trust, faith, relationship with self, access to the present moment, guidance, comfort, ease, feeling centered, empowerment, strength, higher consciousness, love, joy, connection.

Empowered Hearts

Once you have a strong mind-body connection established by listening and acting on what your body tells you, you will have an empowered heart. Now you can begin to use and feel the benefits your heart has to offer you: Love! Truth! Authenticity! The next time you are faced with a decision, you can tune into your heart and trust it—how nice! By feeling into your heart and acting from that place or point of view, you get to be your best self.

Hand Over Heart. Breathe. Your Empowered Heart Meditation:

Bring your attention to your breath and practice circular breathing, creating an exhale longer than your inhale. Connect with your heart on the inhale. Ground your heart on the exhale. Once you feel able to, use your focus. What I mean by this is, direct your attention by engaging your senses. At first you may not feel or see anything during this exercise but that is okay, just keep going (and eventually you will). Using your focus of imagination, pretend there is a ball of light that has unconditional loving energy that feeds you, and gives you everything you need. See it radiating above your head.

Feel this golden ball of glowing energy entering the top of your head. Bring it down into the space that is your heart. Feel its radiating unconditional love resting there. Feel the sense of peace the ball of light brings to you. Now, see yourself . . . you could look different than what you thought—maybe you appear as a bird with big wings or an Amazon woman with powerful biceps. See yourself there resting in your most sacred center—your heart. Feel into this space and make it your own. Maybe you'd like to add a floor of cozy pillows or maybe you'd rather be on a cliff with a beautiful view of the valley below. All of these images can reside in your heart.

Once you feel settled, begin to feel into your body. Feel the peace that resonates there. Are there any burning questions you feel you need answers to? Any decisions that you'd like to make? Would you like guidance about a certain matter? Now is the time to bring these thoughts forward to this moment and make them known.

Then wait in silence. Feel the stillness. Enjoy the peace and quiet. If anything answers you it could come in any shape or form with any of your senses. Sometimes, I'll just start thinking about something that seems random but it leads me right to what I need to know. So go with whatever comes to you. Follow the thread even if you think it's silly. Maybe your knee begins to feel a funny pain or you notice that your chest is tightening. Place your attention there and wait again for what happens next. Repeat this process until you feel you have "heard" it all. The best thing to remember during this exercise is to stay neutral. Don't get frustrated, impatient or irritated with yourself, because this will act to block this communion. Keep a gentle attitude and be okay with waiting.

You are the answer—you, yourself can be your own guide by tuning into your heart.

Hand over heart. Breathe.

I invite you to take a break and let this information soak in. Let it percolate. And while you do this, begin to notice what goes on around you using this new information. Begin to practice living in your heart space. *Simply hold your attention and focus there—inside yourself throughout your day.* Stop and tune in there after you get back into your car before turning on the engine. Place your hand over your heart and breathe for a minute there. Hold your attention there when you communicate with others. Maybe you notice feeling depleted or weak there? This could be a signal for you to fill yourself up with loving kindness; take a break/rest, call a friend, go do one of your favorite activities, or meditate.

Alternatively, you will find that holding your attention there in your heart helps you to realize a new strength within. The shift happens right away. The more you practice this, the more centered in your strength you will feel. Your interactions with others will improve when you decide to live from your heart space. Observe how your friend may shift in her stance as she is talking to you— in response to *you.* Notice how your personal power—*feeling the strength of what's inside you*—can affect your day. Demonstrate this. Feel this. Sense this. Maybe the grocery clerk treats you with respect. Maybe your neighbor offers you some help. Maybe this change will show up in your decisions or choices that you make. Maybe your husband/wife/life partner looks at you differently when they talk to you about their day. Or you notice that your son/daughter doesn't put up the usual fuss about getting ready for bed. You will begin to see that others respond to you differently. It's as if your self-worth is broadcast across your chest. Interactions with others will be more rewarding. *It's pretty amazing —the changes that occur around you once you hold your personal power in your heart. Enjoy living from this place!*

Keys to Reflect On:

- Your heart is your power center—your source for connection
- Get out of your head and into your heart
- De-clutter your heart
- Surrender to your heart's desire and have self-compassion
- Listen to your body to develop a strong mind-body connection
- Empower your heart and benefit from living your life from that space

Chapter 2
Awareness of the Present Moment
Will Help You Focus

*"As soon as you honor the present moment, all unhappiness and struggle
dissolve, and life begins to flow with joy and ease. When you act out the
present-moment awareness, whatever you do becomes imbued with a sense of
quality, care, and love—even the most simple action."*[14]
~Eckhart Tolle

ckhart Tolle's book, *The Power of Now*, gave me a great deal of knowledge to help me deal with my transition. That is why I decided it would be the second spiritual truth in helping you to start over again. The present moment offers so much freedom; allowing us to work with our focus. For what we focus on will create our reality. We can begin to feel better when we learn how to use the present moment.

We can alleviate stress by focusing on the present moment. Often, we're in a mode of moving fast, trying to get things done and we believe we don't have enough time. Add on big changes that a transition brings and it becomes even more important to slow down. What happens when we slow down? We get to experience the present moment! I remember being in the middle of a stressful move from Colorado back to California; the house had sold but we didn't have housing in California yet. I was packing up our things when suddenly it occurred to me to sit down on the couch that was then haphazardly placed in the middle of the room. I heaved a big sigh and that's when it hit me: a happy feeling. Even though everything around me was in total chaos, I felt at peace with the present moment. I felt so content knowing that we had made the right decision and I began to feel very excited about the move.

Transitions bring stress. They just do. However, if we can focus our energy and attention on the present moment, we will find relief. As opposed to letting our mind go into our past or our future, in which case stress is added and causes us to feel overwhelmed. Thinking about the future, we want to make plans. Thinking about the past has us lamenting or regretting, potentially causing us to feel depressed. These are experiences that take us away from our heart center. *Before we know it, we are disconnected from our hearts because our thoughts are buried in the past or the future.*

One of the women in the women's support group I facilitate, *Women Starting Over*, volunteered that she had just been through a heart wrenching break up with her boyfriend of five years. She shared that she felt very emotional and stressed out as a result. However, when she learned that placing her hand over her heart was an instant way to find serenity, she realized she could re-gain her sense that everything would be alright. The action of placing her hand over her heart had a calming effect.

Thank goodness, you have easy access to getting yourself back into the present moment wherever you may be, or with whomever you are with. The simple act of putting your hand over your heart to breathe will put you in touch with the present moment and with what is possible. It will also bring you a sense of potential, as if to say, "Okay, well the past is definitely screwed up and I have no idea about my future, *but in this very moment I feel okay and I feel like I can start over with a clean slate.*" There is no burden from previous emotional baggage and there is no anxiety over making plans for the future. The present moment is laden with your potential to birth something new—or to simply relax and find a sense of inner peace.

When we bring our full attention to the moment we are fully focused, not distracted. We actually have more energy, more creativity and more flexibility!

When we don't stay in the present moment, it's harder to stay connected to our heart. Especially in times of transition, it can be easy to trip inside our minds, to lament, "Why me?" or "Why did this have to happen?" We look back on our past and re-hash it all until we feel sad and frustrated. But if we use the present moment's experience and only focus on that which is right in front of us, then we don't have room to think bad thoughts or complain. It's easier not to fall into the trap of feeling like a victim. By focusing on the present moment, we steer clear of those feelings and stay connected with what *is* present in our hearts.

Learning how to live in the present moment will help you manage your stress. Take a day in your busy life, and observe yourself. When you are cooking dinner, are you thinking about what you have to do afterward? Or maybe you are recalling a conversation you had with your son/daughter. These thoughts take you *away* from the act of cooking—to the future or to the past. Whereas if you were to focus *only* on cooking, your thoughts would be about the water boiling, the pasta in the water getting tender... you'd feel your mouth water when you stir the sauce... you'd smell the aroma of the parmesan cheese . . . This experience is being in the present moment. *That is all there is* at that moment—the past is not occurring nor is the future.

Ha! Easy! You might be proclaiming. Well, good, then let's begin practicing it! Usually what happens is other thoughts will enter into our mind and distract our attention. So, how do we stay focused? *Be* in the present moment—*be here now.* Professional athletes use this mantra as a strategy to win games. Focus on whatever is going on at that moment—and nothing else.

I enjoyed reading former pro-tennis champion Andre Agassi's book *Open.* I liked how he used the present to stay focused on his game and out of his head. Once he realized those mind games were messing with his talent, he used the *now* to stay in his body and ignore those thoughts. The more he was able to play tennis "in his body" versus "in his head," the more he was able to stay focused and win games.

Use Reminders

Sometimes, I will post affirmations on my bathroom mirror to help remind me. I use affirmations: "I live my life with ease," and "One thing at a time," because they help me to stay focused. My energy is directed to where my heart and mind only focus on one thing at a time. When I am in the present moment, I am better able to manage all of my tasks. (And believe me I have a lot as a single parent of three boys!) I'm not only better at managing my tasks, but my mood is better too. When I focus my attention on the present moment, I don't get overwhelmed, which is an easy feeling for me to feel.

In contrast there are days when I allow myself to feel compromised, because I am not staying in the present moment. My mind wanders off too often to recall that I haven't been able to have any time for myself; I can't seem to stop thinking about something that's bothering me, or the list of everything I have to do tomorrow keeps calling my attention . . . On these days my overall energy and mood are lowered. My focus is diffused and my perspective is all about how my needs aren't being met. This is a negative thought pattern going south! Naturally my interactions with my kids will be compromised by my bad mood, my level of frustration and by my nagging worry that I won't get my needs met.

Whereas, during times when my focus is all about what is going on in front of me, I can actually see and experience my son's delight at playing with the cat, for example. Using affirmations I can re-focus my thoughts to the present moment. I have a friend who says, "Change the channel!" I am using this now with my kids and they understand what it means. It's the same process using an affirmation or reminder to switch our attention to the present moment. I can enjoy and take part in the laughter of a friend who shares something embarrassing that happened that day. Or I can truly listen to my co-worker's concerns. In turn these interactions feed me, providing me with more energy in the moment to then give back—whether it's helping with homework, the act of listening or cooking dinner.

Surprises have a way of forcing us to deal with whatever is happening at the time. Ever notice how when someone makes you laugh or smile out of the blue, it shifts your attention? This is an example of yanking you back into the present moment using a bodily response—even better. Consider those times you sneeze... does it snap you out of too much thinking? Or what about when your favorite song comes on the radio? It has the power to re-direct your attention to the song playing, and soon you don't remember what you were thinking about.

You can use various methods to remind yourself of the present moment. Laugh your way back to the present moment! Turn on some music and dance your way into the present moment. Remember the breathing exercise from the last chapter? Your breath is the most powerful way to re-focus and remember the present moment. I know several people who put post-it notes on their computer desktops reminding them to, "Just breathe." These are methods that serve as great reminders.

Hand Over Heart. Breathe. Mindful Emotional Recall Exercise:

Take this moment to realize something right now. How do you feel in this very moment . . . this second? Now let yourself remember something a few minutes ago . . . yesterday . . . and then a few months ago . . . and lastly, a year ago. Notice how you feel now. Did your mood change? What is your breathing like now? Is it shallow or did you hold it for a bit? Come back to this second again to feel your feet on the ground and your breath going in and out. Now take your attention to the future . . . let your mind wonder about tonight . . . then tomorrow . . . then next week . . . months from now . . . and a year from now. Notice how you feel now. Are you clenched/tight/gripping anywhere? How about in your facial muscles, lungs, stomach, gut, or throat? What is your breathing like? Now bring your attention back to this moment. Maybe you hear a voice, a bird's song, a dog barking in the distance. Your breath is easy again. Pretend there is only this moment—there is no last year or a year from now. Can you do that? Practice right now. Enjoy this moment. Pretend it's all you have.

Did you notice that, while doing this brief exercise, it felt like you were traveling around your psyche as you oriented your attention to your past, present, and future? This happens any time you use emotional recall. Now write down the thoughts that nagged at you that you'd like to re-direct. Next to those thoughts make up a new thought or affirmation to counteract or "neutralize" the negative thought. For example, Emotional thought: "I think too much about not sleeping and I fear bedtime, because I'm afraid of another bad night's sleep." Neutralizing thought: "In this moment, I don't need to worry about not getting any sleep. In this moment everything is perfectly fine." Emotional thoughts can carry a sting of emotion that has the potential to yank you out of the present moment. Neutralizing thoughts take the "sting" out of the thought that grabbed you.

Consider how much time you spend in this type of thinking space during your day. Begin to catch yourself. Maybe you begin to realize you spend a lot of time thinking about the future or the past. Step aside and simply bring your attention back to the present moment. Do so without judgment. There's no need to be self-critical, simply observe and re-direct your attention. Be as persistent with your thoughts as your thoughts/memories are persistent with you. This is a new skill to learn so it will take some practice until it becomes a part of you.

Each time you place your attention and focus on a past experience your body literally recalls all the emotion involved with it. Depending on the experience, your brain will respond with any and all appropriate chemical reactions, such as a surge of adrenaline or raising cortisol levels (a stress hormone). If it was a negative event, then you have just engaged your body in a negative stressful response all over again. This gives you good reason to practice being in the present moment.

Where do you place your focus and attention?

Spending time recalling events stirs up our emotions in present time which makes it more difficult for us to stay in the present moment. *When we recall things that happened yesterday or earlier today, we are asking ourselves to transport to a different point in time.* Depending on how sensitive you are, you could be activating all six senses! How exhausting. Unless you are directing this energy or pattern of thoughts/memories into something constructive, it's a waste of time. Why is it a waste of time? *Because everything you need is in the present moment.* Yesterday already happened as did earlier this morning so it's a done deal. If you want to re-create it, use the moment you have now with *new* action and *new* thought. It's as simple as that.

Re-inventing the past (as you will learn in Part Two) is certainly possible. It transforms the present into a re-frame you will *want* to have. However, this is your focus now; living in the present moment. Consider *this very second*, are you feeling capable and having everything you need? If you are truly in the moment, prior to your mind explaining that no you are not because of this and that—you did have a second where all was well. This is the consciousness I invite you to expand.

Hand over heart. Breathe. Take this in while you are in a relaxed state. Let this truth work its magic. Sit with these words for awhile. Think and feel into these statements: Life only gets hard when we remember yesterday's argument, tomorrow's to-do list, a promise we made and haven't fulfilled yet . . . There are so many things that our minds can grab hold of to yank us backward and forward in time. But when we are in the moment, we can use our hearts *and* minds—we have a greater ability to function. *That's right, when our hearts and minds are in sync we have greater functioning capacity in the moment.*

Consider the amount of power you gain in realizing the potential of the present moment. If there is no past then there is no regret. You don't need regret if you have the present moment to make it all better and start fresh again. Would you agree? If you woke up this morning without that "carry-on" baggage of regret, resentment or sorrow, would you feel empowered in what the new day has in store for you? Consider waking up to the day with a clean slate . . . it's yours for the making! It doesn't matter what happened yesterday or last night even. It doesn't even matter what happened during your marriage, your high school years or your last job. You have today with a clean slate. You are free of the past. That's empowering!

Suzanne, a woman in the support group I facilitate, *Women Starting Over,* was separated from her husband. He told her that he didn't love her anymore after seven years of being together. She didn't see it coming, so she was dumbfounded by the news. Her days now are filled with thoughts such as, "What if I had done this . . ." and, "When did he begin to feel that way—was it this year or last year or . . .?" She spent a lot of time wishing she had been aware of his feelings and how/when they changed. And no matter how much analyzing she did, she couldn't figure it all out. However, when she tuned into the present moment, that is all there was . . . so she found relief. She also found her *self.* Many times when she focused her attention on the present moment, she realized that her jaw was clenched or that her breathing was shallow. Her body didn't feel at ease. But this awareness caused her to seek what she needed. She began attending yoga classes and learned how to feel at ease inside her body. Now the present moment feels rich with a new sense of well-being. Her past doesn't matter so much anymore, and gradually her thoughts about her husband lessened to the point where she doesn't feel the need to analyze it all anymore.

The more we practice being in the present moment, the more capable we are of mastering our "monkey minds." A monkey mind is full of chatter. It calls our attention here and there, always distracting us away from our focus. But when we actively participate with ourselves to re-direct, to choose a different focus and call ourselves back to the present moment, we become masters. We train ourselves to minimize the monkey mind and expand the "big mind" where freedom reigns. "Big mind" is all about remembering our ability to choose our thoughts and realize the potential of the present moment.

Planning

Another way we take detours away from the present moment is with planning. When we plan we get to feel a sense of control. So if we are big planners, we like control! Now realize too, that you don't need to necessarily plan for your future. This could be a new idea for some of you. Tomorrow will happen when it's tomorrow. Next month will happen when it's next month. And so on. We can let go of our need to plan. That's a big relief, would you agree?

Sure you can plan for next month or tomorrow or next year... but leave it at that. What I mean by that is, use the perspective that planning is a way to sketch out the future. Knowing that it's a "sketch" will still leave open the possibilities and potential of the present moment. Viewing your plans this way also allows room for letting go of expectations of those plans because who knows what could happen to your plans; someone could be late, the order might get forgotten, your stockings might tear—anything and everything could show up for you and throw off your plans.

This is a great time, also, to introduce this concept: *Simply do the best you can and forget about it.* That's all we can do, right? All we can do is our very best in that moment. No matter how much we planned for it. When that time in the future arrives, let go of the plans, expectations, what's right and wrong . . . to *surrender and trust the moment.* Enjoy what unfolds during that time! You can always make adjustments or accommodations. You can still be you in that moment. You will still have the power of choice. In fact, *that is one of the greatest things about being in the moment: you have the power to choose!*

Parenting three boys under the age of ten (at the time upon a fresh divorce) was overwhelming, as I am sure you can imagine. But staying in the present moment helped me to avoid hopeless thinking. I remember a road trip we took a few summers ago that required four hours of being in the car with a baby, a toddler and an eight year old. However, I had organized the trip so that they had plenty to do and snack on to make the time go by more smoothly. I put together a special goody bag for each boy, with carefully chosen books, activity tablets, pens, and games. Then I had a bag of lollipops. I also had a bag of juice boxes, and dry snacks like goldfish and graham crackers. Oh I was so prepared! The plan I had devised was this—keep them satisfied to keep the complaining down, make one to two stops for bathroom breaks/diaper changes, and pull out the movie on my laptop when things got real bad.

Now, had I viewed this plan as a "sketch" so that I could focus my attention on the present moment versus the plan, then I would have had more emotional space to feel fine when "Plan A" didn't materialize in the present moment. If my focus was about what was happening "now," then I could have allowed one more stop along the way to change a poopy diaper, clean up a whole cup of soda that spilled on the floor, or stopped to help get the battery operated train wheels from spinning and winding up into my two year old's hair! I didn't have the emotional flexibility because I was too focused on the outcome as opposed to all those details that happened in the journey (the present moment) of getting there. Without the emotional flexibility of the present moment, I became upset and was tempted to go into "Why me?" victim thinking: "If I wasn't a single parent I would have more help to deal with this!" or "Why did I have to get divorced? Now I am stuck doing this all on my own!"

The next road trip I used the same plan of action but decided to allow some room for those things out of my control and considered it to be a "sketch." This time I was much more relaxed and was able to enjoy the present moment. I had fun creating conversation and car games with my sons because I wasn't so focused on making the plan work. All my attention was in the moment so that I could laugh when my middle son cracked a joke. I could make another stop on the road to allow for a spontaneous mutual craving for milk shakes! And I could delight in the opportunity to get the lowdown on what's been happening on the playground in my oldest son's fifth grade. Had I been caught up in worrying about the future of getting there on time — or worrying about them getting hungry—I would have missed all of these wonderful things. Had I been focused on achieving my goal of only stopping once, I would have felt irritable and then missed the fact that my youngest son had a new favorite song. Ever notice how you don't really hear your children tell you something when you are caught up in thinking or doing something? We can't hear them when we aren't emotionally present. They really love it and soak it up like sponges when we give them our full attention. And we feel good in return.

"Change the channel"

Now that I have learned this life skill of living in the present moment, I am teaching it to my sons. I hear myself tell them "Change the channel" when they get moody or pouty about our future plans. "Clean slate," I say when they repeat the drama of an hour ago. And they do the same with me! The drama is over and done with and it's time to focus on the present.

Sometimes it's our mood that takes us out of the present moment. The only reason we stay in our mood is because we keep telling ourselves *we are* the mood. When we tell ourselves, "I'm in a bad mood" over and over, well, guess what? We stay in that bad mood. This is true when your little ones get hurt—if they have the tendency to really have a good long cry, it's because they are stuck in the perception that they are in pain about how or what happened. When that part is over, I notice that when I help calm them down and say, "It'll be okay, it's over now," they breathe a heavy sigh of relief and can begin to feel better. While volunteering in my son's third grade class I'd hear the teacher tell the class, "Hit the refresh button!" She told them this when one of them was stuck, distracted or had a "no can-do" attitude, and it worked.

Kids get this message! They really do. It's much easier for them to re-focus their energy than it is for us because we have been practicing our "baggage" longer, and the longer you practice bad habits the longer it can take to transform them.

46

Staying in the present moment can help us with our transition because it supports our intention to keep moving forward. We realize that when we place our attention on what happened in the past, our focus on "the now" is gone. Soon we are back to feeling like a victim of what happened rather than capable and strong in the present moment.

Hand Over Heart. Breathe. The Sponge Meditation:

Here's a quick and easy exercise to do for yourself the next time you're having a tough time being in the present moment. It can be difficult to concentrate if we are still wrapped up in a discussion we had an hour ago at work. Maybe you are feeling depleted or scatterbrained. Not only will this exercise restore your energy, it will clear your thinking as well. Close your eyes and relax your body by taking some nice slow, deep breaths. Slow down and feel the exhale become longer than the inhale. Envision a big fluffy sponge above your head that is intended for only those things that happened previously in your day. Now bring your attention and focus to each thing that occurred beginning with what happened first, say in the morning. Envision taking the sponge and absorbing all of your energy that happened during that time—imagine the sponge soaking up each event thereafter where your energy was involved. Just pretend it's working. Track it to the next thing that happened in your day and repeat. Maybe a certain person comes to mind; rather than absorbing their negative energy, simply intend to soak up *your* energy from that experience. The intention is to reclaim your energy and focus. Rather than spend any time analyzing what happened during the day, simply intend to absorb all of the energy of what happened in your day up until now.

Keep repeating with whatever happened previously until you have reached your present moment. Then visualize the sponge above your head again and begin to squeeze it. Imagine or envision all of the events you have collected going back into your body.

When you are done, you will feel more whole and present.

Resisting the Present Moment

Resisting the present moment can play out in different ways. Maybe you're the type of person who likes to "escape" the present moment. Have you ever been around people who told you that you "space out" too much, or asked you to pay attention more times than not? Some people find solace in their heads so they go there a lot—often they have been called imaginative and spacey—they enjoy daydreaming. Or maybe you're the "on top of it" type; in conversations you're busy figuring out the answers to questions before they have been asked, or thinking up a follow up comment to avoid any "awkward silence." You like to feel in control of the moment. It's less stressful that way, so you plan out your conversations.

Resistance can also show up as feeling judgmental when we don't like the present moment. When we don't accept what is, we are denying the present moment and creating *resistance in our hearts* to what *is* going on. Due to our judgment of what is happening, we stop the flow of the present moment. We have a negative emotional reaction which makes it more difficult to simply *be*. Resistance is the root of all negative thinking. When we are so identified with our mind, its grip has us unable to be present. In judging ourselves and others, we immediately get out of the present moment and become critical inside our minds and resist what *is*. However, remembering our connection to our heart space and letting go of our expectations will help us to let go of judgment and other negative thinking. We can then feel more able to be in the present moment. I discuss letting go in Chapter Six.

Eckhart Tolle, author of *The Power of Now,* is a wonderful teacher. He said, "The pain that you create now is always some form of non-acceptance, some form of unconscious resistance to what is. On the level of thought, the resistance is some form of judgment. On the emotional level, it is some form of negativity. The intensity of the pain depends on the degree of resistance to the present moment, and this in turn depends on how strongly you are identified with your mind.[15"]

There were times during my divorce that I found to be extremely difficult. One of them was communicating with my sons' father. More times than not, the air was filled with resentment and anger. I couldn't wrap my head around the fact that we couldn't be friendly. I always thought that if we did split up, we would be nice to one another. But the reality of it all didn't match my heart's desire. So I resisted every single moment he was in my company. It felt excruciating, until I realized that it didn't make any sense to be so upset about the reality of the present moment. I found it was my reaction to the present moment that was creating my turmoil. By resisting what was just plain uncomfortable communication with my sons' father, my judging it as "excruciating" became my reality. Alternatively, the minute I accepted that, "Okay, this is how it's going to be for a while," I could feel much better. The present moment became bearable. I remembered I had the option to direct my thoughts and focus.

Choose Your Thoughts; Be Mindful

Jon Kabat-Zinn is a well-known stress management teacher. His definition of mindfulness is, ". . . paying attention in a particular way; on purpose, in the present moment, and non-judgmentally."[16] When we are mindful, we are only focusing our attention on what is going on right now. So when we're stopped at a red light, we notice the green hills, the color of the car ahead of us, the sound of the car radio, and the scent of exhaust. We accept these things as part of our reality and we experience them.

When you access your heart center in the present moment, and live from that space of power—YOU get to choose your thoughts and feelings. This is mindful living. You return to self and feel that connection with your heart center. When it feels like you can't, try and try again. Don't give up, "Just keep swimming," Dori from *Finding Nemo* says. Practice makes perfect, so just keep practicing like you are learning a new instrument. It's all just a matter of mastering a new skill!

Living from your heart space in the present moment means using your ability to choose your thoughts. It really boils down to *choice.* What I mean by that is simply choosing each and every thought or experience we have. *Become the director* of your story or experience. No doubt, there will be times when that negative past experience comes to mind and badgers you. But you can counter that by choosing to think and focus on something else more productive or beneficial. When I am having a hard time with this—when the negativity just keeps trying to enter into whatever

I am doing—I direct: "Nope, I am choosing something different." Then I re-focus and place my attention on something else. Plain and simple, matter-of-factly. Sometimes it may seem like you have to do this twenty times a day—for example, to deal with a disagreement with someone you really care about. What's done is done. And there is no use re-hashing it all out on replay because that will not change it. Save yourself some time and space inside your head and keep directing your thoughts. Watch how they can come and go. Notice when they get in there and affect your emotions/feelings. Notice the potential they have to affect your mood, your actions and the rest of your day. It's all very interesting, isn't it?

Be Aware of Your Ego and Direct Your Thoughts

Living from our heart space involves directing our focus away from ego-centered thoughts. This can be very helpful during times of transition. I love Louise Hay and have learned so much from her positive affirmations and mind-body information. She says, "You know, all of life is thinking! No matter what you are doing, or not doing, you are thinking. Your thoughts shape your life! This is why it is so important that we all learn to take control of our thinking. Our thoughts create our experiences."

One of the biggest challenges in taking control of our thinking arises when our egos get in the way. Ego takes us out of the present moment and usually invites negative thinking. Yet, we have so much personal power and potential when we choose our thoughts.

Learning to discern between what thought is originating from our egos and what thought is originating from our heart and soul is really a lifelong practice. However when we practice this process, we can get really good at *discerning which thoughts to listen to and which ones to ignore.*

Wayne Dyer has a very helpful way to decipher what is ego. He says, "Your will is the ego part of you that believes you're separate from others, separate from what you'd like to accomplish or have, and separate from God. It also believes that you are your acquisitions, achievements, and accolades. This ego will want you to constantly acquire evidence of your importance . . ."

I also really like the acronym he uses for Ego: E –Edging, G – God, O – Out.[17] It's another way to realize you've disconnected from your heart.

Sometimes we turn to family for support during stressful transitions. And yet communicating with family members can make it difficult to distinguish between knowing what your ego and heart express to you. A friend of mine, Sandra, shared with me a conversation she had with her mother. Sandra, who was in her thirties, was feeling overwhelmed with a very stressful move and wanted her mother's support. One day, she talked to her mother about needing help with her children and how she didn't feel supported by her husband. Her mother's response was full of judgment. She asked Sandra why she was giving her husband such a hard time. Couldn't she see how hard he worked for her and the family? Sandra immediately felt offended and reacted with anger. She responded to her mother by rattling off a list of things she did for the family to show her mother how important she was. Sandra's reaction was full of ego because her mother's words took her out of the present moment—to defend herself. Had she taken a moment to respond thoughtfully, she could have remained connected to her heart to respond, "Mother, I was hoping for some emotional support because I am feeling overwhelmed right now." Her mother's response also stemmed from ego. Both responses were disengaged from their hearts and trying to prove something. And both reactions stemmed from the past (her mother's comments about her husband's work history) or the future (Sandra's wanting). Had they both stayed within the present moment by directing their thoughts, their hearts would have connected and both of their needs could have been met. With the present moment in mind, you have the self-awareness you need to direct your conversations.

When we observe and witness our own experience, it gives us the opportunity to practice the power of choosing. All of this leads to one very beautiful thing . . . *personal freedom*! When you get good at this, life becomes so much easier. When you get great at this, life becomes a breeze on most days . . . and when you become an expert at it, well, then you have reached Nirvana!

Direct your thoughts by using this helpful technique: "Old Story or New Story?" The next time you feel stressed or overwhelmed, stop and ask yourself if what you are feeling is tied to your past or if in fact, you are acting out of who you are in this moment. In other words, many times without knowing it, we bring our past stories into the present which then cause us to feel stressed. When all you needed to do was offer yourself a reality check to get you back into the present moment.

My friend Kate was a professional dancer and taught dance for fifteen years. When it came time to move out of her home she was faced with what to do with all of those items from that time in her life. Immediately she felt stressed with the idea of whether to keep them or not. When asked if she wanted to bring the past Kate into the present/along with her and her move, she quickly answered, "No! That's not who I am anymore." It helped her see that her stress was wrapped around the "Old Story" thus causing her to feel overwhelmed. Once she embraced that concept she could then feel excited about her "New Story" of moving out of that house and getting rid of those things from her past. Thereafter, she was able to check-in and ask herself, "Old Story or New Story?" each time she felt stressed or overwhelmed. This technique allowed her to direct her thoughts and determine the present moment, and all of the possibility it offered.

When our hearts and minds are in sync in the present moment, we have greater functioning capacity. Will you remain the director of your thoughts? Or are you hearing yourself exclaim, "It's too much work!" placing you back into victim mode. Dr. Phil would tell you, "Fine, then go back to how you were living life before . . . How's that working for you?!"

Know this—that with this conscious self-awareness you get to expand. There is no destruction involved here. You are getting bigger and bigger in heart, mind and spirit. You are on your way to feeling stronger; increasing your opportunities for inner peace.

Do you love yourself enough to keep at it? The following chapter will help you to build self-love to the point that you can say, "Yes, I can keep at it. My work is paying off!"

Keys to Reflect On:

- The present moment can alleviate stress
- The present moment will help us to stay connected to our hearts
- Ego will take you out of the present moment—learn about your resistance
- Direct your thoughts so you can exercise your power and freedom to choose

Chapter 3
A Loving Relationship with Self Builds an "I AM Love" Foundation

"If you want to have the kind of relationship that your heart yearns for, you have to create it. You can't depend on somebody else creating it for you."
~Gary Zukav

Mike's divorce took him completely by surprise. He was planning on spending the rest of his life with his wife. So when she told him she wasn't happy, it felt as if suddenly everything he knew to be true dropped out beneath him. It was as if his insides shattered into a million pieces and washed away with one fell swoop. Who was he now, if everything he felt was real up until that point wasn't actually true? Now, he had to find his footing again. But where did he start? He could find another woman to replace her as quickly as possible. He could mourn the loss of her and their relationship. He could even pack up everything and leave town to start a whole new life. His options felt overwhelming, and as a result he felt lost—where could he begin to figure this out?

He longed for that solid sense of self that he had before when he was married. The hole in his heart felt unbearable. Finally he realized, with my guidance, that what was missing was a loving relationship with himself. Reluctantly, he decided to spend some time on his own. Gradually, he learned to trust his feelings inside his heart and act on them. Later, he felt strong enough to sell the house and begin the journey of starting over again. And all along the way, he got to know himself more and more so that his shaky sense of self disappeared and was replaced by a strong core sense of what he was all about. What was the result? The hole in his heart filled up causing him to feel whole again. He made good choices and decisions for himself that served his heart and *"highest good."*

Now that you are tuning into your heart inside the present moment, you can take your next step toward feeling good again during this transition. Here you will begin to learn how to love yourself. The result will be a deep-seeded feeling allowing you to declare to yourself, "I AM love!" You will feel it deep inside, resonating from every pore of your being. This would be ideal, yes? Once you have this kind of love with yourself, you will feel strong in the face of drama and the challenges that come your way. You can rest assured that once you have this kind of peace within, everything else can begin to flow with ease and effortlessness. Wouldn't that be nice?

Or if you'd rather, you can carry on in life *talking the talk* and express to yourself and others the many wishes you have. Like, "I want to feel good." Or, "I'd like to take better care of myself." Or, "I want to move forward with my life." These are worthy desires. But it all boils down to the *heart* of the matter—do you love yourself *enough* to follow through with your actions? Starting over again takes courage to act when you're afraid. When you have a loving relationship with yourself, you find the courage you need.

I encourage you to take your time with this chapter. It's the largest of them all. So, at your own pace, read and complete the exercises taking breaks when you feel you need to. This chapter could be a book in and of itself!

There is a series of books titled, *Just do it!* shouting to its readers that *action* is needed, not just words. It's also Nike's slogan. But many people get stumped here. They can't seem to bring themselves to *just do it;* then they criticize themselves for not being able to do so. But when you don't have a loving relationship with yourself, it's really difficult to find the courage or willpower to *just do it.*

The other night, three women came to the support group I facilitate, *Women Starting Over,* so excited. Each of them had found the courage to "just do it." They had been coming to the group for several months where each month, we discuss a chapter from this book. That month we were on Chapter Seven (inside Part Two); when they hit on that deep sense of self-love. They happily shared their good news; one had gone on a singles cruise (without knowing anyone), one attended a dance for the first time, and one had begun a new volunteer training program. Each of them had some fear around making these personal leaps, but they could push through it because of the loving relationship they had established with themselves.

When you have a relationship with yourself that is loving, you begin to feel the *true motivation* for acting on your desires. *You want to make good choices for yourself. You want to make decisions that are in your best interest. You stop ignoring your needs. You take care of yourself. And you take action.*

Like Mike in the previous story, I needed to stop and think after my divorce: Did I love myself? "Of course," I said, "Sure I do!" After almost twenty years of study, training and work experience in the psychology field, I felt I had a pretty good sense of who I was, both during and after my marriage.

However, what I didn't expect were all the different aspects that loving myself entailed. I learned that there are many "levels" of this concept. There are certain states of being; actions that we use to demonstrate this for ourselves. For example, there is a superficial layer that we go to first. "I love myself because . . . I buy myself nice things. I like the way I look." Then there is a level of relating to self, based on how we appear to others, or the work we do in our community: "I love myself because . . . I am nice to people. I volunteer at my son's school. I have a good job and provide a good income." This kind of loving yourself centers on what you *do* in the world or whether you like yourself by society's standards. This is how we express our ego/mind chatter that I discussed in the last chapter. We succumb to our mind chatter that tells us for example, "You'd better say no to dessert otherwise your boyfriend will think you're going to get fat." Is that really an expression of self-love? Not really, your action is more about pleasing others and in this case, your boyfriend.

Then there are the *real* markers for whether we love ourselves . . . For instance, when you want to say "No" because you're too tired, do you love yourself enough to actually say, "No"? Or do you end up saying "Yes" and sacrifice your needs? If it's the latter, then you are not showing yourself or the world that you love yourself. When you want to start up a workout routine to lose weight, do you love yourself enough to actually start it? If not, it's because you don't make the time, and excuse yourself to others as well as yourself by saying, "I don't have enough time." Does this response honor who you are and what you want? When the origin of pleasing begins within, that is the real marker. Intrinsic motivation stems from meeting your internal/psychological needs, whereas doing something because you want to look good to your friends or community would be considered extrinsic motivation (that which begins externally, outside of self.) Which type of motivation do you believe you use most?

Transitions are opportunities to create something new and to start over again. However, by choosing to ignore yourself through sacrifice or neglecting your needs, your relationship with yourself suffers. That's what it really comes down to—*when you want to create something for yourself in this world, you have to love yourself enough to create it and receive it.*

If we can't bring ourselves to act on those things we want to change, does that mean we don't think highly of ourselves? Well, isn't that really the same thing as loving yourself? If you think highly of yourself, you know you are worth what you want and you love yourself. Try not to get caught up in semantics and conclude, "Well if I don't have self-worth then I can't have self-love." They intertwine and work together, so that if you work on one, then you will naturally strengthen the other.

To act on those things we want to do or say is *honoring* who we are. To follow through and meet your needs, you are saying you are worth it. For example, if you're home late from work and tired, yet you still have to make dinner for the family, do you love yourself enough to order out/ask someone else to cook/use an alternative? If so, then you are honoring yourself by not forcing yourself to give what you don't have in you to give. How many times do you keep giving when you don't have enough to give to yourself first? Sometimes it will require saying "No" to others in order to love yourself enough to put your own needs first.

Hand Over Heart. Fountain of Light Meditation:

Take some time out and find a quiet space. Set aside five minutes to give to yourself. Just for you because you deserve it. Tune into your breath and begin to manipulate your inhale and exhale so that there is a brief pause in between, and the exhale lasts longer than the inhale. When you are in a relaxed state, focus your attention on the space behind your eyes in the center of your head. Just bring your attention there. Now imagine that you have become a giant fountain of light. Pretend that you can bring in through the top of your head rays of golden light. Bring the golden light down through your head, throat, chest, abdomen and lower spine. Imagine the light running down through your legs and then back up your spine and out the top of your head. Imagine that the golden light continues this cycle. You see it bubbling up and out of the top of your head, spilling over your sides just like a fountain . . . easily and effortlessly. Feel the release and the nourishment it brings. Watch how it circulates back through you again. And again . . . until you are ready to remember the room you are in and that you are enough. You are more than enough. You have filled yourself up so that now you have extra to give to others. Enjoy.

The light in your fountain represents the energy you have and how much you have to give. Notice how the light builds up inside until it spills over the top and ripples over each layer after that? That flow represents how much you have inside of you to give to others. In other words, you have to fill yourself up first. It's the "extra" light that becomes available to give to others. Without the accumulation of light (energy) within, you cannot have enough energy to offer others, and any you do offer could drain your "fountain," leaving you with the potential of feeling resentful, frustrated or stressed out, even empty.

Are You Being Selfish?

Starting over again will challenge how you prioritize your life. Saying "No" to others and saying "Yes" to yourself establishes a good relationship with who you are. Saying "Yes" to yourself more often will give you the strong relationship with yourself that you will need during transition. Our needs are heightened during times of transition. Maybe you have settled into a new town and you are feeling uncomfortable with your new surroundings—you like it, but it doesn't feel like home yet. Okay, so what can you *do* to make it feel like home? What needs of yours can you honor and act on to make yourself feel good? Friendships, stimulating conversation, or a satisfying meal all represent possible personal needs important enough to honor.

It can be difficult to say "No," but if we don't have a solid *no* we can't have a solid *yes*. This is what I heard Dr. Jean Houston proclaim in a women's symposium I attended. I thought it was brilliant! When we don't have the comfort level or the confidence to put our foot down and take a stance, our answer ("yes") will seem weak. Then we don't have the full presence of mind to declare its polar opposite, ("no").

Definitive statements to declare what we want to do will also define what others' reactions will be. There will be some people who will be accepting and others who will become argumentative. In other words, they might not like it—can you stand up for yourself despite that? It can be a problem for us when we hear others' judgment, "You are being selfish!" If we're not feeling strong enough to declare, "No," then we will cave in, acquiescing to what they want just to keep the peace and avoid the argument or confrontation.

Most of us have been ingrained with the notion that if we take care of ourselves first, then we are being *selfish*. This is simply not true. As an example, think of the pre-flight instructions we are given when we board an airplane. We are told, in the event of a crash landing, to use our own oxygen mask first so that we can in turn help the others around us, including our children, with their masks. Otherwise, without our oxygen masks on, we would be unable to help them.

But just like any old stodgy belief, it takes some time to release and open up to a new one. It's okay to be full of self; as opposed to being selfish, we are "self-full." I invite you to try out this concept and stand up for yourself. Use your voice and hold your ground.

Women Meeting Their Needs

Speaking as a woman, I believe women in particular are still living with guilt if they choose to take care of themselves first. This hinders their ability to step confidently forward in transition. For example, look at the working moms who defy this old belief—they go to work in many cases to meet not just their family's income needs, but their own psychological needs. The truth is, there aren't many women, (just as there aren't many men), who can feel satisfied without mental stimulation. Care-taking 24/7 doesn't meet the intellectual needs of most women. There is no sense of accomplishment because the work is never done. There is little reward; rarely does anyone say thank you for folding the laundry, for instance. In the process of taking work outside of the home, women frequently wind up doing it all: working, care-taking, home management, cooking, cleaning, and more! I think it's fair to say that most women keep the schedules of their homes/families. So it's really up to them to create the change they seek, which usually means a more balanced household where *everyone* does their part.

Due to the fact that a large part of our society (I believe) continues to think that mothers are being selfish if they work full time, mothers in particular are still suffering and out of balance. This adds to a woman's difficulty in transitioning from neglecting her needs to fulfilling her needs. If the income isn't needed and a woman wants to leave the house and use a daycare for her children so she can work, she is still called selfish by some people. But what if she is a happier person for working? What if she is much happier and more fun to be around—wouldn't she then be a better mom to her kids? Wouldn't that happiness spill over into her family life? Wouldn't both she and her family be better off than if she remained solely at home taking care of the kids and feeling resentful, inadequate, stressed out, or terribly antsy? For some women, this is the case. The quality of interaction she will have with her children will be much higher and her children will in turn benefit from having a happy and fulfilled mother—daycare or not. Take this time of *transition to put your needs first—despite societal or family pressures.*

"Women need real moments of solitude and self-reflection to balance out how much of ourselves we give away.[18]" ~ Barbara DeAngelis

There are some women who seem very capable of meeting their own needs. They carry themselves without question that suggests they are important. They radiate confidence. Of course there are varying degrees of this, and each woman could benefit from asking herself, "Where do I fit in amidst extremes— forgetting to fulfill my needs on a daily basis or actively putting myself first all of the time?" In observing these kinds of women, we can learn from them and keep in mind, "What is my degree of wholeness?" so that we are consistently able to take care of our needs, despite the demands of work, children, husband, partner, chores, home-making, etc.

There is no definite answer to the question, "What is my degree of wholeness?" because we are always changing. On a given day, our mood might be good, the rest of the family may be cooperating, and/or we might have had a really good night's sleep. It could also depend on what phase of family life you are in. If you have children and they are very young, your hands will be full all of the time; if they are grown and have left the house, your hands will feel empty. Knowing that each stage of motherhood will be different, you can meet your needs accordingly. Sometimes mothers feel desperate to get out of the house, and so going out to do an errand might help. Other times you might find relief in just listening to your favorite song. Asking for help is a good thing—maybe it's time to see if your friends are available or hire a sitter. Empty nesters or women without children can join a book club or explore travel. Meeting your needs will help you to find balance (a degree of wholeness) amongst all of your tasks in life.

What might seem like a new concept to you will encourage you to shift your perspective: *By taking care of your needs, you can best serve and take care of others.* Speaking as a woman, we have a lot of serving to do, as we are usually the hub inside our families; we are the center of a circle of various demands for our attention. However, the center of a circle has to be strong to hold all of the spokes of the wheel together. Feed yourself first and fulfill your needs to maintain this strength. It will eliminate any resentment when it's time to give to others. You will feel full instead of drained.

Men Meeting Their Needs

I must share that in researching this topic for men, the majority of studies and articles revolved around men's needs *inside a relationship, or needs as they pertained to a woman.* There simply wasn't much available on the topic of men saying no, or even on men fulfilling their needs. Some of the research claimed that men don't even know what their needs *are* most of the time! However, I know there are men out there facing the same problem as women: how to say no, how to meet their own needs—it's just not talked about.

Some women might balk and respond with disbelief. They might exclaim, "What? Men seem to be much more filled with a sense of entitlement and ease in fulfilling their needs!" And I have plenty of friends who'd support that opinion telling me they spend hours trying to get their partners to return from a surfing session, for instance, that they said would last only "a couple of hours." Play time for some men, whether it be surfing or a golf game, can easily turn into a half a day, or even a full day. Gasp! Women would argue they have to plead and bribe to get the same amount of "play time" inside their families. But rather than argue "Who has it easiest?" let's keep it fair and earnest, and explain a man's perspective of feeling "selfish" and their ability to say "No." Just like there are all types of women in their ability to fulfill their needs, so too are there men.

Generally speaking, men who have a hard time fulfilling their needs are those who find it easier to take care of others. Just like women who don't put themselves first, neither do some men. These men won't speak up and wind up giving all their power away to others. Soon they feel resentful and wonder why nobody ever listens to them.

One of my clients, Sam, was transitioning back into being single again. It was a very difficult time for him because he felt so emotional about his break-up. But the demands at work were enormous and he wanted to help his boss handle it all. He wanted to "do his fair share." Plus, it helped to fill the hole in his heart. So rather than say "No" when he felt like he needed to go home at the end of the day, he stayed longer and worked another couple of hours. This happened every day for six weeks until he found himself feeling horribly resentful toward his boss. He no longer perceived him as a friend but as a slave driver. And yet, he still couldn't let him down and tell him, "No." Subconsciously he perceived his boss's needs to be more important than his own. Working with me, he was finally able to see that his needs not only were just as valid as his boss's, but even more important at the time. If he had continued at that pace with a newly broken heart, his body would continue to wear down and physical illness could present a new problem. Transitions can be emotionally demanding, which is why it's important to be able to say, "No, I need to take some time out for myself." In learning how to prioritize himself, he was able to alleviate stress and sleep at night.

I have learned by experience that there are also men who find it easier to say "Yes" and go underground with their real desires and motives, than to say, "No" and state what they need. In other words, in order for them to get their needs met they become passive-aggressive (dishonest). By giving a superficial "Yes," or never saying "No," in their minds they are keeping the peace in their relationships. To their partners, families and friends it may *look* as if everything is okay, when in reality these men are meeting their needs secretly, even rebelliously. Meanwhile the dishonesty doesn't seem to be a problem because firstly, they haven't gotten caught yet, and secondly, these men don't see themselves as being dishonest. A minor example would be a husband who sneaks off to the movies when he gets a break and doesn't ever invite or tell his wife about it. A more serious example is a boyfriend who has a drug habit or is having an affair. These men find it easier not to say anything than to express what they are needing out in the open. This type of man needs to ask himself: "Are my actions harming others? Is my effort to meet my needs adversely affecting my relationship? Are my actions jeopardizing the trust in the relationship? Am I not in integrity with myself?"

It's not uncommon for relationships to be riddled with power struggles where partners aren't happy with their roles. One feels resentful because the other gets more "play time." One believes there is no equal exchange in how they divvy up the duties/tasks around the house, child rearing, or income. *It's much better to be honest and forthright with your needs by sharing what they are.* Have the confidence to state what your needs are. Maybe there is a conversation that needs to happen inside your relationship, on the topic of, "How do we *both* get our needs met?" Love yourself enough to initiate this discussion.

The last type of man that I'll discuss is the man who wants to take it all on and be the "hero." This man thrives on the sensation of this kind of power and therefore refuses to delegate. These men almost get a "high" from helping others and placing their own needs last. The "high" is the reward that causes them to keep living this way, until someone, usually their wife, speaks up to say, "Honey, I love that you want to help everyone but maybe you should help yourself first. Your car is looking like a garbage can. You haven't sat down to eat a meal with us in weeks and you could use a haircut, too!" All in good fun, this example shows how these men usually will keep going until someone steps in to intervene. Or worse-case scenario, they contract an illness.

Another type of "hero" includes a man that feels good as a result of helping others. In this case, the high comes from the feeling of rescuing someone, whether it's a damsel in distress who needs never-ending help, a boss, a job that's never done, or a best friend who needs a place to live (without any end in sight). These men thrive on this type of giving and end up neglecting themselves and their families as a result. Wives or girlfriends become jealous of the damsel in distress, or feel resentful of the workplace or best friend. Arguments and separation become the norm and these men really have a hard time understanding why. They rationalize to themselves, "But I am *helping* this person and they *need* my help!" Ah-ha, there is the root of it all; usually these men aren't feeling needed inside their relationships or family.

"There are two questions a man must ask himself: The first is 'Where am I going?' and the second is 'Who will go with me?' If you ever get these questions in the wrong order you are in trouble.[19]" ~ Sam Keen

For men learning how to say "No" and express their needs to others, it's a matter of staying connected to their hearts. *Men, in particular, feel good when they believe they have a purpose and can be useful to others.* They need to check in with their hearts to ask, "Am I feeling useful?" or "Am I feeling appreciated or respected?" or "What is my purpose today?" For men, giving time to themselves will involve the answers they give themselves to these questions. "Play time" (a golf game with their buddies or similar pursuit) is one way for men to stay connected to their hearts and themselves. Without this need being met, they simply don't care, lose their inner power, and can be self-destructive. *"Play* time" for men is equivalent to what women call *"Me* time."

Savor the opportunities you *do* get—whether that's minutes or hours. You can "feed" yourself in small ways or big ways. Or you can create the time. For me, it's rising before my children wake up in the morning. Creating this *"Me* time" helps me to find the space I need to practice yoga, meditation or set my intention for the day. I notice that when I do this, I feel happier and I feel more motivated to help my family meet their needs.

Hand Over Heart. Breathe. Journal: Recovering My Needs Exercise

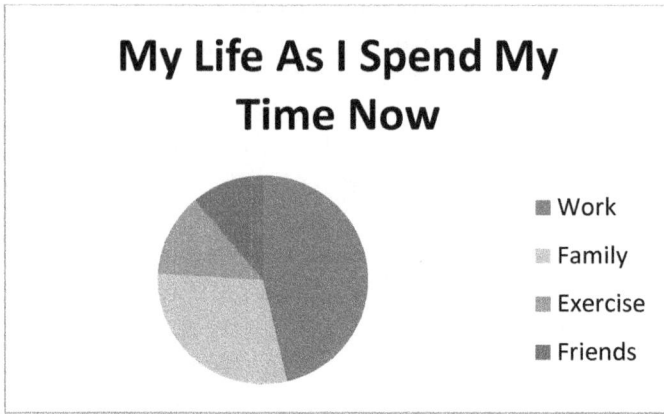

Set aside some time to look at your life as a whole. If you were to rank your needs, what would be most important? Consider a pie chart—for each slice of pie, there is a part of you that expends energy. How you are spending your time these days? Label each slice of pie with your needs such as: health, friends/family, work, hobbies/sports, spirituality/religion, finance, play/recreation, personal time . . . these are suggestions to get you started. Once you have the slices carved out—consider how much time you give them right now (generally speaking). Attach a percentage of time you spend on each.

Now take a step back and look at the pie chart. Notice how balanced or off-balanced it is. What needs do you want to fulfill more? Less? This is your life—how much time do you want to spend on family, friends or work? Next, make a new pie that shows how you'd like to spend your time and energy. You can make several pies: one for your ideal self and one for your current standing; one for who you are now; and one for how you'd like to see yourself in the future. By seeing in black and white how your needs are being fulfilled, this visual will help you find motivation to integrate those personal needs into your life on a daily basis.

Take some time to feel into what your heart wants you to do more of. If it's downtime, you might use reading, meditation, or walks in nature to fill you up. If you've been neglecting friendships or family, make more time. Sometimes I will start off my day with a to-do list that incorporates the pie chart. For example, I make a column for family/home, me, and a specific project. Under each column I list the tasks I'd like to accomplish. This helps me to keep a balance in mind. It also allows me to see that those things I accomplish under the Me column (shopping, yoga, meditation) are just as important as the Family/Home column (outings, laundry, errands, paying bills). So often, we get caught up in the work mode of getting those things done on our to-do list but then neglect ourselves in return. *Love* yourself by doing things on your "Me list." You will feel more balanced.

This exercise would be great to do as a couple as well. After doing individual pies, discuss with each other the changes you'd like to make. Then make a new pie to represent your life together as a couple. Categories could include; intimacy of the emotional kind (reading together aloud), sex, shared hobbies (hiking, dance lessons, cooking), maintenance (checking in with each other to see how the day went, affection, expressions of love), parenting, vacation time . . . the options are up to you. Once you see how your time is spent you can decide what you'd like more or less of as a couple. What better way to get the relationship/love you want!

It may not be easy, but when you begin to incorporate your needs into your daily living you will feel better. This action will ring true as an act of self-love, which means you have increased your loving relationship with yourself. Loving yourself equates to feeling good!

Loving Yourself vs. Betraying Yourself

Starting over again will present more choices and decision making for you to do. Personal responsibilities may have increased. Suddenly priorities become important. Do you put yourself first or last? Now that you know what your needs are, will you fulfill them? *Having a good relationship with yourself includes honoring your needs once you know what they are.* Loving yourself enough to act on what you need, and feeling good about who you are will be the result. But what if you don't feel good about yourself? How do you feel good about who you are? *Feeling good inside will naturally come when you honor yourself and your needs.*

You will notice that when you don't feel good, you can usually trace it back to doing something you didn't feel good about doing. It could be as simple as racing around town to get one more errand in before the kids get home and now that has made you feel exhausted. Or maybe you didn't make it to the gym because you procrastinated, and now you feel guilty and lethargic. It could also be as complex as yelling at your boss or your best friend— yikes! It's usually some act of self-betrayal by unconsciously choosing actions that don't sit well with you. When you unconsciously say *yes* to things that dishonor who you are, you show that you don't love yourself. But when you stop, tune in and listen (as you have learned so far), this self-awareness becomes your new way of living *consciously*.

When we have the conscious intention to feel good about ourselves and who we are, we stop acting in ways that make us feel otherwise. Each action we take becomes a conscious decision based on our self-awareness— will I feel good about doing this? Ask yourself, "Will it honor who I am and what I need?" When we act on our needs, we can continue to feel good about ourselves. *When we don't act on our desires and needs, our relationship with ourselves suffers.*

When we betray ourselves, the deeper result is disconnection and feeling separated from self and the love that is infinitely ours. *That's why it's important to maintain an "inside focus" where your inner self is honored and respected with your attention.* Let those things outside of yourself (external demands) such as work, errands, or even your family be *the effects* of how good you are to yourself.

Famous psychologist, Carl Jung, said that if you live in such a way that you are oriented toward the external world only, your life will not be fully satisfying. One has to spend some time in focused self-exploration . . . consulting with a higher aspect of one's life . . . and then one can live life in such a way that is a synthesis of what is learned within *and* without[20].

I had a client who wanted to work on her eating habits. She was a woman in her fifties living a quiet life with her husband—a transition after raising four children. However, she began to feel bored and she realized she didn't really enjoy her life anymore. Tired of not feeling good about herself and her body, she made a goal for herself to walk a half marathon with a friend. It was a way for her to re-focus her attention back on herself and her desires. She wanted to lose weight. However, she explained that she kept choosing to eat things that were bad for her.

So why was she consciously choosing to eat foods she knew were "bad" for her? Clearly, this was an act of defiance against her better nature. What does that say about her relationship with herself? Was she honoring her need to eat healthy foods? No, so in dishonoring her needs she was dishonoring herself and her intention to get healthy. In repeating these choices—ignoring self—she also continued the disconnection with her heart's desire, and her love for herself lessened. And do you know the ironic layer in all of this? It is that food often serves as a means in fulfilling our need for connection. We all crave connection, so it's no wonder that food becomes the center of our attention when we gather for events.

Think about all the ways we use food: in family gatherings, events, ceremonies, rituals, lunch dates/meetings . . . all of which serve a purpose to connect, whether it be to self or others. So here was my client actively choosing to disconnect with her loving self by choosing to eat unhealthy foods in an effort to connect. Interesting, right? Can you see how ignoring her needs created the feelings and desires to behave in defiance of loving herself? Was she doing this intentionally? On some level, yes—remember there are varying levels of having a loving relationship with yourself. She rationalized to herself that eating ice cream would make her feel good and therefore would be an act of self love. But on a different level, her actions were subconscious because she didn't know or consider that eating junk food was dishonoring this relationship. She couldn't know because she hadn't yet established a loving relationship where she was connected to her heart's desire.

"Pretending that everything is okay and denying yourself of what you need is the ultimate betrayal for all involved.[21]*"* Christa Gauman

On a different note, you may find yourself without a lot of friends right now. Maybe they all left during your divorce. I know often that can be the case. If so, you are not unusual in that respect. But take this time to *become a friend to yourself.* Can you be your own best friend? Show yourself some love! Can you treat yourself with that same kind of friendship in mind? Now is your opportunity to begin practicing it. Buy yourself a bouquet of your favorite flowers, or pick them while enjoying a hike solo. Treat yourself to a movie and notice the difference it makes seeing it alone—you don't have to worry if the other person likes it or not, so you may realize it's even more fun. Visit a place you've always wanted to go and absorb the experience as something that is self-fulfilling, as meaningful and uniquely yours. Learning how to be your own best friend is so important because there will be plenty of times when you're alone in your transition; best-friending yourself will help battle loneliness.

A Deeply Connected Self—The, "I AM Divine Love" Presence

In my experience, the deepest level of loving myself became spiritual.

The ability to stay connected to Spirit on a regular basis will complete the picture of having a loving relationship with yourself. If you believe as I do—that we are each a sparkle of the Divine, then to truly love ourselves we need to honor that sacredness.

"When you lose touch with inner stillness, you lose touch with yourself. When you lose touch with yourself, you lose yourself in the world. Your innermost sense of self, of who you are, is inseparable from stillness. This is the I Am that is deeper than name and form.[22]" ~ Eckhart Tolle

When you begin to handle yourself as the sacred vessel that you are, then you are loving yourself. Seeing yourself as a sparkle of the Divine, you truly come home to love. You are declaring that "I AM love."

Magical moments seem to occur when I am most in touch with the presence that makes me feel that "I AM love." I was having a special moment with my mother and my sons on the beach a couple of months ago. It had been one of those amazing days where the air was so warm—right up to the white water of the ocean. It was the end of the day, almost sunset. Everyone was bursting with joy, feeling the magical effect of the weather and the beauty of the beach and ocean. Suddenly a pod of dolphins swam alongside the shore. They were close enough that if you had been sitting on a surfboard waiting for a wave, you could have reached out and touched them. Oh, they were having such fun! We watched as they swam through the water back and forth, catching some of the waves in, and jumping out of the water on occasion. Then to my surprise, I saw two dolphins synchronize their jump out of the water so that they could cross each other and appeared to make what looked like a heart! It was just like the popular images or paintings you see! I couldn't believe it! I looked back to my mom and cried out, "Did you see that?!" But she hadn't. I looked around but the couple sitting there didn't acknowledge it either. I quickly asked my sons who were boogie boarding—they hadn't seen it either!

So it was my own special moment, my own piece of magic that brought me incredible joy. And I needed to feel that it was enough despite that no one else had seen it. You know how we want validation for when we see something extraordinary? Sometimes we end up discounting the experience if no one else saw it. We tell ourselves, *oh that was just in my head.* And maybe others we tell will say that, too! But when we can accept those experiences as special—still meaningful even though we were the only ones to see it — that's loving ourselves at a deep level. It's honoring our spirit and Divine essence—our soul.

"For miracles do not speak to you in the language of your mind but of your soul. Your intellect may not be able to explain them, but you can intuit their reality." [23] ~Michael J. Tamura

I'll share another story that happened with the widower of a woman named Kate. Kate was a beloved local mother (with two young children) who came down with cancer and fought it for several years. She had such a great attitude that the Ellen DeGeneres Show learned about her and invited her on to share her story. One of the top items on Kate's bucket list was to rent an ice cream truck and deliver ice cream cones to her neighbors in the town where she lived. She did this and told everyone how much fun it was. She also helped develop a line of tee-shirts and sweatshirts before she died. I bought one of these from Kate's website, a sweatshirt that reads "Be Generous" on the front, while the back says "What would Kate do?" with a heart. One day I went to the grocery store wearing this sweatshirt. As I walked in, I noticed a man staring at me intently. I shrugged it off and turned back to grab a cart. When I re-entered the store with the cart, I noticed two kids off to the side and the man still staring . . .

That's when it all clicked, this is Kate's family! Needless to say, I figured this out as I walked past them. I knew Kate, but had never met her husband. And had recently seen pictures of her children. I stood in the bakery shaking for a while. It was very moving. There was no conversation. There didn't need to be. Who knows, maybe he needed that experience of seeing me wear something that she created. Maybe he had been missing her. Who knows, but in that moment I felt touched by divine design and the interconnectedness of us all.

Unless you go about your day with conscious awareness, the everyday experiences will seem ordinary. However, when we're in touch with that "I AM love" feeling, the sense that we *are* love, we have more opportunities to see how we fit into the world. We can sense how everything is connected and life feels more meaningful to us. Living life this way, we have an opportunity to feel that heartfelt sparkle that we represent in the world. But only if we are tuned in or conscious of our surroundings and loving ourselves. With the love we have for ourselves we are then able to love others and tap into the tapestry of love that intertwines our world.

". . . for every time you hold the Harmony and send the Love to your 'Presence,' you glorify It and you glorify the Universe around you." ~ Saint Germain discourses[24]

What does a true heartfelt connection feel like? If you saw the film, "Avatar," you will remember the best part is when Neytiri, the princess of the Omaticaya clan tells Jake Sully "I see you." This is the highest statement of love between the Na'vi; it means they see into one another's souls. Just imagine having this kind of experience with yourself and others . . . it would feel pretty incredible, right?

A heartfelt experience doesn't have to arise from the magnitude of a famous movie. There are dozens of ways you can feel it for yourself. It's that moment between yourself and another that can reveal itself in the gleam of an eye, when recognition takes place. That shared feeling, "I know what you mean." Or, it could be felt through a special *thank you*. When we direct that interaction with ourselves, it feels like an "Aha" moment, when we resonate with an inner peace, or we have an experience of self-gratification ("Thank goodness I decided to go to yoga class!")

Hand Over Heart. Breathe. Heart-felt Connection Exercise

When you go out into the world today, away from the comforts of your own home, I invite you to shift your perspective. I challenge you to go out with this sense that "I AM Love," loving who you are—so that each encounter you have with someone turns into a heartfelt connection. This could look like a moment when you look into their eyes and see the brilliance of who they are despite the "cover" they wear. Every single one of us is a sparkle of the Divine. When you speak to this person, speak from your heart and choose each word to suit the occasion to honor the person standing before you. Relate to them from your own loving heart. Be mindful of their precious heart. This can also be done by giving people your smile. With each smile you give, let it be a reflection of the love you feel inside. I guarantee you will come home feeling amazing.

Make Sacred Space

Loving yourself also includes this one last part—providing time to honor your relationship with yourself in its sacredness. I invite you to develop a consistent time to devote to this practice. For some people, it's a surfing session every morning or maybe going for a run after work. The way in which these activities are held or regarded is sacred—nothing else gets in the way of this time. It doesn't have to involve meditation or going to church. It can be a time to simply be with self and hopefully connect to that Divine space within. For others it might mean a yoga practice or a women's circle. Perhaps it's a walk in the woods. Nature can be like a church for some people. Surfers often regard their time in the ocean as sacred. By honoring your connection to all things you are living from a point of view that "it" all begins with you—peace within will create peace throughout.

Physically creating sacred space is a good idea as well. You can make an altar with all of your favorite things and a special candle or two. Create a space in one of the rooms you live in—or designate a room, just for you to feel sacred and loved. Add colors and soft pillows that make you feel good. Make this your very own personal sanctuary where you can re-connect to your heart and feel into your "I AM love presence."

When Connecting to Self is Challenging

While transitions are busy and clients tell me they don't have time for these things, I suggest they begin by placing their hand over their heart three times a day. And when they do so, I ask them to stop and quiet themselves for a few minutes. What happens when you practice this ritual regularly is your connection to the earth begins to feel stronger and your sense of being becomes more solidly rooted. Emotional roller coasters don't happen as frequently, and when they do, the ride is very short. What used to take you days to get over (strong emotional reactions), maybe even weeks or months, will now only take minutes, hours or a day. This difference makes a wonderful impact on your sense of well-being—nothing can sway you. Your deepest connection—to self—is the same as the connection you have with Spirit. You carry this sense of sacredness in your heart around with you knowing that any discrepancy is merely a temporary contrast or separation from Spirit.

Remember that any discrepancy in connection to self, is a reflection of becoming separated from Spirit. You saw this in the last chapter while learning what happens when you resist the present moment. It's easy to do without knowing it, especially during times of transition. These experiences can take the shape and form of many different things. Maybe it's a hefty fine from a speeding ticket, an unexpected death, a natural disaster ... Drama will still happen in your life—you will still get parking tickets, jury duty calls, maybe even accidents where you or your loved ones are in harm's way. But these things will not loom so large—they will be viewed as "temporary glitches"—"bumps on the road"—times when what you *want* to happen is in contrast to what you *don't want*. My intention is not to minimize these events one bit, but rather to keep the bigger picture in mind. (You cannot always control life so expect the best.) When you arrive at these rough patches in life, the contrast provides you with an opportunity—something new for you to learn and get an even closer connection to self. Conflicts or events where you feel emotionally challenged offer ways for you to learn how to be even more engaged with self and Spirit.

Hand Over Heart. Breathe. Loving Sun Meditation:

Transitions can cause us to focus on what's going on outside of ourselves, so much so that eventually we feel out of touch and lonely inside. Once again, I invite you to go back to tuning into your heart to help facilitate this process. Usually we don't take the time to stop and tune in within, do we? But after a while we can do this practice pretty quickly and it becomes second nature. In just a few minutes, we can have access to a sense of inner peace. Close your eyes and use your breath to relax your body. When you are ready, imagine a giant sun large enough for you to feel its power and small enough to fit through the top of your head. Regard this sun as unconditional love. Begin to move it down through your head and neck into the space around your heart. Feel the warmth from this golden ball of light giving you unconditional love. Let this method guide you to your heart and spend some time there in peace and quiet . . . Surrender and allow this time to happen for as long as you need it. Use your breath to inhale warm fuzzy feelings. Use loving memories if that helps you. Think of it as giving yourself love. That warm sun is feeding you love, comfort and joy. Use your exhale to anchor those loving feelings there. Feel and sense your essence that resides inside your heart; your truest self—your soul. Stay here as long as you like, until you feel ready to open your eyes and continue your day.

Loving Ourselves Gives Us Inner Strength

When we exercise our conscious awareness to take charge of our lives we are using our inner strength and we feel empowered—even in the face of adverse circumstances. This progression occurs when you have a loving relationship with yourself and you can realize why this union is so important.

Past experiences *will* enter our lives again to challenge us—do we have enough inner strength to meet those moments? If I have a good, strong relationship with myself, I can handle it. For example, now that I am divorced from my sons' father, I am still required to interact with him for important reasons (our children). There are conversations and shared events I need to have. In other words, now that I'm connected to my heart, I can use my inner strength to interact with him. I have the means to be present with an empowered sense of self rather than a disempowered sense of self.

Having a strong relationship with yourself will feed you the inner strength to be authentic in your interactions with others—even those you feel hurt by.

Having a loving relationship with yourself will provide you with the awareness or the desire to honor your needs and integrity during tough times. And when you act on your "I AM" Divine knowingness, challenges pass even more smoothly. When you find yourself under personal attack, you can reach inside for that safety blanket to proclaim, "Sticks and stones will break my bones but words will never hurt me!" (Grin) Staying connected to your heart/Spirit will help you when life happens. You will have the inner strength you need to get you through.

Realizing that we are personally responsible for our life will help us facilitate good results. We can use the power of our own thinking and consciously choose to re-direct our thoughts. *Remember that it's not about why something happens, it's what you decide to do with it and how you will handle it*: Will it be a huge drama? Will it last long and ruin your vacation or time together? Will it put you in a bad mood for the rest of the day? Will it change you for the better or for the worse? Or . . . will you make the most of it by turning it into something rewarding at the end? Yes, it's making lemonade out of lemons and turning crisis into opportunity.

Always expect the best outcome no matter what and you will make it so. When you feel in charge, you will take charge and direct your experience to the best of your ability with whatever you have available to you.

Inside this chapter you learned how to build a loving relationship with yourself by taking care of your needs. You were invited to learn about your "I AM Divine love presence," and how powerful you can feel when you build a *loving relationship with yourself.* You realized the benefit of *inner strength* that blooms as a result.

Keys to Reflect On:

- A loving relationship with yourself will enable you to fulfill your needs and honor who you are
- A good relationship with yourself includes maintaining a level of high self-awareness
- When you don't act on your desires and needs, your relationship with yourself suffers
- Maintain an "inside focus," knowing that you are a spark of the Divine
- Make sacred space—provide time to honor yourself in your sacredness
- Loving ourselves builds inner strength and makes it easier for us to manage drama

Chapter 4
Managing Emotions Will Allow
for Self-mastery

"Feelings come and go like clouds in a windy sky.
Conscious breathing is my anchor."
~Thich Nhat Hahn

Starting over again, whether it be with a new job, a new city, or being with or without someone we love, can make us feel overwhelmed with emotion. Hopefully when you combine what you have learned so far—living from your heart space, living in the present moment, and having a loving relationship with yourself—there is good news: your ability to stay on top of your emotions has increased! Managing your emotions is the gateway to personal freedom and empowerment. Therefore you will also have clarity of thought, mind and heart.

Frequently, transitions can leave us feeling disconnected from our hearts or bodies so we don't feel such sensations as hunger or discomfort. We've conditioned ourselves away from being self-aware. We use work as an excuse to keep going and ignore the emotions rising from our transition. It's easier to take care of others and their problems so we focus on them and what they are feeling. The moods of our friends and family are prioritized over our own. Soon we have completely lost ourselves because all we are aware of is how the person we live with, for example, is feeling. So it's simply a matter of turning on the light switch again and becoming conscious of your feelings. You've already begun this process by taking action—practicing hand over your heart and tuning into your breath. Now, you can maintain self-awareness of your emotions.

You won't be able to realize your opportunities to manage your emotions if you aren't aware of your feelings first. Did you have any trouble realizing the present moment in the previous chapter? Maybe it was difficult to bring all of your attention to the present because you were overcome with emotions and didn't feel like you had the ability to deal with them?

Increase Your Emotional Awareness

Once you have conscious awareness of your thoughts and feelings, you can begin to manage your emotions. In chapter two you learned about the power of the present moment. Having this awareness prepares you to check in with how you are feeling. Be aware when you have your conversations with others. Listen to your body and how it responds to people or situations. These are opportunities to be self-aware, inviting you to practice self-care during this time of transition.

Simply observe and take note of where you stand with this.

Begin to consider to what degree your feeling awareness ranges:

- Are you aware of your feelings on a daily basis?
- How about on an hourly basis?
- Do you know when you are hungry or do you not realize it until your stomach growls?
- Can you tell when you feel tired while talking to a friend?
- Are you aware of your choice to change your plans if you're not feeling up to it?
- When you make decisions, do you "feel it out?"

Hand Over Heart. Breathe. Witnessing Self Exercise:

I like to use an exercise with clients when we first start working together. I call it "Witnessing self." Sometimes during transitions, you will feel "lost" or unable to have a sense of self-awareness due to emotional triggers or certain people you find difficult to be around. This exercise will especially help if you find yourself in that situation or if you're feeling emotional more times than not. When you "witness self" you are stepping outside of yourself, so to speak. Take a day to become "an observer" and watch yourself as you carry on conversations and perform tasks throughout the day. Your intention is to separate yourself from the situation so you can see what's going on from a higher perspective. Do not be a critic; that will cause negative feelings. Simply observe with a gentle, neutral stance. I like to use the word "wonder" because it provides such a nice, neutral feeling: "I wonder what that was about?" instead of "What the heck was I thinking?!" Take some time to journal what you observed. Writing it down will help you remember. Record your reactions to people, places or things. Make note of how you felt during a staff meeting, a conversation with a friend, your workout at the gym. Did you react critically about your workout? Did you respond positively to your co-worker? Was your stomach in knots during the staff meeting? The objective here is to gain self-awareness, not a bunch of self-criticism. By stepping outside of yourself, you can also provide an opportunity to learn more about what you are feeling. It's not about finding blame or fault. Rather it's a learning experience teaching you to become more consciously aware without self-blame.

Emotions Are Energy

Here is a concept you might not have considered before: *Emotions are energy in motion.* Energy flows and is designed to move. In Chapter Ten, you will learn how we can use energy to create our reality, but for now I'll introduce the idea that emotions are a type of energy. Use this knowledge to help you with your new feeling awareness.

The secret is to let these thoughts/feelings pass without attaching yourself to them. Let the energy of the emotion call your attention and continue to flow.

When emotions come on strong, remember that they will pass through you if you allow them to.

In her book, *A Stroke of Insight*, neuroscientist and stroke survivor, Dr. Jill Bolte Taylor talks about how automatic reactions such as anger trigger a physical reaction that lasts only 90 seconds. After those 90 seconds have passed, we are free to turn our attention elsewhere. "If I remain angry after those 90 seconds have passed, it's because I have chosen to let that (neuro) circuit run.[25]" Try counting 90 seconds right now so you can get a feel for how long that is. Now do you think you can sit through 90 seconds of anger? Yes. The energy of anger can feel frightening but knowing this, maybe it will enable you to let it flow. There are healthy ways to use this powerful emotion.

Anger can be used to empower yourself. Consider a time you felt angry and whether it made you feel strong or not. Most likely it did. Rather than taking it out on others, let the anger fuel your desire to feel strong and capable. Transform it by speaking up to use your voice or stand up for something you believe in.

One of the women in the support group I facilitate, *Women Starting Over,* was having a very difficult time after breaking up with her boyfriend of several years. She was overwhelmed with all kinds of emotion; loneliness, sadness, anger and fear were constant companions. It took all of her strength to get up and go to work each day. She wasn't always able to contain it. Sometimes she needed to excuse herself to the ladies restroom to have a good cry. Other times, she'd take her lunch break early because she felt as if she were going mad from all of her obsessive feelings. We have all probably felt this way at one time or another. The more her emotions were triggered by external things, such as hearing certain words or songs, of facing certain friends, the more she tried to control herself. But trying to gain control seemed to make it worse. She desperately needed a sense of calm originating from within herself. Rather than attempting to change what was going on outside of herself, she needed to cultivate peace from within.

She found relief using the hand over heart exercise because it made her feel at home. She began to place her hand there each time she felt emotional or overwhelmed. It gave her a sense that she was connecting to a calmer place that could give her some peace. It was a signal to her body, mind and spirit, "I am listening now." And she could find her breath again. Using her breath she was able to release the emotion that was bothering her. In learning these tools to manage her emotions, she began to feel better and more at peace.

Hand Over Heart. Breathe. "Third Eye" Meditation:

Here is another way for you to practice finding a sense of calm in the "center of the storm." First, remember your breath and let it guide you to find yourself inside your body. Simply close your eyes to bring all attention and focus behind your eyes, so that it feels like you're in the center of your head. It will feel like a still point. You might even create a symbol or image there to validate that you are now centered and still. Stop reading right now and let yourself have three minutes to try this out. Keep in tune with your breath. Bring your attention to the point between your eyes, then move your focus back so that you are behind your eyes—as if you could watch a movie on a screen out in front of you. It's a good place to be when you practice meditating. It will make you feel "centered." If it feels good, stay longer! Practicing your "third eye" will make you feel calm and peaceful. Try holding this space as you move throughout your day. You will experience a lovely sense of calm and remember your inner spirit. Some say your third eye is "your seat of power." I like to use this practice for receiving intuition during my meditation.

One of my favorite teachers, Michael J. Tamura said in his most recent book, "Centering your awareness behind your eyes means you are taking up residence as a spiritual being in the driver's seat of your body."[26]

Take Charge and Be the Captain of Your Ship

Knowing that emotions are energy and finding a sense of calm amongst the intensity will help you take charge. Some of you may be feeling out of control and exasperated from the struggle you've been having with your emotions. This is very common. There is no need to feel badly about it. You're having a normal reaction to a major transition in your life!

I invite you to step into the role of playing captain of your ship (body) so that you, not your emotions, can be the one to call the shots. You get to direct your energy! Strive to be the best captain of your ship by navigating all those thoughts and feelings (of the ocean) so that you can have smooth sailing. It's like the ocean; the waves (emotions) will keep coming … but you can learn how to ride them! Let them rise and wash back out to sea again. Allow your emotions to swell, crest and break. There will always be an ocean of feeling. Your job as captain becomes one of navigation; directing where to steer your ship and waiting it out until the waves decrease in height. Use the opportunity to get good at riding out your feelings so that you can become an awesome sailor.

Tough transitions such as divorce or the death of a loved one challenge our ability to cope with our emotions. Lucky for you there are steps you can take to help manage them! I'm going to walk you through how to manage your emotions so that you can get a solid sense of what that feels like.

The next time you experience a powerful emotion, gently sit with this question for a while: "What do I need?" Observe non-judgmentally (this is key) what shifts or happens next. It needs to be a light-hearted effort—your approach is gentle and supportive versus critical and judgmental. Answers simply don't come using a self-critical approach. Simply say, "This is interesting, why am I feeling this way?" (To eliminate the word "why" because that word can call forth criticism by its very nature, say, "Hmm, I'm feeling _____. I wonder what this is about?") Maybe it will lead to a deeper feeling or issue. Maybe it will lead you to an action or decision. Use your feelings to guide your way. Once you have heard the message or felt the message from your body, take some time to sit with it. Does it resonate with you? How so? Where does it lead you—to a new action you'd like to take? Is this feeling serving you in a good way? If not, is it time to release it from your body? Use your exhale to sigh it out. Stand up and shake it off.

Next, I invite you to be open and willing to hear the message inside the feeling/emotion. This experience will be something new and different—just be, relax, breathe and observe more. Notice with a light heart what image, words, or different feeling comes up for you. This is how your body speaks to you! This is how to become completely informed of who you are, what you want, and what you need. Wait and listen to what comes next. Then ask yourself about that: "Hmm, that's interesting. I didn't realize that bothered me. Do I need to do anything about it?" Sometimes the answer to this question is a simple "No" and you are ready to move on. Other times it's an action step.

Make the decision to deal with your emotions. Here's how:

Here are my "Six Steps to Manage Emotions":

1. The minute you feel yourself getting riled up, imagine that you sink into your body and bring your attention to your heart. Just place your attention there—inside of your body as opposed to your head/mental/mind stuff. It can help to physically put your hand there.

2. Next, inhale and begin to take charge of your breathing so that you expand the inhalation, bringing your breath in more slowly ... now do the same thing with the exhale. Do this until you can feel your body relax. Are you tuned into your breathing now? If so, then you are in your body and out of your head. See how easy that was? That was the objective.

3. Now that you have separated yourself from that powerful emotion that had you so riled up, imagine that you can have a conversation with it. Sound weird? It does, but notice how that emotion doesn't have power over you anymore? Ha! That's right! You have just begun to manage it by taking on the managerial role. You are the boss now because you have separated yourself from your emotion. This is key!

    As manager of that emotion, drop down into your body and bring your focus to your heart: home base. Ask yourself, "Where in my body am I feeling this sensation?" Locate the area and ask what it needs from you, its manager. "What do you want [Anger, for example]?" "What do you need [Anger, for example]?" Then listen. Be patient. Stay relaxed and open.

4. As its manager, experience the emotion as it tells you what it needs/wants from you. Pretend it's one of your best friends as you listen and meet it with compassion and understanding.

5. Make your decision about the feeling/emotion and the information it gave you. Is there a step or action you need to take? "Okay thanks [Anger, for example] I get it" would be a good start. Then take action; it's probably a personal need you've been ignoring.

6. Final response: Exhale! You can release that emotion! Then breathe a sigh of relief. You are free again! You can go on to the next thing knowing that you have dealt with an emotion that threatened to ruin your day. Good job! You didn't attach yourself to it, did you? It didn't get stuck inside your body and give you a stomach ache or a head ache, did it?

Here is a quicker way to remember (a condensed version):

1. **Heart**: Bring your attention to your heart.
2. **Breathe:** Use your breathe to get out of your head.
3. **Converse:** Ask the feeling what it needs/wants.
4. **Experience:** Let yourself feel the feeling and listen.
5. **Decide:** What action is needed?
6. **Exhale:** Release the feeling with gratitude.

Once you get the hang of this, imagine the potential you have to feel good. With practice, this process becomes quick and easy. The possibilities are endless . . . with what you eat, how you exercise, your health, or your new love interest. Once you get the hang of this you will begin to feel better. The more practice you get with listening and attending to your emotional needs, the more trust you will have in yourself. Trusting self = personal freedom! Doubt, fear and anxiety will lessen or go away. Most importantly, you can be self-reliant. You won't be swayed by your emotion or act in a certain way when it's not in your best interest. Your mood will be more positive too. The key is to listen.

Let Go of Your Attachment to Your Emotions

When you manage your feelings and emotions you are practicing this concept: You are not your thoughts. Take some time with this idea and let it sink in. This is one of the most powerful statements you will practice and one of the most enlightening experiences. Clients first learn about this concept when I ask them to practice "witnessing self" (recall earlier exercise).When they can step outside of themselves and observe their reactions to others, they begin to see the degree to which they are letting their emotions get the best of them. They begin to see how much their emotions run them.

Realizing you are much more than your thoughts will put you in touch with your spirit. You are resonating with your sacred heart and finding peace within. You can hold a space for being this type of consciousness, that you are not your thoughts or feelings—you are much more than that. You are a spirit, soul, essence of Spirit first and foremost. After you accept that notion, your reality is centered around your body versus your head/ego. Jesuit Priest and philosopher, Pierre Teilhard de Chardin, said, "We are not human beings having a spiritual experience. We are spiritual beings having a human experience."[27] The human experience is being with our emotions that poke and prod us, the drama that unfolds in our lives . . . and the transition that got you here.

The opportunity with this conscious self-awareness then becomes a decision or choice: you can say, "Nope! I don't want to get all riled up about this, I am going to choose to relax and take a deep breath instead." You begin to sense that you have personal power during those tough moments. Hopefully you feel empowered now that you are able to catch yourself. Use these moments and the freedom you gain by remembering you have a choice in how you want to feel based on your thoughts.

This type of decision-making grants you so much freedom. Simply remove yourself and become an observer of your thoughts and interactions with others. Know that you have this freedom within (to exercise) at any given moment when you feel a need to exercise it. You have the ability to clear out all of that mind chatter, all the conversations that occur inside your head that are not you. You are so much more than that.

During emotional times, it's also good self-awareness to realize, "Okay, I am dealing with more than what I thought," and to allow yourself plenty of time and space to go through it. Knowing you have a full plate of emotion will help you to accept your circumstances and create a more loving attitude with yourself.

Of course, there may be times when you feel stuck in emotion. When that happens consider this: if you decide to view your feelings as signposts along the road of your life journey, you can stop, look and listen—then keep going. Treat them just like actual traffic signposts. If we were to stop and read a signpost marked "Lonely" and stay there, we'd cause a traffic jam, right? We'd be stuck. We may even need a tow truck or help from others to get us going again. This is what happens when we attach ourselves to a thought or feeling: "I feel lonely, therefore I am lonely." The attachment causes more attachment until soon you are stuck in that feeling. You feel helpless and disempowered to do anything about it. Soon others around you are affected by your mood and wonder why you feel that way. You end up dragging that feeling into every action—work, cooking, cleaning, talking to people. You are stuck because you have declared (it) for yourself, "I am lonely." Our brain cells run on this loop and message us endlessly until we decide to stop it by choosing something different.

We do this by realizing what we're doing, stepping outside of ourselves, getting perspective and willing ourselves to declare, "I want to feel better" so we can feel better. This newsfeed has to register in your brain as a new loop to run, so it's important to hold that focus! Then act accordingly.

Randy was a client who was very sensitive and didn't want to hurt anyone's feelings so he kept his emotions bottled up inside. He wanted to be able to tell his friends what he really felt, but whenever he tried his throat would constrict and his chest would tighten. He felt so much emotion inside that he didn't know how to manage it. In the process he'd get attached to the feeling. The result would be to push the words out in an effort to feel better, but this caused his words to be mean and full of anger. It was interesting that being so sensitive of other's feelings actually resulted in hurting their feelings—the very thing he wanted to avoid doing.

After I coached him, Randy was able to first realize that his emotion could pass. He could release the emotion by getting in touch with the bodily sensations his emotions created. Then he could use his breath to soften and relieve the tightness and constriction. Once he was in tune with his body, he could ask what was needed for him to do. Then he could choose to speak from his heart. He could be mindful of his words and use a tone of voice that didn't offend people.

The Benefit of "Feeling Your Feelings"

"My own approach has always been to push intense emotions down and attempt to deal with them later."
~ Alanis Morissette (Singer, Songwriter)

I believe most people avoid feeling because they are afraid. They're afraid that once they allow it (the feeling/emotion) to happen there will be no going back. Subconsciously they think it could be the death of them! No doubt, it can feel threatening to let an emotion run its course. There's also the simple fact that people don't want to feel badly. They rationalize in their heads that by not feeling (to keep going), they can avoid feeling badly. But doing this always catches up with them. When we avoid feeling our emotions, we experience emotional build-up. Then we feel depleted. This happens when we don't stay connected to our bodies. That relationship between body and mind needs to be present so that we can stay on top of our feelings and remain in charge of our experience. The minute we separate from self and our connection to Spirit, we are operating from ego and mind chatter, letting our negative emotions get the best of us.

There are benefits to acknowledging your feelings. These emotional times are heartfelt opportunities to learn more about yourself and what you want or need. When you take the time to ponder them, you get to realize, for example, "Oh, I'm resentful because I haven't asked for help." You understand that neglecting a need (to ask for help) has caused you to feel resentful. Maybe you said, "Yes" when you really had wanted to say "No," and now you feel guilty for not honoring your previous engagement. By learning that you feel guilty, you empower yourself to change your mind: "Oh, I'm sorry but I just remembered I have to do this errand first." Now you have taken action and honored your feelings: score!

Another benefit in the act of acknowledging the feeling and the issue it brings up is that acceptance brings automatic compassion for self. When this occurs, a transformational shift in energy happens and the feeling goes away or lessens. This will be your opportunity to release, so it's a good thing—the emotion will lessen so that you can move on again. In other words, shed the tears for as long as you feel them coming on, if you can. Try not to get interrupted and shut them off. If you need to cry for an hour or a whole day, so be it! This is your opportunity for a much needed release. I heard Dr. Joan Borysenko speak at a women's conference the other day. She said that it's important for us to have a grieving song. She sang hers for us. It was full of melancholy and deeply soulful. She said you cannot have a time of change without grieving for what you have left behind. And as I have learned with the passing of one of my soul mates, Leigh Binder: *you cannot move forward with a heavy heart.*

Once we experience the emotional release, our feelings can pass and we can move forward. We feel lighter, as if a heavy weight has been lifted that we might not have even known was there. We feel a new sense of energy rising in us and we feel motivated to do something. Our perspective shifts and we can see the whole picture again, we realize that that feeling had tugged us down into narrow thinking. Now that we are unattached to the emotion we have clarity again. Our hearts can expand and even let a little joy in (grin). This practice of letting go is one aspect in the bigger picture of this spiritual truth. In Chapter Six you will learn more about letting go.

Addictions can develop when we don't manage our emotions

What happens when we don't want to "feel our feelings"? One thing that can result is an addiction. The act of experiencing the "high" reinforces your need to feel good so you do it again. Soon you have conditioned this new behavior and it becomes a habit. It begins with the desire to escape your feelings by smoking a cigarette, drinking several glasses of wine every night, eating a whole bag of potato chips, or spending the day in front of video games. Most people weren't taught how to manage their feelings and emotions so they escape them or numb them.

Addictions have become very common because of our inability to know what to do when we experience emotions we are not comfortable with. This is true especially in a time of transition— we are more vulnerable to falling into patterns of drinking or smoking—anything to escape our feelings!

Tim had been laid off from a 20 year career with a company he started working for straight out of college. Now that he was home, he had entire days to himself. He watched and felt jealous when his girlfriend went to work. He felt ashamed when he got together with friends because he was the only one who didn't have a job. Whenever he talked to his mother, he was overcome with a need to break down and cry. But instead of feeling these emotions he drank and took up his old habit of smoking cigarettes. "It's only temporary," he rationalized to himself.

Once he followed my "Six steps to manage emotions" process, he learned how to release those emotions and use them to take needed action. His jealousy of his girlfriend going to work was pointing to his need to get active again; to busy himself during that time of day when she left the house so that he could feel purposeful too. His shame led him to open up to his buddies and simply say, "I feel like such a loser! You guys are lucky to have your jobs." He felt better after expressing his insecurity to them and could then receive their support and feel accepted again. Finally, he let go and cried when he talked to his mother. He needed this release so he could relieve the sadness and the heaviness that was weighing on his heart.

You'll find that once you begin "feeling your feelings" rather than finding an escape route (addictions), your need to avoid them won't be as great. With continued practice, it will be easier for you to refrain from making choices that numb you. You'll feel more capable too. It's like the cat and mouse chase game—once you become the cat you don't need to run away and hide anymore because you will have the upper hand.

How do you know when you need to seek professional help? Are there many times when you have, for instance, used drinking alcohol "to unwind" when you get home from work? You know it's a problem if you decide to stop but can't or when that routine feels more important than anything else. I've made this quick self-check list. Ask yourself the following:

How will you know if you have a problem or an addiction?

- You decide to stop but you can't—it feels like your willpower is weak.
- You spend time thinking about it—looking forward to it, using your thoughts of it to make you feel better ("I can't wait to get home and open up a 6-pack of beer or

bottle of wine.")

- You make excuses for it to others and you feel the need to explain it
- Rationalizing: You make the behavior okay so that you can feel good about it. "I can stop when I want to, I just don't want to yet." Or, "I don't do it every day."
- It's time-consuming and interferes with the normal ebb and flow of your day—you hear people complaining that you spend too much time on it. (Cigarette breaks are inconvenient to others!)
- You depend on it to relieve stress. (You feel tired from work, so you decide to go shopping to perk yourself up, but you spend more money than you can afford. A tough week of work is good reason to gamble the weekend away.)

There is nothing wrong with accepting help when you need it. There are mentors, therapists and support groups out there, who are more than willing to help you out. It's really important to take this step now more than ever because transitions are so stressful and can push you over the edge if you don't have help.

Transitions can lead to addictions for two types of people— those who already have a bad habit or those who begin one. Vanessa was a client who left her hometown to move out to California with her sister to start a new life. She was a recovering alcoholic so she had a sponsor—only this person was back in Texas. Without taking into consideration the stress of a new job and a new move, Vanessa began drinking again. She wasn't prepared for making these transitions. She had lost touch with her sponsor and didn't know about the AA meetings that were available here. Had she planned this out better, ahead of time, might she have prevented another relapse? Support systems are very important during these times.

Without support (both emotional and physical), our emotional selves can fall apart more readily. If you have friends or family you can call when you need to, your ability to feel better is increased. I remember calling my parents every day during my divorce and they were absolutely unwavering in their support, a huge help! If you don't have that kind of help, then seek it out and find a support group. Groups where you are allowed to share your feelings can be very healing.

You can choose a healthy way to release all of those pent–up feelings from work: go for a run or a walk, spend some quiet reflection time outside in your yard, or place your attention on your pets. There are healthy rituals you can choose to engage in so for your heart's sake … stay connected. I know it's so easy to disconnect by watching TV or getting buzzed from a couple of beers or glasses of wine. I also know that the first step to change is to become aware. What's your choice of escape? How often do you do it? Take responsibility for your emotional self and decide to make good choices to meet your needs. As a result your energy will feel more positive and you will feel better. You'll also be honoring who you are, which as you've learned, builds a loving relationship with yourself.

Isolation

Some of you might be feeling isolated from others at this time. You may be finding it easier to be alone because you are so emotional and you'd rather not run the risk of "losing it" in front of your friends, co-workers or family. It's okay to retreat with the purpose of healing yourself and allowing time to feel your feelings. But when it becomes a way of life and you have rejected so many overtures to get you out of the house that now nobody asks you anymore, or people start using the nickname "hermit" to describe you, then it's time to get out or ask for professional help. It's definitely easier to be alone than to be with others when you feel this way. Yes, this is taking care of yourself but there also comes a time to get out and be with people.

Humans are social animals. We benefit from socializing and interacting with others. Well-being is highly influenced by our relationships and interactions with others. It's something to keep in mind the next time you come across an event that interests you and you decide to pass. I believe we all have the innate need to connect with others. I think that's the reason the online group format "MeetUp" is so successful. There are MeetUps in every city and all kinds of different people with different backgrounds are getting out and joining others as complete strangers at first in order to participate. Meet-ups consist of groups that hike, cook, date, paddle board, seek spiritual discussions, backpack, run... you name it.[28] It's one resource you can use to come out of isolation.

You may find yourself needing to make new friends, but you don't feel emotionally strong enough. You can start by finding groups of people in your same situation. That's why I think support groups are so great. It's much easier to meet someone and form a friendship when you share the same interest or are going through the same situation. Check in now, how am I feeling?

<u>Hand over Heart. Breathe.</u> Did you forget to read the road sign: "I'm angry!" Or "I'm lonely"? Did you create a traffic jam or do you need to call for a tow truck?" (Grin).

Change Your Mood

Now that you know how to manage your emotions using this six step process (aha!), you realize you have the power to change your moods. We don't need to be victim to them. What a relief! When we tune into the present moment, it becomes clear what we are feeling. What about the times, however, when you become emotionally present and don't like the way you feel? And you don't have any desire to change it? You feel stuck, apathetic, uninterested.

How do you change your mood if you don't have the will do to so? Feeling into that statement feels like dread, a very heavy weight because if you don't experience free will (the desire/drive to change), what do you have? Not much! The present moment will give you free will. Sometimes simply believing and having the will to feel better can start to transform hurt and negative emotion. It's simply a matter of changing your focus. Use the present moment to acknowledge, "I am willing to feel better" or declare, "I am feeling sad now, but I want to feel happy." Repeat your desire to feel better over and over again until it registers in your brain. Once you are running a new "tape" your body and feelings will respond in kind.

Hand Over Heart. Breathe. Change Your Mood Exercise:

You can direct your thoughts using the present moment to change your mood. First, start by claiming aloud, "I want to feel better." Then again, "I want to feel good." Keep repeating with as much conviction as you can until you find yourself really meaning it when you say it. Stay in touch with your body and the sensations that arise. Then watch what happens. Something has shifted and there is some lightness of being now. Your heart might feel less heavy. Keep going. Now, find and remember those things you do have that are working for you. Build upon those until you have a list of at least five things that are working for you. If you have to start with the basics, like having a roof over your head, so be it—there is nothing wrong with that because it's true. If you didn't have a roof over your head you'd be sleeping outside in the cold and how awful would that be? Maybe you are indeed homeless, but you know you have a nice laugh. This is true because people have told you so in the past. Simply start wherever you are and build on it. Focus your attention only on those things that are working. Stay with this focus for at least 10-20 minutes if you can—the longer the better, so that your brain has a chance to register this new blueprint.

Have you ever noticed that when you are feeling depressed but are also granted an opportunity to help someone and do so, that it produces a good feeling? It's the quickest way to get out of feeling depressed because you are literally getting outside of yourself/ego/perceived problems by focusing and placing your attention on helping someone else. You have directed your thoughts toward helping others.

Use your heart's compassion to get out of the house with a new focus like helping others. If there is a place needing volunteers—go. Sign up for the day. Just go there and visit. Usually local homeless shelters are staffed to handle walk-in volunteers. If not, the worst that can happen is that you have gotten out of your self-pity for a while. Here is another idea: go to the nearest animal shelter and spend some time visiting with the dogs and cats. The intention here is to give to these furry creatures; your attention and affection will help them to feel better. Once you have let yourself forget yourself for awhile you will notice that those depressing thoughts are gone. Your mood has shifted and you can see the bigger picture again.

This method works because depressing thoughts are narrow focused—they make you feel as though you are trapped inside a hole or stuck inside a fog bank. The sense you have is that you can't see out. Once you change your focus and place your attention on others who need your help, it will feel like the clouds lift and you can see clearly again. Your world expands (including your heart) and you can see the bigger picture.

For those of you who might be starting over with friendships, keep in mind there could be some behaviors that trigger strong feelings. Let's say you have been burned more than once by friends in the past. Now you are transitioning into picking out good people for friendships. There will be times when a new friend might challenge your idea of what friendship means . . . you could find yourself feeling emotional because they didn't return your phone call or canceled plans at the last minute. Your emotions from all previous experiences with bad friendships are now brimming to the surface. All of the old feelings are coming up. Here's a perfect opportunity to realize "you are not your feelings" and to let them rise, crest and fall away. Remember your heart space and connect to all that is. Divine love is there for you to fall back on and find comfort in this re-connection. Choose your thoughts by directing them away from "I want to tell her off!" Tell yourself instead, "I'm going to give her the benefit of the doubt." Create space in the present moment to listen and allow these old feelings to speak to you. Realize the need your emotions are making you aware of. Then take action. Change your mood by beginning a new tape inside your brain, "I want to feel better about this now."

If that still doesn't help to shift your mood/energy level, try skipping ahead to Chapter Seven to use the "Body Dialogue Exercise." You will learn another way to listen to your body and trust its wisdom.

This could feel like "work" but once you practice these methods enough times it really doesn't take much effort at all. It becomes second nature and eventually you will find yourself doing these things automatically. So much of what we do is simply a matter of re-training our brains.

Now, doesn't that make you feel like you are your own master? That you are free and capable?

Keys to Reflect On:

- Be self-aware and "witness self" to get in touch with your feelings
- Emotions are energy in motion
- Learn the "Six steps to managing your emotions" and practice them
- There are benefits of feeling your feelings
- Addictions can develop when we don't acknowledge our emotions
- Realize your power and change your mood

Part II:
You Are Not Your Past:
Learn How to Transform Your Experience into Something That Serves and Benefits You

Chapter 5
Perspective is Powerful

"Bless your difficulties and ask to see their hidden guidance."
~Caroline Myss

Now that you have learned some new life skills to add to your journey of starting over, you can feel confident in your ability to transform your past. It's not uncommon for people to get stuck in their past, especially when they've been hurt.

Some of you have experienced trauma in your past or during your transition. Events such as discovering your spouse is having an affair, getting fired on the job, or hitting rock bottom as an alcoholic, can leave you feeling full of regret. I have news for you: you are not your past. Using the power of perspective, the fifth spiritual truth, you will remember who you are, before the trauma took a hold of your focus. More than likely, your sense of self was there before this past experience bogged you down. Using all of the life skills and spiritual truths you learned in Part One, you can now set your emotional baggage down. It's all about opportunity—you get to move forward by making some huge steps to release and let go!

The opportunity is here for you to review your past with new eyes: a different lens. Take off the glasses you were using before. This is a new ride. I am going to give you a whole new perspective to view your past. No need to hold your breath, really! Here it is, it's simple ... There are gifts to be found.

Finding Gifts

In trying on a new perspective, you become able to see that your past includes a gift. This seems to be a perspective that successful people have incorporated into their lives. For example, in Al Gore's acceptance speech for winning the Nobel Peace Prize in 2007 regarding his work in exposing global warming, he said, "Seven years ago tomorrow, I read my own political obituary in a judgment that seemed to me harsh and mistaken—if not premature. But that unwelcome verdict also brought a precious if painful gift: an opportunity to search for fresh new ways to serve my purpose."[29]

Referring to the presidential race and the many accusations of unfair practices in counting votes, he decided to realize the gift he was afforded from that traumatic event: an opportunity to search for fresh new ways to serve his purpose. In seeing his life unfold this way, he was able to take new action that rewarded him with a huge amount of self-fulfillment and a pleasing way to view his past.

I invite you to place your hand over your heart. Your past is full of gifts. Breathe. Your past is full of gifts waiting for you to find and open. Here is where you will begin your treasure hunt. There are gifts to be had, yippee! Okay, rather than have you believe I am nuts, I will explain first! I am about to pass on some very sage wisdom because it's what saved me. Yes, I do mean it when I say it saved me while I was going through my divorce. I was seeing my friend Christa for some coaching and energy work. On many occasions as I sat there sobbing, she would look into my eyes point blank and ask me, "*What is the gift?*" She asked me this each and every time I fell into my holes of fear, doubt, sadness and grief. And, oh! There were some deep holes, let me tell you! However, this question grabbed hold of me and pulled me out.

All of a sudden I was faced with another way to look at what I had perceived previously as a horrific and tragic situation. A gift? There I was sobbing, "I'm not going to be able to see my baby!" (Divorce = custody arrangements = less time with your children and at that time, my youngest had just been born and was barely three months old!) Another day, I cried out, "How am I going to keep up with the house?!" I was gripped with fear and overwhelmed with responsibility. Then later I'd cry out, with anger wrenching my heart, "This is not fair!" However, the answer was always the same, only it came with a Swedish accent, in the form of Christa's question: "What is the gift?" Aaaaarrrrghhh! Sure, I became frustrated with this question. However, it forced me to flip-flop my whole way of thinking! The way I had been interpreting my situation was challenged. Flip-flopped and turned upside down, it was a classic yin and yang situation—what is the opportunity here in your crisis? Are you beginning to see the other side of the coin now, as I was asked to?

I listened to an interview Oprah Winfrey had with Elie Wiesel on Super Soul Sunday.[30] She asked Mr. Wiesel how he dealt with losing 15 million dollars to Madoff during that investment scandal in 2008. It could have made him feel like a victim (helpless, unsure and depressed). He had, after all, lost the entire fund for his non-profit, his pride and joy. Surprisingly, he said to Oprah that he and his wife looked at each other and declared that, "It could be worse—we have had worse!" (They both had survived the concentration camp in Auschwitz). The next thing he shared was the wonderful gift of it all (notice his perspective). He and his wife learned how generous Americans are: They received a ton of mail with heartfelt notes and small donations inside. They were astounded and felt so blessed. He wrapped it all up by telling Oprah that he refused to see Madoff, as an example of our human nature. He considered him to be just another human, thus proving himself to be a victor, as opposed to a victim of this man.

Victim or Victor?

By searching for the gifts in your past experience you are declaring yourself a victor; someone who has overcome adversity. Why is this important? It's the victor stance that will make you feel strong and capable. It is this perspective that empowers you to move forward in starting over with clarity.

I invite you to expand your awareness beyond feeling like a victim to the bigger picture of how it all relates to who you are and where you are going in life. When my divorce began to unfold, I was overwhelmed with hurt and betrayal. It was so tempting to wallow there, and I did—but not for long. I had a very strong desire not to be a victim of it all. I wanted this experience to fit into my life so that I could come out a stronger person for it. I wanted to come out of it bigger and better than I was before—like a victor! I wasn't sure how or what that was going to look like. All I had was my desire and my perspective. I wanted to be the new single mom in town who would show everyone how good life can be after a divorce. I wanted to show other mothers, in particular those who were in unhappy marriages, that it's definitely do-able—and you can be happy doing it. I wanted my kids to be happy. I didn't want them to feel sorry for me or see me crying all the time.

To be fair, it's healthy to acknowledge and recognize "the victim" in us all. It's a natural response at times to feel cheated, betrayed or that life isn't fair. However, what you will learn is that it doesn't serve you to feel like a victim. Furthermore, it doesn't benefit you to act like one.

Do you see yourself as a victim? Let's be clear about what that looks like. Caroline Myss explains in her book, *Sacred Contracts*[31] that the "victim archetype tells you that you are always taken advantage of and it's never your fault." In your effort to recognize this self-defeating attitude, ask yourself the following set of questions:

- Do I blame others for the circumstances of my life?
- Do I spend time in the pit of self-pity?
- Do I envy others who always seem to get what they want out of life?
- Do I feel victimized by others when situations don't work out the way I wanted them to?
- Do I tend to feel more powerless than powerful?

The Room

The room speaks
to the emptiness
inside of it
Her ears open wide
eyes soften
Her cat using the
sun beam on the rug.

The pictures on
the wall
are framed memories
spoken only when
looked at
Piano rests
for tiny hands
Fingers pushing
pedals to strings ...
but it's silent now

Blankets drape the
side of a chair
—won't be unraveled
just yet
Missing bodies to
warm

Walls standing
ready
to embrace and
hold the space

But the light is dim
and darkness touches
the windows
Cold glass felt
from within

Stillness
for now

~ Karen Croley

There is a method to this madness. In finding the gifts of your past experience, you become empowered, the bruises begin to heal and you end up feeling like a winner—a victor, who is victorious. The following examples explain how I used this process to transform my own pain/hurt. First I will list the exact pain/hurt, and then I will show you how I realized the gift. That way you can learn from it and then apply this format for yourselves.

"The wound is the place where the Light enters you."
~ Rumi

Here we go ...

Hand Over Heart. Breathe. Finding the Gifts Exercise:

Your past is full of gifts waiting for you to open. I'm going to start off with the most hurtful experience from my past. You don't have to do the same—you can start out with a less hurtful experience and gradually work your way up to what hurts the most. First describe your experience and feelings; the part of you that feels like a victim. Then flip it over, turn over a new leaf to uncover the gift; the lesson learned, the benefit, the part of you that strengthened as a result. Use my example to begin:

Hurt (Victim): My greatest wound is that my children can't be with me all of the time. They come home for a week and then leave to spend a week with their father. This was one of the consequences of my divorce. I am lonely without my kids. Beside is a poem I wrote to help me express these feelings.

Gift (Victor): Now I have time (days and nights), when my sons are with their dad. At first, the house felt unbearable and empty to me ... so I decided to get out and go to the gym instead of wallowing around in it. I had just had a baby, yet I didn't have much weight to lose due to the stress I was under. What I needed to lose was the stress! I went to the gym a lot. I poured all of my grief into the elliptical machines there. I was further rewarded for my efforts with a toned body that made me feel strong. It helped me keep my spirits up too; exercise will do that for you. The endorphins that your body releases during exercise act like a parachute landing. It was also comforting to have some place to go. I didn't have family living nearby. In fact, they lived four to twelve hours away. The gym was a part of my support system. It also helped me form a new mantra: strong body = strong mind! I was building strength inside and out. What a gift!

<u>Gift thinking:</u> I have more time to myself to do the things I've always wanted to do, like going to a yoga class three times a week, traveling on the weekends, or making jewelry again!

<u>Victim thinking:</u> Why me? Now I only get to see my boys half the time—half of our lives! This was such a depressing thought, not fair not fair not fair!

Which statement will serve me best? Which statement will produce good feelings, energy and hope? I chose the former statement to live by and it has worked for me! Sure, I get those pangs at times and fall into a little victim thinking—"Not fair" or just plain grief from missing them. But the key is that I don't spend much time with those thoughts. As you learned in the last

To illustrate this gift I'll share a journal entry here:

I was turning thirty – seven years old and all of a sudden I had all of this glorious energy! I was free to hold a party in my house! I invited friends that had been in my life and knew the circumstances and they showed up for me.

My yoga teacher came ... my friends who had known me from when the boys were babies came ... and my best friends at the time played host. I sat there like a queen as strawberry margaritas were poured in my honor.

To top it off, I was given a birthday cheesecake with candles for me to blow out as my sons gathered around me cheering me on, "Make a wish Mommy!" It was a great way to start off the next year of my life as a single woman.

106

chapter about managing emotions, I let those feelings come—and then I let them go! I remember that I have a conscious choice here—to feel good or to feel bad. Feeling bad won't make me productive, on track with my goals, motivated or happy around my kids; feeling good will.

~ Hand over Heart. Breathe ~

Hurt (Victim): I no longer had a partner in life. I didn't ask to raise a family on my own or to be a single parent.

Gift (Victor): Now I had more energy. I no longer had to give energy away to my partner. I no longer needed to focus my energy on doing what he wanted to do and using so much effort trying to make him/us happy. Now I had that energy back, now I really could have fun. I no longer had to worry about whether he'd want to or not want to go to the beach with the kids. I could take the boys out for a nice drive up the coast without checking with him first ... All of a sudden I truly had more energy to give to the boys and myself, because I wasn't working so hard to make the relationship work anymore. I was without the burden of his moods, his stress, his needs . . . I was free to make my own decisions. I had a new sense of freedom that felt really good! Another gift!

I decided to throw myself a birthday party just a few months after my husband moved out. My life was in a shambles. The thought of passing the days underneath the covers did occur to me. However, I didn't let the thought linger for very long. I had to be (and wanted to be!) fully present for my children.

This new way of looking at my life—as someone who now had more energy and someone who now felt like she could have a party for herself—was victorious. The victim would have had a pity party, and decided not to do anything for her birthday. She'd wallow in the confusion of why the horrible break-up happened, why he behaved the way he did, and why I didn't get out sooner.

The awareness that I was completely in charge of my family (a realization that is was my three sons and I), allowed me to not only feel free but capable as well. So many times I had the three of them asking for something, needing something ... and what I realized was that I could do it! I could meet their needs as a single parent and truly be there for them—unlike before, when half my thinking was tied up in what time my husband would come home, where he was, or what mood/stress he'd be under. It was nice to have a simpler focus: my sons, and make them top priority. It was most important to me that my sons continue to experience me as a good mom. I knew that my role in their lives was taking on a new shape and form. It seemed to me, I didn't have any other choice than to be there for them emotionally and physically. In fact, I believed this so much that my focus didn't allow for much of anything else in my life. In my mind, there was no opportunity to feel depressed and stay in bed. My kids really needed me. It was up to me to provide a stable environment for them. This gift made me feel empowered and capable. The victim would be obsessed in thinking about the fact that her ex-husband was busy moving his girlfriend and her two kids into his home and how easily replaced I had been. But the victor in me could feel a new inner strength!

I invite you to place your hand over your heart now and breathe.

Hurt: I felt betrayed by his lack of commitment. Dishonesty shattered my world and what I thought my life was about.

Gift: Had he not shown a lack of commitment, then I would probably still be in that marriage. New perspective: thanks to him, I am not! His actions forced me to take action that was in my best interest—a new commitment to myself. I realized I had lost touch with my needs and wasn't honoring them; I had been betraying myself. He taught me that I alone am responsible for my life. It all comes down to me with each and every choice I do or don't make. He also showed me I had been ignoring a lot of choices and decisions up until then. I bought a ring to signify this new commitment to myself first and foremost. It's a turquoise band I wear on my right hand, and I never take it off. I am an empowered woman committed to my personal growth.

I looked at dishonest behavior and added it to those things I never wanted to experience again. Rather than lament over why he was dishonest and spend time wallowing there, I could shift my perspective to those traits in men that I wanted to experience. Now, I had a chance to be with a man who treated me with loving kindness and appreciation. The minute I saw or felt one of those qualities I didn't want in a man such as dishonesty, I could recognize it: another benefit! I could recognize that quality because I had experienced it. The difference was this time I could say, "No thanks!" How great is that? Had I not experienced a lie, for example, I might not know what one feels like—and that would hamper my ability to recognize it. This in turn would lead me into another undesirable experience. Having had those experiences that I didn't want to be part of my future allowed me to stay true to who I am and what I want, by picking and choosing the next one more carefully. Clarity became my steering wheel, my road map—its strength was getting stronger and truer every day.

I invite you to place your hand over your heart now and breathe.

I hope this has helped you to see what finding a better perspective is all about. Now it's your turn to transform and shift your perspective. Here is help for finding the gifts of your hurtful experience. Ask yourself these questions and spend some time journaling:

Find the lesson presented that you can learn from and build new understanding for the next time. (Ex: Holding onto resentment tears people apart).

Find out how the situation is building your inner strength.

See how it's showing you very clearly what you *don't* want which then makes it easier for you to see what you *do* want.

- Expand your awareness to the bigger picture—how does this experience relate to who you are and where you are going in life?
- Did this experience teach you something about yourself or others? If so, what?
- Did you experience something (new) that you wouldn't have typically experienced during "normal" times?
- Were you forced to begin again or start your life over? If yes, can that be exciting or adventurous? How?
- Did you get pushed into something that forced you to stand up for yourself/for others?

- Did you get a new outlook about life? How so? (Ex: Did you take things for granted before and now you have a new appreciation for life?)
- Did you get in touch with feelings you didn't know you had before? If so, which feelings?

After you consider these questions, it can begin to have an effect on you. Hand over heart, breathe. Now that you are in touch and connected, what do you notice about how you are feeling? Are you lightening up? Is the weight shifting, becoming lighter and lighter? Can you get a sense now that your perspective about what happened could be a good thing for you? Can you see that what happened is giving you an opportunity to learn? I encourage you to spend some time journaling now.

Find the lesson presented to you that you can learn from and use to build a new understanding. This task can feel heavy, like work, but it will truly benefit you and how you go about your life thereafter. Many people will go to psychotherapy to figure this out. If you do so, however, I advise you to refrain from getting caught in the trap of trying to figure out "Why?" or to fall back into thinking of yourself as a victim. So be careful here when you answer these questions. Stay positive and light. Be and embody the victor that you are. Use your sense of humor and review what happened with a light heart: a wise heart. Pretend you are older and you are looking back on your life. Or as my mother used to say, pretend you are up on a ladder or a mountain way up high and you are looking down on your life. This is the kind of detachment you want to have when doing this task.

Rather than feel victimized by the person that hurt you, see them as one of your best teachers. What do I mean by that? If life is like school, where we learn lessons (Gary Zukav, author of Seat of the Soul, calls it "earth school"), then who are your teachers? Can you learn from people who have hurt you? You sure can! Flip the hurtful feelings into lessons learned. Wrap up your past so that it serves you.

PERSPECTIVE

"You have the power to heal your life, and you need to know that. We think so often that we are helpless, but we're not. We always have the power of our minds ... Claim and consciously use your power." ~ Louise Hay

In other words, now that you have taken the time to review what you learned (who you were back then, those lessons learned and those gifts found), how would you like to re-tell your story of what happened to someone you meet? Let's say you have met someone you feel is worth your time sharing your story. Here is your opportunity to start fresh and share your story in a new light—one that demonstrates who you are today: a victor, strong and capable with lessons learned and a new understanding of how you'd like your new life to be!

I encourage you to take a break here if you need to. This next exercise is also very powerful and a little time consuming.

Hand Over Heart. Breathe. Re-write Your Story Exercise:

Now I invite you to re-write your story. I was able to summarize mine in 784 words the first time I did it, which is a little over a page. The challenge for me was in separating myself and seeing me as a character in a novel or autobiography. The next challenge was to review the turning points—without re-living the painful events. It will feel challenging to summarize briefly with few words while staying positive and the winner (victor) of the situation. Don't let yourself get bogged down with the details of what happened. Stay light and positive, focusing on what you learned about yourself.

What if you had to tell someone you just met your story? You simply cannot launch into 784 words to tell that person what happened . . . Well, you could, but it would probably scare them off! Take some time now to write one brief paragraph to sum up your story. It gets a little more challenging, right? You might need to spend some extra time with this exercise. Most likely it will feel overwhelming and impossible at first. Re-work it a few times until you get your story to the point of liking it. Consider what you'd like your best friend to say about her past hurt; you'd want her to appear happy and strong. Consider how you'd like to appear to that person you just met. Wouldn't you like them to see you as strong and capable? Realize the person you are now and make sure it comes across in your statements. If you find that there is blame or defensiveness, then you are on the wrong track. Statements such as, "He cheated on me so I am afraid of men now" are not empowering ones. On the other hand, "I learned that he had other ideas about our marriage that weren't good for me, so I decided to end it and start over again" is much more powerful. It's a victorious stance. Notice the personal responsibility present in there?

There are statements you do not want to say, because they focus on your weaknesses. For example, "She stopped talking to me, and I have no idea why. I wish I had never met her in the first place." Again there is blame, victimhood and whining. Now see how this statement is much more powerful and positive: "We are no longer friends, which is too bad because I really liked her. But some friendships aren't meant to last forever and I'm okay with that." See how strong you seem? Be sure to show off your strength in these new statements because they are also your new beliefs. These statements become like affirmations because the more times you recount this new story the more times you are telling yourself these things—building a stronger and stronger you each time!

My Story (condensed): I married my husband when I was very young and unsure of myself. We both went to school and spent time building our individual careers. I felt anxious and doubtful about the relationship the entire time we were together but decided to start a family with him anyway. I believe we were meant to bring three beautiful boys into the world. Despite some anxiety and depression, I began listening to my heart and acting on my inner voice. The truth of who I was needed to unfold. Betrayals from my husband helped me see how stubborn I had been and forced me to stop betraying myself. Our divorce gave me the inner strength I had been missing and allowed me to return to the spiritual path I had abandoned.

Amy, one of the women in my support group, *Women Starting Over,* had been through a difficult relationship break-up. She was nearing her sixtieth birthday and feeling insecure about where she was in life. After some re-writes, she was able to sum up her story in just a couple of sentences. She wrote, "I decided to simplify my life and focus on my personal growth/internal development. This has led me to want to make a career change to a field where l can be of service to others." She flipped the heartache around so that her break-up enabled her to step into a new phase of her life.

Practice Sharing Your Story

Begin with close friends and notice the language you choose. What words do you use to describe what happened? Are you telling your story like a victim or a victor? Is there a hero or a heroine? Remember you didn't need rescuing—you empowered yourself! Are you smiling? Is your posture still erect and grounded or do you have your back and shoulders slouched? Are your breaths steady or shallow? How about your tone of voice—is it strong and clear or wispy and wavering? What kind of response are you getting from the person you are sharing it with? Are they telling you, "Wow, nice attitude!"? Or are they saying, "Oh … you poor thing!" Are they offering words of encouragement or offering sympathy?

Depending on your story, you might have to weather some reactions from others. In other words, there are certain subjects, such as divorce, that have been burdened by societal stereotypes or assumptions. I remember there were times when I found myself having to really go that extra mile with my tone of voice or choice of words to make my story fly. Just so that I could try and avoid the old, "Oh you poor thing, you sure do have your hands full!" I didn't want anybody's pity and I didn't want people to place me in a victim-type category. So I was a bit sensitive to others' responses, feeling like I had to account for their reactions. There were many times when I ended my story with, "It's so much better now!" or "It was all for the better!" or "I'm so much happier now." Occasionally I'd get a funny look or a miffed reaction, but all that mattered to me was that I was doing myself justice in telling my story as a victor not a victim. I could leave the conversation feeling good about myself.

Your story will get more positive and shorter with passing days, months and years. You will eventually have a much shorter version of your story, and you will tell it without hesitation and heavy feelings. It will be one of many life stories that you decide to pull up and out to share with others at will. You may even get some laughs out of it. The women in the support group I facilitate, *Women Starting Over*, are a great example of this. Each time we have a new woman join the group, they share their story. And I can actually say, it's a beautiful thing to witness!

Hand over heart. Now breathe that in! Feels amazing, doesn't it?

I'd like to congratulate you, that was a lot to go through and you did it! How are you feeling now? Are you feeling more capable? Free? Empowered? Yes!

I had the extreme pleasure of meeting one of my favorite women, Dr. Clarissa Pinkola Estes, author of *Women Who Run With the Wolves*. I attended one of her workshops in Colorado. She said, "I hope you will go out and let stories happen to you, and that you will work them, water them with your blood and tears and your laughter till they bloom, till you yourself burst into bloom."

You will use your imagination in this next exercise, which is designed to help you release even more hurt/pain from your past experiences. The previous exercise helped to shift things in your head space and now this exercise will help to create some shifts in your body. The more you can incorporate a mind-body connection in learning and applying new information, the better!

Hand Over Heart. Breathe. Visualize Your Hurt Transforming Meditation:

Your imagination can be a wonderful tool for you. That's right. Yet everything that you have been told about your imagination up to this point has been minimized, right? You have been told, "It's your imagination!" and it can feel like an insult when someone tells you this because it minimizes your experience. Most of us were told while growing up, that our fears were just our imagination—in the negative sense. Now you will begin to use your imagination in a positive light. Think of your imagination as a gateway to where you'd like to go—a hallway—a tool to get from one door to another. Here you will be closing one door and moving through the hallway to open up a new door.

Create some quiet space for yourself. Consider a time that you remember was hurtful to you. Conjure up the memory now. Breathe. Are you feeling the hurt inside your body? If not, then you need to remember more details, otherwise you cannot move onto the next experience. Once you have an experience that feels hurtful to this day (meaning right now), open up the door and say hello to all of those feelings . . . yuck, I know they don't feel good but just know you are not going to stay there long with the door open. Okay, now that you are reacquainted with that experience and those feelings again, you are going to look at it with fresh eyes. What do I mean by that? Keeping in mind that you are exercising your choice to feel these emotions again will remind you that you are in charge here—you are no longer the victim of this hurt.

You are taking charge to shift and transform these hurtful feelings right now. See the experience in your "mind's eye" (that space inside your head behind your eyes) and imagine a doorway opening. Now, as each hurtful experience presents itself, use your power of choice. For example, "Yes, that (experience) hurt, but can I let it fade into the background now?" Or, "Yes, I still feel hurt by that but I can also sense something different—maybe some hope for getting over this." Or, "I feel the pain of this (experience) but I also have room now for wanting to feel better about it."

As you say these things, watch how the image or picture changes inside your head. Allow yourself to bring in some new light; maybe you can see the sun shining now and the fog begins to clear. Maybe the image in your head just feels lighter. If nothing is changing, create the change yourself: bring in a rainbow, or brighten up the blue sky. This is your visualization, your life, so begin to shape it according to how you'd like to transform your hurt into something beautiful. Check in with your breath, is it easier to breathe now?

It may take some time and patience; stick with it. Start in small doses—bring to mind a smiling friend who takes your hand ... add a beloved relative that passed away. This is your meditation, your visualization, so create this transformation in a loving way. See yourself with your arms overhead declaring a victory for yourself. See your body grow stronger. Maybe you are shedding some weight. Maybe you see a smile begin to form on your face. See your ability to move on, forward into your next life event. See your capabilities and talents. You are getting brighter and brighter; feel your potential now that you have been released from being a victim. When you feel better after having practiced this visual, you are ready to come out of it and bring your attention back to the room. Feel your feet on the ground and open your eyes knowing you can repeat this visual whenever you need to.

After my client Sarah used this meditation, she said her world opened up. She took this experience and applied it to a recent break-up with her boyfriend. She realized she had put herself in a jail of sorts—a mental prison where she was confined by her own negative thinking and couldn't get out. "Why doesn't he love me?" she would obsess. "What's wrong with me?" she wondered. Realizing there were other thoughts that could come to her rescue—new perspectives that could bail her out—she began to feel much better. New thoughts helped her shift her focus. Maybe he wasn't the best person for her … maybe she could be happier with someone else … maybe she had been ignoring her own needs in favor of his which explained why she felt so tired around him most of the time. She could see her past relationship in a whole different light. Having new perspectives that she understood helped her see the bigger picture. She loved the idea that she was a victor—strong, capable and free! In addition, she prided herself on the fact that she could learn from her mistakes. Her new focus allowed her to move forward and make better choices.

Changing your perspective will help you to open up to other possibilities—thoughts that will benefit you rather than bring you down. Realizing you were looking at life from a victim's perspective helps you to find its opposite—the victor—so that you can begin to feel victorious over what you went through. Your sense of empowerment increases as your clarity grows stronger. Your self-esteem builds, your confidence level rises and you know what you do and don't want. It's such a great way to wake up each day. To go through your day with this kind of clarity is to empower yourself and the life you want to live.

Learning how to connect with your body by tuning into your heart and other body parts (via this exercise and more to come) helps you to integrate this change in perspective and solidifies the link between mind and body. Perspective is powerful—knowing we can realize a different one that serves us in life will help us transform hurtful experiences. We begin to understand that when we take 100% responsibility for our thoughts we take back our power and potential.

Keys to Reflect On:

- Shift your perspective by finding the gifts in your experience
- Use a perspective that empowers you
- Notice and direct your perspective so that you are a victor as opposed to a victim
- See the person who hurt you as one of your best teachers
- Re-write your story from an empowered stance and share it as the victor that you are
- Use visualization to help transform hurt into a new feeling-state that helps you to move on and relinquish the past

Chapter 6
Letting Go is Finding Acceptance

"In the end, just three things matter:
How well we have lived
How well we have loved
How well we have learned to let go"
~ Jack Kornfield

This was a limiting thought that I had after my divorce was final and the custody arrangements had been made:
~ I don't like that my son's baby teeth are at two houses . . . with two different tooth fairies! ~
It was limiting because of the way it made me feel about my sons—trapped without the possibility of my being there for them at one of the most special times in their life. Although the reality of it rang true, it didn't serve me to consider my new life this way. My children would now spend half their time at their father's house. The energy I had wrapped up in having no control over what happened in "the other house" was bringing me down. I needed to let go of this painful thought. Not so much to forget about it, but enough to accept this change, and let it be. Letting go is finding acceptance: this is the sixth spiritual truth to help you start over again.

 ⮬ My son's baby teeth are shared between two houses and two parents who love him with a caring tooth fairy who blesses this rite of passage regardless of where he sleeps at night. ⮬

Letting go of old beliefs to create new ones that better serve you (like the one I used above) is one of the things you will learn in this chapter. Now that you can see how a new perspective helps you to accept your past experiences, you can move forward more readily. Past relationships, jobs, living arrangements, addictions . . . those times are over. It will serve your transition to let go of:

- Asking "why"
- Old hurts/wounds
- What you don't have control over
- Expectations of others
- Old definitions of self

Later in the chapter, I'll discuss how to find and re-claim those parts of you that got lost in the shuffle of your transition. In doing so, you may find parts that don't serve who you are today, so it's time to strengthen the parts of you that will create a stable future. This chapter has the most exercises/meditations (there are seven), so be kind to yourself and don't do them all at once (grin).

Letting Go of Why

First off, let go of asking *why* this experience happened, and instead, view this moment as an opportunity to find acceptance. Believe me when I say that I have been "a victim of *why*" for many years. I used to believe that once I figured out *why*, I would feel better. Oh, so many restless nights and bouts of insomnia! Oh, the trick our minds can play on us in thinking we can find the answer if we just figure out *why*, or find a reason . . . Truthfully, letting go of *why* was the single hardest thing to do in my life. I was such a firm believer in "the quest for *why*" until I realized that seeking *why* didn't make me feel any better.

Asking *why* keeps us trapped in our head and leads us to believe that we can find an answer. We have a false belief that we will feel better after we figure out *why*; that figuring out *why* will make us understand. We are fooled into believing that we can feel comforted by having the answer. Wrong! Wrong, because answers are infinite—there is no right or wrong. There isn't *one* answer that will suffice—that's an illusion. Our thoughts change all the time, and our new thoughts impact the answer we think we've found. Each successive thought could easily produce a whole different answer the next day—and then what? You are back on the treadmill once again trying to figure out *why*!

If you're a big thinker like I am, you believe it's getting you somewhere, and you won't want to let go of thinking so much. It's stimulating! It feels intellectually good to ponder, to analyze . . . It takes care of that need we have to figure things out. Are you programmed that way? Did you enter the world this way? Just know that it's a need you have, and the good news is that you can fulfill this need in other more fruitful ways. You can read an intellectual book, do research online, take a class, learn something new like how to play an instrument, or engage in debate or other thoughtful conversation. It's okay to let go of *why*. Learn how to entertain your mind in other ways—and practice.

Instead, use your power of different perspective (see previous chapter) to help you let go of figuring out *why*. A new perspective will help you find a positive outlook and will provide clarity. For example, "I don't need to figure out *why* (something happened), because it doesn't matter in the long run. The event is over, and I am learning from this experience. I know what my mistakes are, and I will not repeat them." There are a billion reasons *why*, so it's actually beyond your control of realization.

You may be wondering: But how do you know your mistakes if you don't review the experience by asking *why* it happened? You may want to beat yourself up asking rather critically, "*Why* did I do that?" Recall if you will, Chapter Five's set of questions around finding new perspective. They didn't involve *why*; they focused on your experience and what you gained from it. In other words, you can learn from your mistakes using this type of focus. You do the inner work rather than placing your attention outside of yourself on the other person to figure out *why*. The answers are found within by feeling into your experience! You are the answer!

Hand Over Heart. Breathe. Hammock Meditation:

One thing that is good for us to remember each day is to practice letting go, to surrender to what is and let go of the effort of trying to control the outcomes. You may not even notice your body tensing, your shallow breathing, or your jaw tightening. If you haven't had time to release stress or meditate or attend a yoga class, there is always your hammock! If you don't have one, close your eyes and imagine one. A hammock is suspended in the air and yet it embraces your body and holds you up. It's literally a "safety net!" Once you lie down in one, you can completely let go. Add a little swinging motion to it and you can even get the same sensation you had as an infant.

I propose that our bodies registered those early sensations we received as an infant and can instantly recognize them when they occur again. This is another reason to get into a hammock: for self-soothing, and to help your brain stimulate early memories of comfort. The next time you feel fearful, worried or anxious; get into your hammock. It's your safety net for self-soothing comfort and letting go. Spend some time there and allow those sensations to take over and do their thing to restore your sense of well-being. When you get up and go again, you will feel ready and refreshed.

Letting Go of What You Don't Have Control Over

Here's a fun story. My client Rose had been struggling with finding a sense of peace in her home now that her kids had grown up. Her days felt empty and meaningless. Frequently she'd find herself wandering into her kids' rooms lamenting over their things and missing their presence. When she sought my life coaching service she was depressed. Clearly this transition wasn't going well for her. She was still holding onto the past when her house was full and her role was Mom. The present moment didn't feel good to her because she was filled with loneliness and sadness over her empty nest. In addition, there were times when she felt frustrated with her inability to control her kids' decision-making. She thought they were making all kinds of mistakes.

Soon after some perspective sharing with her, she began to see some possibilities waiting for her in her new life. With new thoughts about how this could be an opportunity to do what she's always wanted to do (open up an online store for her craft making), she began to feel better. With my support and encouragement, her thoughts focused more and more on her new career opportunity rather than her loneliness.

After some time, she got the hang of it and put 100% of herself into her new business. Her husband and kids appreciated it too; they didn't like feeling nagged all the time and could enjoy her for who she had become: a happy *entrepreneur*!

There are plenty of issues to let go of once you divorce. One of the biggest ones that I have come across is our belief that we can protect our children at all times. Once custody arrangements are made, we as parents have to accept the new reality of not having our kids around all the time like we used to. We have to let go of whatever happens at the other house. I touched on this fact in the beginning of this chapter, and now I'm going to go deeper. We don't have control over what they watch on TV, how much time they spend playing video games, what foods they eat, whether they are getting their homework done or making sure they get a good night's sleep. Sometimes it feels worse when our children bring us stories of what happens at that other house. We want to support them and let them know it's good they tell us these things, but sometimes what we hear will make us want to go through the roof! We realize we don't have control over these things, and it rouses a lot of negative emotion in us. Our first instinct is to call the ex-spouse angrily and demand an explanation.

The better option is for you to let go of what you don't have control over. Stop and ask yourself, "What would it accomplish to yell at my ex, demand they tell me everything, or ask for my approval? Would it serve everyone's highest good to call over there and chew them out?" The answer is probably not, so take the high road and keep your mouth shut unless there is evidence that what goes on at the other house is affecting the kids' moods, school work, or health. In other words, if there is harm done then you most definitely need to speak up for your children's sake; otherwise let it go.

You can always state your desire. For instance, "I would like it if you called to let me know when they are sick and home from school." They can't argue with that. They can discount it by replying, "I don't care what you want! Stay out of my business and stop trying to control me!" But the point is that you are honoring yourself; you aren't betraying your desire to protect your kids. By doing something about it, you are taking care of your needs and making an effort to take care of your children. It's much easier to let go of things you don't have control over once you take action and make yourself heard. You can then tell yourself, "I did the best I could; I did everything within my power to change things."

If you don't make this effort, you will most likely not feel good about it. Remember that chapter on loving yourself? Honor your needs. Your children might sense that you aren't doing that and will begin resenting you for not saying anything. They might even lose respect for you. By speaking up to state your desire, at least you are staying true to who you are and your need to protect your children. It will also enable you to let go of the incident. By letting go of any control you'd like to have, you surrender to the present moment. You do have control over the moment you decide to use your voice. Speak your truth to express your needs and you can let go of all the rest. We all have fears, but we're much better off letting go of them by focusing on what we do have control over: what goes on at our house, our powerful parenting, the very fact that we do have influence when our children are in our presence.

Focus On What You *Do* Have Control Over

You have control over your emotions. The grief over the loss of a loved one, a broken heart, moving to a new city, or the loss of a job can be felt and then released. I had a huge amount of grief to release around the belief I can't protect my kids 100% anymore. There were many aspects of that truth that made me feel scared. Fears ran through my mind: What is he teaching them? What if they are learning bad habits from him? Can I have any influence at all?

Then of course there were irrational fears such as: What if he shuts me out completely and talks trash about me to our sons? What if he moves out of state or stops contacting me when it's his turn to have our sons? What if he neglects them to the point they get hurt? These were thoughts that kept me up at night. However, to find some relief, I could use what I knew about managing my emotions.

Suffering is alleviated by letting go of fear and having compassion for ourselves. When we find ourselves having a really tough time . . . let it happen. Suffering is okay. It will pass. Remember, emotions are energy, so don't attach yourself to them. Let yourself cry; it's another form of release and letting go.

"Tears are a river that takes you somewhere . . . Tears lift your boat off the rocks, off dry ground, carrying it downriver to someplace better."
~ Clarissa Pinkola Estés

Perspective can change and lift you up in the morning. Each and every day is a new day to let go of the past and begin with a clean slate. It's for you to choose your focus; will it be . . . :

- Victim or Victor?
- Confusion or Clarity?
- Head space (thinking too much) or heart space (connection with your Divine self)?
- Letting your emotions run your life or taking charge by managing them?

Focus on what you do have control over. You do have control over your own thoughts. I had to let go of the thoughts that weren't serving me, so I learned to re-direct them. I could even delete them at times. My thoughts needed to serve me, not bring me down. By re-directing my thoughts to those things I do have control over, I was able to help myself feel better. Use the present moment to be mindful of your thoughts and choose wisely. It's comforting to know that you have this kind of freedom available to you at all times.

Using your ability to choose a different perspective will help too. The last chapter helped you to find relief using a different perspective. A simple twist of a negative thought can transform into a positive helpful thought. A new encouraging thought helps us to let go. The example I use here with losing my ability to protect my children at all times can be seen in a new light with this perspective: They are learning how to become independent, self-reliant human beings.

Let Go of Past Beliefs

Thoughts that don't serve us can be grouped into a bigger concept: a belief system. We all behave according to our beliefs; they are the underlying reason we communicate, act or think. A belief system is a group of beliefs and thoughts that support our reason for behaving the way we do. When we are in the midst of a transition and trying to start over, it's a good idea to examine the beliefs we are carrying into our new lives. In other words, realize which beliefs are hindering you rather than benefiting your ability to move on. It's time to release them.

When you release old beliefs, you also release old wounds. For example, in my case I had to release my belief that single mothers don't get the support they need, either emotional or physical. Each time I acted from that belief it was registered in my lower back as "lack of support." This belief also created horrible hurt feelings such as: "I am tired, I can't do this alone, I will always be alone, there is nobody to help me, I don't have the energy to do this on my own." These beliefs would accumulate in my lower back and cause me physical pain because our bodies carry our emotions. Letting go of these hurtful thoughts and feelings allowed me to begin again, this time with a clean slate. Then I could access the possibility of the present moment and use what I know how to do, which is manage these thoughts and emotions. Remember, "Six steps to managing emotions" in Chapter Four? Now is the time to use them.

Not only do we benefit emotionally from releasing old beliefs, we also improve our behaviors. In other words, we stop repeating the same mistakes. Our behavior stems from what we think about and those beliefs we hold in our hearts. The previous example, of my belief that "single mothers don't get the support they need," proved just that because my actions followed suit. I over-compensated. I never asked for help, and when I did I felt guilty, as if I wasn't enough. I ended up putting out too much effort and accomplished more than I actually needed to. It caused me to feel too tired at the end of the day. My belief acted like a chip I carried on my shoulder, but I thought I had to be Superwoman. I had to do it all. The price I paid was to feel worn out and on my way to experiencing a physical ailment known as adrenal fatigue. What also happened, was that my friends and family interpreted that I didn't need help because I appeared so capable and strong.

Once I turned this belief around by becoming conscious of it and letting it go, I was granted a much better belief that allowed for freedom and ease: I am supported with help whenever I need it. This new belief made me feel good and realize that there was potential for getting my needs met. It also helped me to ask for help, because I didn't have to be Superwoman anymore. Letting go of the chip on my shoulder, I could accept help when it was offered, and when I didn't receive it, I could ask for it. I could also rest when I needed to. This change made me feel good again:

I felt supported for once in my life!

Hand Over Heart. Breathe. Create New Beliefs Journal Exercise:

What are some beliefs that you now realize don't work for you? Do you have a certain belief that causes you to hit the "replay" button over and over again? When I'd think to myself, "Single mothers don't get support," my belief created my behavior. My behavior led to repeating the same mistakes, trying to "do it all" rather than asking for the help I needed. Now that you are getting conscious of your thoughts and behaviors, you probably have realized some of your own limiting beliefs. Write them down here so you can keep track of them when they come up. Once you are aware of them you can make a conscious effort to let them go and replace them with new beliefs.

For example:

Old Belief	New Belief
Single mothers don't receive help	Single mothers are supported with help when they need it
I don't have enough energy	I have all the energy I need in the present moment
There's never enough time	I can create time
I'm not enough	I always do my best and that's enough

Hand Over Heart. Breathe. Visualize Your Old Beliefs Dispersing Meditation:

Using your imagination, release these feelings and beliefs to make way for new ones that benefit you . . . visualize this happening. Bring to mind everything that goes along with your limiting belief. Pretend you are in that belief with all of your emotions attached to it, as if it's happening right now. Notice and observe how your body changes and feels holding this belief. You know for sure without a doubt; this belief is not serving your best interest. Once you have tuned in and can feel strong in your knowing, you can take the next step: let it go!

The final piece of releasing, and just as important, is finding a place for it to go. I like to visualize the old belief and everything it entails leaving my head, going up into a ball of light that I imagine is big enough to hold it. Watch the ball of light transform the negative energy into a brilliant golden light and then delight in the magical rain that comes out of it. Imagine golden drops of new life spreading back down onto the earth. Dispersed and gone. If you are not a very visual person, grab a hold of something instead: take a rock and bury it or throw it into nearby water; burn a fire with those things you want to let go of (maybe photos?) There are so many ways to symbolize this release. Feel free to try out as many as you like until you find one that truly feels like the job is done.

I like to imagine a vacuum cleaner sucking up the negative energy in my body. Other times I need to write down what I am releasing and then light the piece of paper on fire, watch it burn and turn into ash. I know others have buried things in their yards or at the beach. Then again, some people swear by simply screaming it out.

Hand Over Heart. Breathe. New life, New Belief Meditation:

Now that you have a new space that has opened up in your body, how does it feel? For some it can be freeing, as if a weight has been lifted. For others it might feel empty, void, vacant; without the happy feeling they expected. That's why the next step is important; fill yourself up with light and love. Again you can do this using visualization or using something more concrete like an actual picture cut out from a magazine. You might choose to symbolize it with a stone that you found, a beaded necklace or a ring band (something you wear).

Bring into your being a new sense of what you'd like to create and sit with it. Maybe your new belief is about honoring yourself first from now on, fulfilling your needs on a daily basis, or making time for something that matters to you. I wear a turquoise band on my finger to symbolize that I am now committed to my *self.* Infuse the new belief/physical symbol with all of your positive emotion. Feel the lightness and warmth of new possibilities take hold. Enjoy how good it feels. Spend enough time so that your body registers it as something permanent. You have created a memory. Each time you re-visit this meditation it will get stronger. It will be like "logging in" (no password necessary).

Let Go of Expectations of Others to Find Acceptance

I had the good fortune of working with Jennifer McLean (author, speaker and healer) prior to her success with *Healing with the Masters,* a regular online teleseminar series featuring well-known teachers in the field of personal growth. She said that when you change, others will increase the volume of their behavior. However, there will be some people in your life who don't understand. Rather than please them, stay true to who you are becoming. It's an opportunity for you to decide to let them "fall away." If they cannot resonate with your new energy vibration, they need to go.

Letting go of a hurtful experience also includes letting go of the people involved. Or at least their "bad" behavior. But were they really being "bad?"

Here's something to consider: what if those people in your life (with whom you find yourself getting routinely upset) were doing the best they could? If you seriously believed this were the case, would that alleviate some of the sting you feel toward them? When you take away your expectations of this person (They should know . . . or, why can't they . . .) all that remains is the person. If they are doing all they are capable of doing then can you really be upset with them? See how letting go of expectations invites compassion into your heart? Try doing this the next time you are frustrated by someone's behavior and see for yourself how much better you feel when you let go of the expectations that only serve you disappointment and hurt.

Ready to go a step further? What if you stopped and spent some more time in wonder to look at this person from this new perspective? That they are doing the best they can. Give them the benefit of the doubt. It doesn't harm you to do so. It releases you from the burden of thinking that they can do better. It also reduces the negative feelings that follow when they can't. Using this perspective will make you feel better.

Want to go even deeper? Let's say, you had the ability to see into their heart space. Let's say you do this, and you can see their heart is all clouded up, confused or detached. Now that you can see their "blocks," do you feel even more compassion rising up inside yourself? Can you at least regard this person differently? Now that you can actually see (or imagine) they are incapable or that they are doing the best they can, are you capable of letting go of what you want from them? Can you let go of having them meet your own expectations for what you think they should be doing? Now you can also see that your frustration and disappointment starts and stops with you. Yes?

In other words, now that you can see they are incapable of doing what you want, you are left with your feelings and emotions around it. It becomes a new issue: what do you want to do? Accepting others as they are then requires some emotional maturity on your part, right? Because now you have to figure out what to do with the anger, frustration or disappointment you are feeling about this person. You are back to caring for your own needs. And after you deal with these emotions, then you have to figure out what to do next because as long as you keep expecting this person to meet your expectations, you will stay stuck in that dynamic between the two of you; you will keep doing that dance.

The interaction may be serving you in one of many different ways: it allows you to stay mad and resentful so that you don't have to address your own feelings; it enables you to stay stuck in confusion so you don't have to change and do something about it; you get to stay safely passive; and it helps you to continue to ignore and neglect your own needs. This way, you can stay focused on the other person instead of yourself—it's much easier that way, isn't it?

Isn't this interaction tiring? Does it really serve your best interest? Don't these expectations make you feel bad? Once you are able to accept this person for who they are and what they are incapable of doing, then the opportunity is there for you to change. That's exciting because that part you do have control over.

This perspective transforms our view of this person from someone who is behaving badly into someone we can accept for who they are. What if nobody is ever behaving badly, they are just doing what they know how to do? The range of emotion behind each belief tags our thoughts and they can be transformed as well. We can go from feeling hate, resentment, anger . . . to compassion, acceptance, maybe even love (depending on how good you are at this (smile)). Doesn't that feel much better? The object is to let go so you can feel good again.

You may wonder about the disappointment you'll feel once you decide this person isn't capable. For instance, if you bring your judgment into the picture, you will find yourself exclaiming, "That's terrible! What an awful person . . ." If you begin thinking they are wrong because they are not able to fulfill your expectations, then you are judging who they are. Once again, judging others starts with you. Do you have to make them bad? Or can they be who they are? Can you accept them for what they keep showing you and not judge them in return? Is it in your best interest to spend your energy feeling angry at them?

Blaming them is not the answer either. Blaming others will only make you feel angry and resentful. Let's look at nature. As Vietnamese Buddhist Monk Thich Nhat Hahn explains, "When you plant lettuce, if it does not grow well, you don't blame the lettuce. You look for reasons it is not doing well. It may need fertilizer, or more water, or less sun. You never blame the lettuce. Yet if we have problems with our friends or family, we blame the other person. But if we know how to take care of them, they will grow well, like the lettuce. Blaming has no positive effect at all, nor does trying to persuade using reason and argument. That is my experience. No blame, no reasoning, no argument, just understanding. If you understand, and you show that you understand, you can love, and the situation will change."[32]

Maybe it feels like you need to forgive them. It could be that after so much disappointment, you have taken their actions personally and it leaves you feeling like you need to forgive them in order to have them remain in your life. We'll be addressing forgiveness in the next chapter. You can visit that now if you like, but then come back here to this point and pick up where you left off. Otherwise you'll be skipping part of the process of transforming the past.

Hand Over heart. Breathe. Find the Root of Your Expectations Exercise:

Use the following list to help you to see the "root" of the issue that's upsetting when you encounter it in others.

Sometimes it can be difficult to identify what it is about others that causes you to feel disappointed. Once you can pinpoint those behaviors in others that upset you, you will be able to move forward with your transition: you can let it go, use a different perspective, find compassion or have forgiveness.

The chart below can also provide you with an opportunity to learn something about yourself. For example, using the second one "Returning phone calls": Let's say you find yourself routinely upset with a person for not returning your phone calls. Reading the chart you can see they have issues around follow-through, respect and reciprocity. Using this information you can acquire a new understanding of what that person is capable or is not capable of. You can also learn what their weaknesses are or which areas are challenging to them. Recognizing these issues will help you to let go of your expectations.

Here's another example. Let's say you recently moved into a new living situation and find yourself continually being let down by a roommate who can't pay rent because they don't have a job. They say they want to find a job but never take action to find one. Based on this chart, you can realize they are probably dealing with these issues: confusion and lack of motivation. Knowing this about that person will help you decide what to do next. You can let it go, use a different perspective, find compassion or have forgiveness.

<u>What Are They Capable Of?</u>

Behavior/Quality/Trait	Root Issue
Taking Action	Having clarity, heart, motivation, mind and body connection
Returning phone calls	Following through, respect, reciprocity
Saying yes and doing what you say you will do	Keeping your word, integrity, honoring, respect, honesty
Saying I love you	Expressing love, showing affection, giving, feeling gratitude
Giving a hug	Showing affection, expressing self, giving, seeking connection, expressing love
Eating healthy meals/food	Taking care of self, loving self, honoring self, consciously aware, feeling good
Taking care of business: paying bills, house cleaning, chores	Taking care of self, self-discipline, honoring self, paying attention to personal needs, feeling grounded
Active in sports/athletic/active	Expressing bodily desires, kinesthetic, physical and mental strength, mind-body connection, coordination
Playing	Letting go and having fun, experiencing joy, light, spontaneity, humor/laughter
Spending/earning money	Interacting with give-and-take energy, balance, high self-esteem, abundance, free, open

You could also regard these issues as qualities that you value. For example, I value a good hug, so I would find myself feeling let down by a significant other who didn't. The root of the issue is that they aren't capable of showing this type of affection. I can get upset because they don't meet my expectations, or I can let go of my expectations and figure out how to fulfill this need within myself.

I can then tell myself, "Okay I need to let that go and appreciate something different about this person." Or I can question whether I want to be with someone who isn't capable of something I value and find it somewhere else. The point being, that once you can respond with this conscious awareness, it's easier to let go because you can see the underlying issue that leads you to an action step. This chart is intended to help you get clarity so that you can move forward and avoid getting stuck in drama that doesn't serve you.

Here is another example. Let's say you have just broken up with your romantic partner and you would like to remain amicable

Breaking Point

When we are so close to
who we truly are,
there is a nakedness
about how we carry
ourselves throughout
the day.

Having vented
everything to this
person who listened
so well,
I began to feel stripped
of all false pretenses.
I wondered, why bother
with artificial sentiment?
I am letting go, to be
purely who I am in this
moment.

Too bad that most
moments are
disappointing.

We are at a point now
where he never says
sorry anymore.
In part it is appreciated.
Yes, we are real now,
we've released our pain.
But it also adds to the
disappointment.
When there is no
remorse,
you are left with words
that sting,
and you reel heavy with
emotion.
Words soar like an
arrow cutting the air
with a sharp tip,
aiming for the heart
with great precision.
Ouch. Pure hurt. Pure
pain.

But it is what it is.
It's been released.
And it's real.
An opening
for finally closing
the door,
to open up a new one.

~ Karen Croley

so that you can continue to share a pet, handle mail, and other responsibilities that you once shared together. You'd like to take care of business with this person, so you can accomplish these tasks. But this person isn't cooperating; they're not returning your phone calls, they're not friendly when you do get a chance to talk, and they're not responding to your requests to get your things back. How do you let go of your expectation of this person to act in a caring, responsible way toward you and your needs?

Dealing with people who are being difficult or challenging can be a tricky task—not to mention an extremely frustrating one. But rather than use up all of your energy feeling angry and resentful with them for acting that way, you can take a deep breath and realize you have choices. You always have choices, even when it feels like you don't. In this case, your choices include surrendering your need to get business done right away. You may need to wait a while and let time do its part to work its magic, whether that's a matter of hours, days or months. Depending on how badly you need your things back or for the correspondence to happen, it could mean just waiting it out. Letting go of time or your need to get it done right now could help the situation.

Another choice is to ask for help—maybe a professional counselor could play mediator or a friend could act as a liaison. A third choice is to take the high road and extend an overly-friendly hand to this person. With all the authentic intention you can muster, relate to this person as if you want what is best for them too—not just yourself. You want the both of you to get your needs met during this closure.

Eventually all of the behavior that we make allowances for, all of the behavior we settle for adds up and takes energy away from us—energy that is there for us to feel good and feel fulfilled. *It's our birthright to feel good.*

I wrote this poem (see side bar) at a critical time in my marriage. We were at a crossroad where we decided to finally let go of all false pretenses. This allowed us to take our next step.

Don't Take It Personally

Something else I have found very useful in letting go is to adopt a perspective from one of my favorite books, *The Four Agreements*. It is, "Don't take anything personally." It aligns nicely with letting go of expectations. When you decide not to take someone else's actions personally, it's easier to let go of your expectations of them and vice versa. We get some emotional separation from the circumstance, and we can see that person more clearly, realizing they are acting out of their own past history or experiences in life. Those things include everything from relationships with family members, past trauma, to the mood they're in that day. We don't need to take their actions personally; we can let go of our hurt feelings. That feels better, doesn't it?

Hopefully you are getting the idea now, that everything can get tangled up together: threads of hurt and disappointment twist with letting go of expectations and taking other people's behavior personally. You'll find that once you weed out one thread and come to peace with it, other threads will get lighter and be easier to transform/heal as well. It's natural for these threads to be intertwined. Such is the matrix of life itself because everything is connected. The most important threads remaining will be the ones that lead back to you.

Letting go of what involves others and their behavior allows us to shift our focus back to ourselves. This inner work is what helps us to move forward with what we do want in our lives.

Finding Self

Now we have an opportunity to see ourselves in a new light! The final stages of letting go lead us back to ourselves and re-connecting to the true essence of who we are: our souls. We have the chance to see that we have evolved; we're not that person from our past anymore. However, another important piece is that we own up to our role in what happened. We'll achieve clarity once we can see our part in the past experience.

Hand Over Heart. Breathe. Past-self Review and Recovering Your Heart Threads Journal Exercise:

Set aside some time when you are feeling relaxed. Light a candle to set up the sacred space for you to honor your past experience. Have a journal ready to write down your thoughts. Bring to mind and heart those past experiences. Review those events and ask yourself:

- What you liked/didn't like about yourself
- What you wanted (wished)/didn't ask for
- What you needed/didn't ask for
- Who you were then and who you are now
- Reflect on the "gifts" you gained from the previous chapter.

For instance, I am a lot stronger than I thought I was! I had no idea how much inner strength I had until my divorce happened. Another big realization about who I am was that, for the first time in my life, I felt smart. There I was 38 1/2 years old, and people were telling me that I was intelligent. That just hadn't happened before! This helped me to let go of my fears of feeling incapable and own up to being the best single parent I could be.

Get to the heart of who you are now. Find the common thread of those personality traits that remain in you today—those parts of you that you have held onto that I like to call "heart threads" where your soul resonates most. For me, it was recovering my love for photography. It will feel like you found a thread of who you are, and when you tug on it, the thread will lead you to the full essence of that part of you and your soul. It could be your sense of humor, your passion for running, a hobby, or an outlook on life. Maybe it was a gathering with friends once a year that you forsook. Remember those parts of you first that have stayed strong and steadfast.

Let yourself feel empowered by this exercise. Sometimes you will come across memories from your past to help you realize a heart thread (that deeper sense of who you are). Now go back and reclaim those parts of you that you lost or gave up along the way due to a job, a relationship break-up or an addiction. Was there a spirituality inside you that weakened? Did you let relationships with friends or family members slip away? Did you stop going to the gym? What needs do you still have today that you have forgotten about? What's most important to you? Write these thoughts down and follow them until you reach some of your own answers.

For example, (and this shows how interesting life is!) while I was on a break from writing this book, I decided to straighten up the room downstairs. I found something I created eight years ago. It stood out for me to see loud and clear. I picked it up, and it was a photograph I had taken while on a trip in Yosemite with my then husband and two sons.

I had taken many beautiful pictures during that trip. It felt wonderful to capture the beauty of the valley in all its shapes and forms. There were ancient redwood trees with wide canopies reaching into the deepest of blue skies, waterfalls spilling from heights you never imagined water could come from, and gentle deer that grazed in wide open meadows beneath huge boulders of granite cliffs. I was feeling the power I had within to capture beauty and share it with others. I went home and made cards out of some of the pictures and felt really good about it.

I remembered a theme that emerged out of the photos I took during that time. I had an interest in paths, so I focused the viewfinder of my camera on these paths: ones that wound deep into the forest; other walking paths that led visitors through nature; and some paths naturally made by deer and elk. Have you seen the photo series of doors? I felt drawn and attracted to that theme as well. I think they're mostly European doors with architecture so simple yet unique, and colored turquoise or burgundy. I got to thinking . . . paths and doorways are both symbols of transition! My soul was yearning for a path out of my current situation. I was longing with desire for these paths and doorways that led away from where I stood.

It was easy for me to see it several years later. I was divorced and living a whole different life than I had before. I spent many years looking at these "images" rather than stepping through the doorway or making steps on a new path. And yet, in remembering my love for photography and for Mother Nature, I felt alive again as if I had recovered a part of myself that I had let go. I had uncovered a major heart thread. I decided this part of me is very much a part of who I am and too significant to ever let go of again.

Hand Over Heart. Breathe. Spring Cleaning Exercise:

It doesn't have to be spring necessarily, in order for you to clean out the clutter in your home. Clutter inside your living space can add to any feelings being of overwhelmed you may already have. If you aren't keeping a steady flow of things coming into your home and things leaving, then it's possible to have things pile up. Feeling overwhelmed leads to apathy which can look and feel like depression. Noticing this, you might wonder to yourself, "When did I stop caring . . . about my yard, my bedroom, my living area?" It can be deceiving—the stuff you accumulate in one sense makes you feel safe and secure, almost like a warm blanket against feeling lonely. If that is the case, when you begin to clear out the stuff it could remind you of being alone and that things have changed.

On the other hand, if you leave the clutter in place, it can make you feel heavy and pull you down. Clutter can make you feel trapped, as if you cannot move forward.

I encourage you to motivate now and get rid of your stuff! A good rule of thumb is that if you haven't used it in the last year, then you don't actually need it—get rid of it! Team up with your neighbors or do a solo garage sale. If that doesn't appeal to you, make a donation to the Goodwill or any local thrift shop. In order to be successful with this exercise you will need to first motivate (reward yourself with something), get organized (three piles—one to keep, one to toss, and one to give away), and move swiftly (don't get caught up in what you find and re-think too much about getting rid of it).

One of my friends revealed to me that her husband expected her to clean and cook and care for the children while all he expected of himself was to work/provide the income. This way of living never felt right to her. And yet she continued to meet his expectations. (She had let go of her own desire for partnership.) Meanwhile, he was free to come and go as he pleased while she was stuck with keeping the house clean and all of the parenting. They were also living beyond their means because her husband came home regularly with a new "toy."

One day, she found herself in their garage surveying all of his toys. In doing so, she realized she had neglected her own love for sports. She had one bike compared to his: windsurfing equipment, three bikes, skis, and racquetball equipment. All of a sudden she realized she had let this part of herself go. She said it was empowering for her to regain some sense of self back. And do you know what? She said he never even used any of his stuff, he was so busy working. She got bold and began selling it all. It became the act and turning point that served to fuel her decision to move out the following month with the money she made from selling their things!

Although this example is kind of extreme, it shows what we will do when we suddenly realize we've been neglecting ourselves for a very long time. Measures to re-gain self can become drastic if there have been years and years of neglect. In some cases, it's a threat of divorce, a trip to Bali, or going on strike and refusing to perform any more housework. Sound familiar? The thing to keep in mind is to never lose yourself in relationships, jobs or addictions.

Never let go of what's important to you. But if you have, it's never too late to find these and bring them back! Tug on your heart thread until you reach your soul.

Keys to Reflect On:

- Let go of asking "Why?"
- Let go of old beliefs and adopt new ones that serve and benefit your emotional well-being
- Let go of expectations of others to find acceptance and compassion
- Use a different perspective to help you let go: "Are they capable?" "Don't take it personally."
- Re-focus and shift your attention back to self
- Realize your "heart threads" to reconnect with your soul.

Chapter 7
Forgiveness is Liberating

"Forgiveness means letting go of the past."
~Gerald Jampolsky

A Revelation occurred to me while writing this chapter of the book. You see, I had been stuck. It's a perfect example to share—how a belief can hold you prisoner, costing you energy, focus and drive. As I was getting ready to complete this chapter of the book, I had the belief that I needed to have forgiven what happened and have it all wrapped up, neat and tidy, so I could go on to the next chapter. With this last chapter's focus on forgiveness, this issue in particular made the process seem more challenging for me. I kept asking myself, "Am I really all done forgiving my sons' father?" The answer would always come back quickly, "No." So then I felt stuck and unable to move forward to write the next chapter of the book. This book had been sitting untouched for eight months.

Then I had a conversation with my friend Christa and shared with her my troubles in finishing this chapter. For some reason I so easily heard the words roll off my tongue as though they were poised and ready for that very moment telling her about this predicament: How can I move forward with the book if I haven't been able to complete the process of forgiving my sons' father? In that moment, I realized I had wanted to close the chapter up like a locked door keeping my vulnerability safe. However, my friend Christa challenged me as she always so lovingly does, "Is that really possible? Isn't forgiveness more likely to unravel and expand as the years go by? As you begin living this truth, so does your ability to forgive," she said. Well, the lights began going on like I had hit the jackpot of realizations. It made so much sense.

Forgiving another (especially if you have a long history with them) is a multi-layered and multi-faceted process. There are bound to be new and interesting things for you to look at during this process of unveiling. With each new grievance, so too arrives a new "gift" or strength to add to your repertoire.

I invite you to take a moment to pause and place your hand over your heart. Take a nice deep breathe in to connect to your heart. And a nice long exhale to center yourself there.

Forgiveness is an important piece of the puzzle for transforming your past. This chapter builds on what you have learned from previous chapters with the purpose of setting you free to feel gratitude for what you have been through.

I think the absolute best example of someone we all know who has been successful in practicing forgiveness is the late Nelson Mandela. I'm honored to share his achievement now because when I first wrote this, he was nearing the end of his days. Who better to teach us how to forgive than someone who has been imprisoned and tortured in South Africa for 27 years for his public rejection of Apartheid? Nearly his entire life was taken away from him because his beliefs contradicted those of his nation's government at the time. Yet he was able, upon his release, to unite his country—even befriend the very men who imprisoned him.

Through his actions, he taught that forgiveness, generosity and respect were just as powerful in winning political persuasion as any gun could be. Imagine the hostile environment he confronted. His country was fraught with tension and political unrest. Yet his talks for reconciliation with his captors, and then President F. W. de Klerk, led to the end of Apartheid and established a democratic government where he, Mandela, would reign as President. (And also earned a Nobel Peace Prize with de Klerk in December of 1993.) Mandela "... showed it is possible to be a great human being and a great politician at the same time; that showing respect to friends and enemies alike can get you a long, long way; and that nothing beats the combination—in Mandela's case, the seamless convergence—of magnanimity and power[33]." We have been blessed with his example of forgiveness. What an amazing teacher he was!

Forgiveness Is Like an Onion

First off, forgiveness is not a spiritual truth you will understand overnight! Rather, it's a process of unraveling layers. Consider an onion and how many layers of skin it has. Each peeled off layer leads you closer to the pure essence of the onion. And the tears? Well, they come on stronger as you peel them off, don't they? Just when you think you are done forgiving that person, another layer of hurt is unveiled. However, the good news is that each layer can be healed. This includes both forgiving another and yourself. What seemed raw and unnerving about your past won't stay that way as long as you address it. Forgiveness is a process of healing.

The idea of dealing with layers of forgiveness may provoke a sense of fear, and naturally so. It can seem heavy and foreboding. That's okay and understandable. When you are ready, simply make the decision to forgive. This chapter will guide you through the process.

Second, know that forgiveness is an experience of letting go. By forgiving someone, you have the opportunity to release a lot of pent-up negative energy that is causing you hurt and sorrow. Is that confusing or misleading? Like most people, you are probably wondering, why do I need to befriend that person again? Well, the good news is that you don't have to! Forgiving is really all about giving yourself a gift: the gift of freedom. Freedom from what, you may be wondering? *When we forgive someone, we are freeing up our hearts to feel good again.*

When Phyllis Rodriguez and Aicha el-Wafi got together, I don't think they expected any miracles. I watched them give their talk about forgiveness (a video on TEDWomen recorded in May of 2011.) Phyllis had lost her son in the 9/11 World Trade Center attacks. Aicha's son was found guilty for playing a role in those attacks and is serving a life sentence. A year after this tragedy, they met, already aware of their mutual bond: the love for their sons and suffering for their loss. One of them reached out (Aicha) to break the ice and begin the process of forgiveness. Gradually, a friendship was born despite their initial fear of one another. Since then, they have traveled through Europe and the U.S. to share their story. They formed the Forgiveness Project, "Exploring the possibilities of forgiveness through real stories." To learn more, you can visit http://theforgivenessproject.com. Another amazing example for us to learn from!

There Are 4 Steps to Forgiveness:

1. **Be willing to choose to forgive**
2. **Use what you have learned thus far**
3. **Take the leap of faith**
4. **Have courage**

Step One: Be willing to choose to forgive.

Consider how much time you spend each day with hurtful memories and feelings caused by a person or past experience. Now that you have begun practicing the present moment and have gained more awareness about what you're feeling and thinking every day, you probably have a much better idea about this than you did before. Feeling those feelings and thinking those thoughts are dragging you down and zapping your energy. However, when you own your part in it—choosing how you'd like to feel about it, then you can free yourself from your emotional turmoil. You can see that it really has nothing to do with that person at all. Forgiving is all about you and the choice you make to feel better. By releasing the need to hold onto the hurt, you are giving yourself a wonderful gift of space in your heart to feel good again.

I use my example to demonstrate what it's like to go through the steps of forgiveness. We are divorced now, but because we share three children, there are times when my sons' father and I need to interact and share the same space. There were times when I was dealing with hurt feelings, and there were points of contention between us not to mention the heaps of emotional pain that caused our divorce to begin with. However, any difficulty or discomfort was an opportunity for me to release more resentment I'd been holding onto. Fairly fresh from our divorce, he began to coach our son's little league team, so I had plenty of opportunities! Despite hurt feelings from our past together, it was my job, as my sons' mother, to attend each and every game—but also, to put a smile on my face and endure watching the spectacle of their father putting on such a good show, right? I didn't necessarily have to enjoy these times, but I at least wanted to feel okay about attending the games, so I could focus on watching my son.

By having self-awareness, you can feel how a non-forgiving attitude is affecting you. At first I noticed the resentment and anger settle into my body, and how awful it felt during each game. These emotions triggered the realization that I had more forgiving to do. I decided that I didn't want to "feel these feelings." I wanted to feel good.

"To forgive is to set a prisoner free and discover that the prisoner was you." ~ Lewis B. Smedes

Hand Over Heart. Breathe. Affirm Forgiveness Exercise:

Now, I invite you to consider these powerful words intended to start your journey in forgiveness. They will help prepare you to take the first step in finding the willingness to forgive.

Here are some statements for you to relate to and speak out loud (feel free to substitute any word or emotion so that is fits you best):

- "I release the need to remember (name them) with resentment in my heart."
- "I release the need to view (name them) as someone that hurt me."
- "I release the need to hate (name them)."
- "I release the need to think of (name them) as a bad person."
- "I release the need to talk about (name them) using profanity, bad names, or shame."

Repeat saying these statements out loud until you feel them resonate in your body. Notice how you feel after repeating these statements. You have begun to own your powerful emotions about your past or this person. By feeling the emotion that comes up, you are giving yourself this release. Can you begin to see how your role in forgiving is all about you and your willingness to do so? When you are done, notice if your energy has shifted from an unwillingness to a willingness to let go. Repeat as necessary until you feel a difference in how you are feeling.

Step Two: Use what you have learned thus far.

Use a different perspective, let go of expectations, manage your emotions and use the present moment. I used my awareness of the present moment and directed my focus—where did I want to place it? Did I want to place my attention upon the negative feelings I had about my sons' father, or did I want to place it upon "what is working" in this scenario? I wanted to place my focus on what I did have control over—how I perceived the situation. "What is working," was that he was providing a great activity for my sons that made them feel loved and supported.

I noticed that after directing my thoughts and using this perspective, I began to feel better. My heart opened up and it wasn't so difficult to put a smile on my face anymore. When I looked out onto the infield and watched my sons' father, I changed my perception and let go of our past together. I allowed myself to view him as a loving father who made the time and effort to coach his son's baseball team. I began noticing and appreciating what a good job he was doing. I even could feel some connection with him when our son practiced a new skill like pitching to the other team for the first time. The emotions of anger and resentment released when I practiced this. Forgiveness gives you the freedom to be yourself and return to the self that is naturally happy and content. And it simply feels so much better to be in your own skin without that layer of negativity, doesn't it?

<u>Hand Over Heart. Breathe. Emotional Release Journal Exercise:</u>

The following questions will help "chip away" at that fossil of hurt you've buried for so long. They will also raise emotions that you need to deal with. Part of the process of forgiving involves managing emotions and using a new perspective.

I invite you to ask yourself:

- Do holding these emotions in every day make you feel good or bad? Explain.
- Do you see your grudge against this person or what happened as "emotional baggage?" If so, describe.
- Do you view this emotional baggage as weighing you down or as uplifting you?

- If so, how would it feel to put it down, to let it go?
- Does it serve you to hold onto the hurt, sorrow and anger (by not forgiving)?
- If so, how do you benefit from holding onto the hurt?

Try a new perspective using a "What if . . . ?" question about this person such as:

- "What if this person was doing the best that they could?"
- "What if this person came into your life to teach you something?"
- "What if this person was never meant to be in that type of relationship with you?"
- "What if you could appreciate them for what they showed you or revealed to you about yourself?"

Do any of these perspectives help to shift the emotion? Do you feel lighter? Write down your thoughts and which perspective you decide to use. Tape them to your mirror if you think that will help you to remember. It will also help to encode them into your brain and begin the process of incorporating new beliefs and perspectives that serve you rather than harm you.

This exercise is not about liking this person again. You can still choose not to be in the same room with them, but wouldn't it be nice to feel like you could stand it? If you had to share something with this person, wouldn't it feel much better if you had no more ill will toward them? It's a heavy load to carry anger and resentment. Perhaps you don't realize it yet because you haven't let it go.

Maybe your anger or resentment has become comfortable like a cushion... so much so that it's a freaky thought to give it away and not have this cushion anymore. Simply ask yourself: Do I want to feel better? That's what it came down to for me. I simply wanted to feel better. This became my drive and what motivated me to forgive. Take care of yourself by treating this process gently—make it a sacred act—light a candle to signify that Spirit is with you and supporting you. Use the following exercise to help you with powerful emotions that seem unwilling to release.

Hand Over Heart. Breathe. Body Dialogue Exercise:

Upon finishing this exercise you will have a new tool to use that connects both mind and body. And you will have a new perspective that originates from your body vs. your mind. By tuning into your body, you can receive information to help you get a better perspective. And when you actively participate in your own healing, you are telling the universe you are capable and self-sufficient! Now, that's a great thing! As for my clients and myself, I use this exercise to get in touch with those emotions that are calling my attention by showing me physical discomfort.

Ask yourself, where in your body do these feelings (for instance, anger and betrayal) register with you? Is it your heart? Your lungs (because your breathing has become interrupted or shallow or constricted)? Maybe these feelings are tightening your gut or your stomach? Does your head feel heavy, cluttered or achy? I name these places because these are common body parts that register negative emotions.

When we repress these emotions they can get stuck there until we open the door to let them out, so to speak. Using our imagination, we have our own unique way of getting in touch with our feelings inside our bodies. For some, these feelings may register to us as a color, shape or form. For me, there have been times when my feelings looked like yellow bile . . . black goopy slime . . . or a large red shield. It really doesn't matter what shape or form you decide they are, just as long as you are in touch with them intimately. Use your imagination or even pretend. I know that may sound strange, but if you aren't used to this kind of thing that is where you begin. After some time using this method, it will become easier for you and will notice your ability to imagine or visualize what's inside your body.

Once you are in touch with how those feelings have registered in your body, simply listen. Pretend to have a conversation. Most of the time hurt feelings get lodged in our body and act as a protection mechanism. It's like your body has added a new layer of armor to guard against further hurt. So if you were to imagine a conversation with your body, an example could look like the following:

After tuning into your body and what you are feeling, you might realize the feeling is coming from your chest area. You bring all your attention there and wait until you sense that it's actually

148

your lungs. Use your imagination to see what it looks like—if it's healthy looking or not. If not, what is there? Black sludge, hard metal, or is it bound with wire? Your lungs are calling your attention.

Here is an example of how a body dialogue might present itself:

"What is it that you need?" you ask your lungs (anger).

"Attention," your lungs (anger) reply. *"You keep ignoring me,"* the lungs (anger) adds, *"And now it's hard to breathe easily."*

"Okay, I am here now listening. Tell me more," you say to your lungs (anger).

"To be free and function well, I need this hurt here to be paid attention to," the lungs (anger) say.

"Okay what is it that I need to know?" you question. (This is the key question to ask!)

"Stop and listen, be gentle with yourself and acknowledge your anger. Feel it and release it instead of stuffing it here," your lungs (anger) reply.

"Thank you lungs (anger). I will do that now. Thank you for protecting me this way. How would you like me to get rid of (the large metal shield you're wearing, for example)?"

To close, we go in with a pretend vacuum cleaner and suck up the muck/mess, soften, or un-bound/open up the space so that our body can feel whole again. But there are other methods for clearing the body as well such as; imagining a waterfall of rushing water to cleanse and send the muck down into the earth to be neutralized. You can soften the space by imagining a swirling of colors to whip through ties/binding. Or if you are skilled at Acupressure, EFT (The Tapping Method) or Reflexology—these are also excellent techniques for releasing. Again, don't hesitate to call on a professional for additional help.

When I work with clients with this exercise, they get a new appreciation for their bodies and the power they can access to work with them. With the new connection between mind and body, they find they have made a step toward wellness and well-being. You can experience what it's like to be a master of your own body, and its healing process. You may also find that doing this for the first time can feel awkward, frustrating or leave you feeling clueless. That's okay too—anytime you try something new you will have these feelings. Then with practice or each time thereafter, it gets easier and quicker. I love this saying I heard today, "Your hand cannot block out the sun . . . it will always be there." The same is true for your feelings, you can try to block them out to make them go away. But wouldn't it be more beneficial and productive for you to deal with them instead? Like the sun behind your hands, let your feelings pass through and they will no longer be so irritating.

As time helps us heal, so too will your ability to forgive. It's a process that takes time, but it will happen more quickly if you use what you have learned so far. It doesn't have to be wrapped up in a nice neat package so we can say we're done forgiving. Like so many other things in life, it is a process and takes time.

Step Three: Forgiving others asks you to take a leap of faith.

You aren't "letting them off the hook" by using these statements; they will still be held accountable for what they did wrong—just not by you! It's not your job to see that justice prevails with this person. In other words, it's something you can let go of and let Spirit handle for you! It sounds like having faith, doesn't it? Maybe you're reminded of the Serenity Prayer . . .

> God, grant me the serenity
> to accept the things I cannot change,
> the courage to change the things I can,
> and wisdom to know the difference.

Can you have faith that this person's karma will catch up to them? The Law of Karma states that, "As you sow, so shall you reap." What goes around, comes around, and we don't control karma. Knowing this allows you to trust karma and release them, so you can feel free to move on.

Hand Over Heart. Breathe. Twin Hearts Meditation:

I have a very special meditation to share with you. It has helped me enormously to forgive—so much so, that I have incorporated this mediation into my daily morning routine. I was introduced to

Master Stephen Cho's work and teachings when I met my soul sister Helen on the other side of the world in Ireland. She is a Pranic healer and received her certification from Mr. Cho. Here is a section from the meditation for you to practice on your own. Once you are in a relaxed state with your eyes closed, bring this person to mind and silently say to them: "We are all evolving, we all make mistakes, I have learned from my mistakes. God's peace and love be with me. God's peace and love be with you. I hope you have learned your lesson. You are completely forgiven. Go in peace. May you be blessed with peace, love, inner healing and spiritual maturity. So be it. I release you. You are completely forgiven."[34]

Step Four: Have courage.

You must have the courage to take the leap of faith and therefore, the willingness to forgive. Have courage to know that when you release these negative feelings you will feel better. Do you trust that you will feel better after having forgiven someone? How do you trust that? You use your courage to begin to practice by willing yourself into action and by making the decision to forgive. With each action toward forgiveness, you will be rewarded with some relief; this is what builds your trust—the satisfying completion of each step.

"Forgiveness is a virtue of the brave." ~ Indira Gandhi

You might also notice and observe emotions that haven't shown up until this point. The key is trusting that you are on the right path and that you have the courage to keep going. You can handle each emotion—use the "Six steps to managing emotions" in Chapter Four. Use your tears as a way to release each layer of the onion so that you can feel better.

Hand Over Heart. Breathe. Put Them On Stage Exercise:

Here is a visualization to begin embodying forgiveness. It's one thing to use your mind and answer questions using the previous journal exercises—your mental life is important. But to get you fully engaged, you always need your body to be present too. Embodying as many senses as possible will always integrate your new action or the change you desire.

Get comfortable and give yourself at least ten minutes. Tune into your breath and remember the fact that your spirit loves it when you do this. You are re-connecting right now. You can forget about everything else for ten minutes. After you have done enough rounds of inhaling and exhaling, bring your attention to the space behind your eyes—front and center. Pretend you are behind a video camera and you are looking out through the space between your eyes. (This is what they call your "Third Eye.") See a stage with an audience full of loving people. Now place that person you want to forgive on that stage. Only do one person at a time. It could even be yourself! Put them in a comfortable chair. See yourself offering them some water with a smile on your face. It may not feel genuine to offer them comfort, but that is okay. Fake it for now. Now using the "gifts of perspective" you found earlier in this book, bring those to mind. For example, use "This person taught me a lot about myself."

Look into their face and say, "Thank you. Thank you for showing me something that I needed to release (i.e. anger, resentment, fear) so I can feel good again. Thank you for the gifts I've received from that experience (i.e. inner strength, clarity, your next step)." See yourself put your hand over your heart as you watch their expression of gratitude for you, light up the stage. Watch them receive your forgiveness. Feel the happiness in the room—the audience is applauding and your heart feels like it's growing bigger. Take your time to feel this positive exchange between the two of you. When you are done, turn to the audience and take a bow to show them and yourself that the person you just forgave gives you permission to forgive yourself as well (i.e. your decisions). Feel the audience applaud you. Use this moment to feel your heart expand with this new sense of freedom. Feel their love for you as you walk off stage with your head held high.

When you are ready, bring your attention back to the room you are in, knowing that you can re-visit that stage whenever you'd like. Bring those feelings of love, gratitude, forgiveness, freedom and strength into this moment right now. Repeat this exercise until it feels real. It may take more than a few times to reach this point.

Struggle

Some of you have been hurt by things like: infidelity; an addicted partner; having been fired from a job; or the death of a loved one. Forgiveness feels complicated if there were unresolved issues, or betrayal by a friend/family member or a business partner. If you were accused of things you didn't do, or if you were taken to court, you will find it difficult to forgive. In response, you may have neglected your feelings or forgotten your needs; maybe you blame God or the illness. I mention these to set the stage, so to speak. Now consider the amount of emotional pain you carry with you from the time you wake up in the morning until the time you go to bed at night. Be honest in this appraisal and take some time with it. Reflect on your thoughts, your nightmares, and how many times you repeat the story to others. Are you ready to release it all?

Forgiveness isn't easy to do—I don't pretend it doesn't require some work. I struggled with my own thoughts, such as, "Okay, so if I let go of thinking of him as a bad person or release the resentment in my heart toward him, won't I forget and possibly make the same mistakes with him that I made in the first place?" It's a classic worry, right? Anxiety does create some struggle with forgiving. We worry that if we forgive that person then they will be able to hurt us again. Most of us were raised to hold onto past hurts so we could know how to navigate the potential for future emotional pain. However, as you have learned about living in the present moment, you will have the awareness and freedom you need to make the decisions that are right for you. Simply be in the present moment and you will feel it when things don't seem right. Then act on them and deliver a "No" if you need to. Trust yourself. Maya Angelou (a favorite of mine) said, "When you know better, you do better."

Trust that we do make progress. Even when it feels like you're taking steps backward, life is like a corkscrew where the spirals in motion look as if they are going in reverse when in fact the next rung brings you to a higher level. In fact, visualize a strand of DNA—its shape is similar to a ladder twisted lengthwise into a corkscrew shape. It's our personal evolution!

Public figures in our national history have struggled with forgiveness. Dare I mention Hillary Clinton and her ability to forgive husband, former President Bill Clinton for his infidelity? She gave this response in an interview back in 2010 regarding whether she has forgiven him. "I have. I have. It wasn't easy and I don't pretend to be any kind of example of forgiveness. I think we all do things to people, sometimes deliberately, sometimes inadvertently, that cause pain. You can either go down that road or you can ask yourself, what is it that I want to achieve, and be, at the end of this process? Do I want to stay married? That is why we went into counseling, and why we worked at it. I take marriage very seriously, as does my husband. I highly recommend forgiveness."[35]

Maybe you don't trust yourself enough to believe that your forgiveness will set you free. Are you afraid of what will happen if you forgive? Vietnamese Buddhist Monk Thich Nhat Hanh explains, "People have a hard time letting go of their suffering. Out of a fear of the unknown, they prefer suffering because that is familiar." What's the worst that could happen? Remember, you are in control of who you choose to let into your life and who you choose to keep out. You also learned a great deal from that hurtful experience.

I like to use Nature for advice. Nature has its own cycle of death and re-birth. When you consider a plant and its growth, it has to shed its old leaves in order to grow new leaves. The process happens like this: The older leaves harden, and eventually fall off. The plant doesn't think, I can't let these old leaves go—I need them! Instead, it lets the last stage in its cycle unfold. This provides space for new growth. The plant cycles like this naturally, with beginning and ending growth periods. Everything depends upon the amount of nurturing provided. With the help of the sun and its warmth, water and good soil, the plant is nurtured to do its best to meet its highest potential. The same holds true with forgiveness—we release the pain and hurt to make new room in our hearts for happiness and new experiences.

Transforming Victim Consciousness

Another layer of the onion: You may find yourself attached to the grief of what has happened. Some of you may be reeling from a new diagnosis of cancer, a new physical disability, or the loss of someone dear to you rather suddenly. To the outsider, we want our lives to look as if "things aren't really that bad." The reality is we feel less than capable, like we're not a whole person anymore. To get by, we incorporate a super-focused frame of mind that maintains "Everything is okay" despite our tragic circumstances. It helps us to hide from our wrong-doing—the blame we feel for this affliction. Our hyper-focus is all about making it look as if we're okay, so that no one can see that we are hurting. Everyone else is going about their business while our way of living life has transformed into something totally and completely different. We feel alone, so we pretend the pain isn't there. The grief feels paralyzing, and it causes victim consciousness. This is a state of mind that is isolating. It separates us from others unintentionally because of these feelings. Our victim-like thinking is that we are alone in our grief because nobody else could possibly understand.

Your anger and frustration with "God," "the world," or "just plain life," has you buried in a type of grief that causes you to feel weak and suffer from thoughts like "Why me?" And while no one can blame you for thinking this way (it's completely natural), these thoughts are keeping you stuck in victim consciousness. It's true that no one else can understand what you are going through. Still it feels like they all are looking at you, judging, worrying, trying to help, or hiding from you . . . So we get really good at pretending, but where does all of that pain go? Inside our bodies . . . eating away at the very core of the strength we need so desperately.

Yes, it's painful and your heart aches—so give yourself plenty of space to feel your pain. Have a good cry to release it all. Then realize that you still have the freedom of choice. How long do you want to feel this way? Remember, you're still in charge of your heart, mind and body. Of course there is no rush or time limit governing the amount of time you want to grieve. The unforgiving part of you holds this state of mind—that the grief is most important, that you are the victim and always will be. However, when we allow ourselves to forgive it will transform our experience into something we can feel good about and allow us to re-join the human race. Once you allow yourself to feel the pain, you can transform it by asking yourself, "What is my next step?" Don't expect the answer to come right away because it probably won't. But you have just cleared the way for a new path. Now that you have owned up to your experience, you have taken charge of yourself. When we take charge, we no longer feel like a victim instead, we feel empowered with strength to do something about it.

As I wrote this (on another terribly foggy day), a hummingbird flew right up to the window and hovered there for me to see him. "I bring you joy," he seemed to say. Joy is what you feel when you forgive others and yourself. You bring joy to yourself by doing so. Like the hummingbird, you raise your energy, so you can buzz around again. Realize that grief is an emotional process that you are moving through. There is no need to attach yourself to it. Let it flow so that it moves through you. Choose the victor stance! Reject the tendency to go back into victim thinking consciousness. You don't want to wake up years later asking yourself, "Why did I waste so much of my life grieving?"

I had a client, Cary, who was going through a divorce because her husband had been unfaithful and was addicted to gambling. Not only did he gamble all of their life's savings away and cause them to go bankrupt, but he cheated on her while she was pregnant with their second child. He didn't show any remorse either—he said it was all her fault and that she had caused him to act that way. She told me it felt like she could never let go of that hurt. That hurt consoled her like a blanket, comforting her anger. I taught her that as long as she felt hurt and betrayed, she would continue to be a victim of her husband and his behavior. Well, she figured out quickly that she didn't want him to have that kind of power over her. No way! She wanted her own power back. Once she made that declaration, "I am a victor and feel powerful and capable when I'm around my ex-husband," she was on her way to feeling good again.

However, she realized that once she forgave him for one thing, another thing would come up for her to forgive. With the amount of contact she had to have with him due to sharing the kids and their kids' lives, new things to feel hurt about would happen. "Oh, the agony!" she'd exclaim. There was always going to be something for her to feel hurt by as long as he was in her life! "How depressing!" she'd cry. But these were victim-like feelings and thoughts. As long as she kept these thoughts running in her mind and heart, she could never win. Knowing these thoughts were running her down, it motivated her to learn how to forgive and accept him as the person he consistently is with her. It was that or the other choice she had, which was to constantly be upset by his behavior. And what kind of life is that? Not a fun one— and she wanted a fun life. She didn't want to hold onto the resentment, anger, and hurt residing in her heart and mind. She wanted to feel good, so she initiated the process of directing her thoughts and focused her attention on a new perspective.

Ho'oponopono (*Ho–o–pono–pono*)

Have you heard of something called Ho'oponopono? It's a very powerful ancient Hawaiian healing prayer. Within this prayer lies the theme of forgiveness. It's believed that in saying these words "I'm sorry. Please forgive me. Thank you. I love you." you are petitioning Spirit from a conscious state of mind to transform memories from our subconscious to be voided or nullified. Not only that, but you acknowledge 100% responsibility for the memories and realize that in replaying these memories you have been keeping these problems alive in your subconscious mind.[36]

I have tried this myself, and I can tell you it works miraculously! It takes some gumption, in that you have to really suck it up to take the high road and say these words. However, the results are shocking. I practiced this prayer for a few days using my sons' father. It felt odd and inauthentic at first, but after a lot of repetition the words began to sink in and feel real. I had to keep the bigger picture in mind and use my strong desire to feel good again. I kid you not, the next time I saw my sons' father I felt literally as if it were the first time I laid eyes on him! It was so bizarre because as I watched him help the boys out of the car, there were no negative feelings *whatsoever*. He looked to me like the person I had met twenty years ago: He didn't have all of those layers of negativity I had given him. I was so surprised, I even asked my son if he thought his dad looked different. He just looked at me funny and said, "No, Mom . . ."

Hand Over Heart. Breathe. Ho'oponopono Exercise:

I encourage you to try it, especially if you didn't have much success with the "On stage" visual exercise. It's just a matter of picturing that person in front of you and repeating the words over and over again. The repetition helps you to begin feeling the words' meaning. ("Fake it till you make it" applies here.) Be aware of all emotions and thoughts that rise to the surface and write them down so you can put them aside and focus your attention here.

Repeat out loud to the person you'd like to forgive (imagine them in your mind and use their name):

"I'm sorry." (This is where you own your part—your reason for doing what you did.)

"Please forgive me." (For your part in the conflict.)

"Thank you." (Thank you for showing me what I needed to learn.)

"I love you." (Spoken from your heart.)

It could take several repetitions for you to feel a shift in your emotion. You will know there has been a shift when you feel your body soften and emotions begin to rise.

Forgiving Yourself

One of the women in the support group I facilitate, *Women Starting Over*, realized that she couldn't forgive her husband until she forgave herself. Darleen had lost her husband to a heart attack, a loss complicated by the fact that years prior, he had tried to commit suicide. She still had not forgiven him for the attempted suicide when he died. She became aware of the enormous amount of guilt she felt in her heart for the anger she felt at the time of his passing. She realized that the anger and guilt she felt was preventing her from forgiving her husband. After using one of the exercises in this chapter ("Body Dialogue"), she felt like she could breathe easily again. The constriction she felt in her lungs released and her heart opened up. Today, she is frequently stopped by friends and acquaintances and complimented about how good she looks. She attributes this to how good she feels inside, and the resulting glow emanating from within her.

It's very significant to include our own hearts in forgiveness. Can you be your best self without this type of self-love (forgiveness)? How many times do we forget the importance of this? But oh boy, can we be hard on ourselves! Sometimes we just want to let loose and feel sorry for ourselves, wallow in our disappointment, or feel deep sorrow. There is nothing wrong with that, but at some point we need to find self-compassion.

Take advantage of those times when you feel deep sadness, because these moments are precious—you are super in-tune with what is going on inside. Use this space you have created to explore these feelings. Then add some self-compassion. Admit to yourself, "I have been through a lot lately!" or "Wow, I have a lot on my plate right now!" Consider taking it easy. Pat yourself on the back. Show yourself some love. Ask for a hug from others. Take a hot relaxing bath. Maybe go back to re-read Chapter Three on self-love.

Be willing to release the anger you've kept for yourself because you didn't meet your own expectations. Let go of the part of you that feels like a failure because things didn't work out the way you wanted them to. Release your need to punish yourself for not doing what you said you would do. Release the need to blame yourself. If you can believe that we are all doing the best we can, then there is no blame.

What happens when we don't forgive ourselves? Let's chase the blame game for a minute using myself as an example and see where it goes. If I were to believe in blame then I would blame myself for the divorce. If the divorce then were all my fault, I was to blame. And if this were the case, I wouldn't have a lot to feel good about. Therefore I would have a lot of reasons to feel bad. I could spend lots of my time punishing myself with bad thoughts and actions. These in turn lead to . . . ? More bad thoughts, actions and feeling very bad. I would then be depressed, maybe even suicidal. I may develop an addiction in order to escape my bad thoughts/depression. My kids would then suffer because they would see me suffering. They would no longer receive good care or the love and support they need. I would be completely absorbed in myself and my misery, and my kids would be neglected. The point being, that blaming myself for my divorce would make it all justified. I should be unhappy. I should deal with the consequences of addiction, suffering, depression . . . My kids would be an afterthought because I would be consumed in my own problems. My health would be suffering as well. Maybe I have gained weight, stopped exercising, or developed an ulcer from all the stress I feel. But it would all be justified—I could hold my head up high around people because I would be blaming myself for my divorce! I would believe I don't deserve to feel happy. I don't deserve to feel good. I deserve suffering—and if that affects my kids and family so be it! Silly, right?

So, how long do we need to suffer? What's the time frame we are looking for here? Who says when we can stop blaming ourselves? Will it be a new lover? A therapist? A good friend? Or will it be ourselves? Because blaming ourselves takes a lot of time and energy. And eventually we will want to feel good again, true?

Maya Angelou said, "Wouldn't take nothin' for my journey now!" And she has been through a lot! (I recommend reading her autobiographies.) Well, you might be wondering, how do I get to that point? How do I arrive at that declaration, to be able to say that my journey and my past experience are meaningful and holds many blessings?

"Nobody's life is entirely free of pain and sorrow. Isn't it a question of learning to live with them rather than trying to avoid them?"[37] ~ Eckhart Tolle

You do the work. Don't just read through or skip the exercises in this book. Apply what you learn by using the exercises. When you do the work, things get easier and gradually joy and inner peace can enter these doors you are opening to your heart. With each open door, a new perspective sheds light that will make you sigh and grin. I remember there was a time when I did a lot of sighing. So much so that my sons would ask me about it; "Why do you sigh so much, Mom?" I told them that it helps me to keep my heart open.

When you are outside, you will notice that a spider's web glistens in the morning sunlight because each thread shines—even the weaker ones. The web is interconnected to reveal the whole design with shimmering clarity. Appreciate the beauty in that— weaker threads, broken threads and new threads. They are all a part of the whole which creates a beautiful design: your life.

The next chapter, which deals with appreciation, will help you to incorporate this concept. It'll feel like a nice way to wrap up this part of your life, and help you to see that your past has definitely served you well.

Keys to Reflect On:

- Forgiveness is returning your heart back to love and joy
- Forgiveness is using courage, faith and trust to release both parties—yourself and another
- Use perspective and your emotions to help you forgive others and yourself
- Step out of victim consciousness to feel forgiveness
- Forgiving yourself will create inner peace

Chapter 8
Appreciation Increases Energy
and Launches Positive Change

*"Appreciation is the highest form of prayer, for it acknowledges the presence
of good wherever you shine the light of your thankful thoughts."*
~Alan Cohen

Now you can have appreciation for your journey thus far. This is the last step in transforming your past so that it serves you. Just like when a rainbow appears after a storm and you gasp to admire how beautiful it is. When a rainbow appears you feel as though Spirit has smiled at you as if to say, *Appreciate all that life has to offer*—both the good and the bad times. I'm hoping by now you can get a sense of that—that everything you have been through has been a blessing in disguise. That awareness intends to support you. You feel a much greater sense of inner strength and stability so that now, you can take a moment to appreciate *all of it*.

*"Gratitude is not only the greatest of virtues, but the parent of all the
others."*
~ Marcus Tullius Cicero

I have learned that being in a state of appreciation is a little different than gratitude in that the energy it embodies is the purity of what you are—Spirit energy. (Remember Chapter Three; "I am love"?) Esther and Jerry Hicks, of *The Teachings of Abraham* fame, explain that a state of appreciation is "me being in sync with the whole of that which I AM."[38] Whereas the energy of gratitude holds a slightly different feeling of overcoming struggle carrying the perception of what was missing in your past. Appreciation is a pure "I am turned on" feeling. There is no hint of what you were lacking. Appreciation just is what you are at that moment—super-connected to Spirit. You can see how this concept is more powerful in aligning your energy toward finding peace with your past.

So, the eighth and last spiritual truth inside of Part Two is about appreciation. (However, I will begin with gratitude so that you can benefit from the many wonderful quotes by famous teachers and authors on the subject.) Gratitude is a feeling-state that is considered to be one of the highest, in the same realm as joy and love. A high feeling-state is just that—a state of consciousness where you feel loving and blissful. But don't worry, just because it's a high state doesn't mean it's difficult to get to (grin). You have already paved the way by reviewing your past with a new set of eyes and in turn have transformed it into something that benefits you.

"Gratitude makes sense of our past, brings peace for today, and creates a vision for tomorrow."
~ Melody Beattie

In previous chapters you learned how to release your past experiences and shift the energy around them using perspective, the act of letting go, and forgiveness. In the final step of the process of forgiving, you gained an awareness of the freedom you can have inside your heart. You re-framed your past so that now you can feel some sense of appreciation for what you went through, right? Feeling appreciative/grateful is a highly transformational feeling. Therefore, you are reading about this spiritual truth at the perfect time! For when you leave one area of your life to rest, it's best to do so with gratitude and appreciation.

You can't create happiness from a conscious state of unhappiness without action, right? The following section of the book (Part Three) is all about creating your future—so, ask yourself—can you build your future based on the feelings you have now? All creation begins with a *good* feeling-state. If you can feel appreciation in this present moment then you will be granted access to feeling good which also helps you to create more good feelings—this is the basis for the beginning of creation and the foundation of the Law of Attraction.

Gratitude is very much a part of the process of creation. Imagine a wheel if you will, where there are spokes—each one contributes to the ability of the wheel to turn. Gratitude is one "spoke in the wheel" with just as much significance as the other spokes in the wheel. Setting intentions and using the Law of Attraction (Chapter 10), will help to create the motion of moving forward in your transition.

But we can't move forward very well without first having gratitude in our hearts. Gratitude brings us joy. These ingredients are necessary to free our hearts of past emotions (like grief and sadness) that weigh heavy on our hearts.

In an article posted on The Huffington Post website, Ocean Robbins cited scientific research which proved that expressing appreciation and thankfulness raised overall well-being and happiness. Expressing gratitude was also associated with fewer health complaints, and a willingness to help others.[39]

There is also this finding: Several studies have shown depression to be inversely correlated to feeling thankful. It seems that the more grateful a person is, the less depressed they are. Philip Watkins, a clinical psychologist at Eastern Washington University, found that clinically depressed individuals showed significantly lower gratitude (nearly 50 percent less) than non-depressed controls. An old saying explains that 'if you've forgotten the language of gratitude, you'll never be on speaking terms with happiness.' It turns out this isn't just wishful thinking.[40]

More than likely you have heard of a "gratitude journal," wherein you write at least five things you feel grateful for—in the morning upon waking or at night before going to sleep. I encourage you to begin one during this time of your life. Participating in this act will shift your attention to what *is* working for you. That way, when recounting or remembering your day, you deliberately choose those things that worked for you as opposed to those things that worked against you. You begin to shift your attitude from a negative one to a positive one by appreciating those things each day. If, after completing your list, your mood lightens and something inside you shifts, you will feel good. This is because once you feel into each of the activities, you began to feel a deep sense of appreciation. This in turn might even provoke you to begin thinking about giving back—this is why it's powerful and contributes toward the cycle of creation. I invite you to begin using this practice daily, so you can reap its benefits.

My client Peter, forty-nine, had experienced an awful lot of heartache when he was "a drunk" (his words.) He spent many years going from woman to woman and job to job and lost his family, until really there was nothing left. It wasn't until he hit "rock bottom" that he could turn it all around and start over again. But having spent so many years hurting himself and others, he found it difficult to live in the present without all of those memories haunting him. He had learned to forgive some parts of his past, but he still felt unsettled by it all. Once he learned to appreciate those years for what they were (some of them were fun, a lot of them made for good stories), he realized he could use those memories to help others. He established some peace of mind. He also found that his heartache transformed into a heart that was full of learning experiences he could share with others. This transformation helped him to feel good again and to feel grateful. He just needed me to remind him whenever he stepped back into feeling depressed about it all—that he had this new gratitude about his past.

Gratitude is an amazing feeling and does help to reverse those times you feel depressed about your past. You can know this for yourself right now.

Hand Over Heart. Breathe. Summoning Exercise:

Take a few minutes to relax your body. Then bring to mind a time when you felt so thankful for something that happened. Recall a time when you wanted to jump up and down, and you thought your heart would burst. Maybe you found your wallet in a public place after you had lost it. Or your loved one gave you a special thank you. Perhaps it was a beautiful vacation. It was a time you were filled with feelings of thankfulness. Immerse yourself in that memory using all your senses. Let yourself feel it happening all over again. When you are ready, open your eyes and notice how you feel—did your mood lift? It's good practice to summon uplifting times in our lives. Use the present moment to summon those experiences that filled you up, gave you hope and inspired you.

Alternatively, think of a person in your life whom you admire. Summon the energy you get from them and use it for yourself— use their inspiration to create the same energy within yourself. It's the same experience you get when you're feeling tired while you're at the gym or in a class. You just don't feel motivated. But then you look across the room and see this person full of energy, thriving at what they do. You admire them and feel inspired. The next thing you know, you've got more energy, and it feels like a switch inside you has been turned on. Use that. Summon your appreciation.

Appreciation

Now I'm going to shift into higher gear by introducing appreciation. Remember that appreciation is an all-consuming high vibration, a tuned-into Spirit feeling. Now, let's continue the previous exercise using appreciation. From your state of gratitude you will increase your feeling-state to the point where you are completely feeling it—engage all your senses toward a state of consciousness in which you can exclaim "I am appreciating (fill in the blank). It's actively happening now. Consider more examples— Maybe it's when you re-united with a loved one. Maybe you received thanks for helping someone or witnessed a beautiful sunset. Now you can recognize, in any case, that your heart expanded and felt full of life, yes? Your energy felt high and full of joy. You were so appreciative; it filled you up with the same energy as Spirit. You were so aligned with Spirit energy that you felt it in your bones. Now, how are you feeling after recalling this experience? Appreciation automatically makes your spirit soar!

The words "Thank you" carry a high vibration—just as the words "I'm sorry" and "I love you." Do you recall the last chapter's exercise using *Ho'oponopono*? The affirmation is repeated aloud using these key words and is believed to transform resentment, anger, or desire for revenge into an appreciative feeling or sense of gratitude. Doing that exercise lets appreciation rise to the surface.

Like the phoenix who flies out of the ashes, or a lotus blossom that takes root in the mud—use appreciation to begin again.

Perspective

Just as there are several ways to include and develop a sense of gratitude in your life, so too are there perspectives that will increase your appreciation. When we are in transition, it's so easy to get caught up in all of the new stressors: new towns are difficult to navigate; relationship break-ups leave us feeling alone; losing a job makes us feel insecure; new child custody arrangements bring on new fears . . . But beneath these layers of stress, we can usually rely on having our most basic needs met. Things like your home, your ability to buy food, a good friend, a sunny day are still there for you. When you begin to reflect on those things to be appreciative of, you may also realize that you have been neglecting to see how good you have it. This will look different for each person, but most of us drive a car, for example. When was the last time you got into your car to drive to your destination and paused to appreciate the car? Our cars provide so much for us; safety, transportation, comfort, enjoyment. (Personally, I've noticed when I get overly negligent of this fact, my car starts acting up, and soon I have auto repairs on my hands.) When was the last time you stopped to appreciate the electricity in your home? Or recognized how fortunate you are for having plumbing/running water every day? I remember learning from one of my favorite teachers, Louise Hay, to seal a big thank you on my envelopes when I mail in my utility bills—or any bill payments for that matter. Now that most bill payments are electronic, we can still take a moment to pause and make this acknowledgment of appreciation, without the physical act of writing out the check and sealing it into an envelope. This helps us to create a positive vibe between ourselves and our bill collectors. Can you see how this perspective could help create better feelings about our past and future?

There are all kinds of "necessities" in life—even our body parts, which could break down (and occasionally do), right? Ever notice how when you get the flu, you feel incredibly glad that you are healthy most of the time? If we break an ankle for instance, and all of a sudden we have to use crutches in order to walk, boy do we feel like we have taken for granted our ability to walk unimpeded! Once we experience what it's like *not* to have (past), then we grow a new appreciation for what we *do* have (present).

Experiencing this sort of contrast to what we do want, keeps the cycle of creation going. Would you have as much forward motion if you didn't ever experience times when things didn't go as you would have liked? There are benefits in duality as long as we appreciate them.

Hand Over Heart. Breathe. Journal Exercise: Perspective - What *Is* Working?

Take some time out to contemplate what is working for you. So many times we get caught up in the cycle of complaining about things or other people—our focus and attention is placed on what's not working. But what if you turned it around and took notice of *only* those things that *are* working? When you catch yourself feeling down or tired, ask yourself, "Okay, what *is* working for me?" Maybe you are so full of stress that you have to start simply by acknowledging that the sun is shining, that you have a roof over your head and food to eat. See if you can build on them and appreciate five more things. Consider the stranger that smiled at you when you walked across the parking lot. Perhaps the experience of laughing with a friend lifted your spirits. Or maybe you made a plan for the weekend that makes you feel excited. Appreciate these things—let them fill you up with a sense of warmth, love and joy. Your perception will be forever changed if you keep practicing this.

Acts of Appreciation

I love to share my appreciation with my children. Why? Consider how much direction we constantly give them, yet we rarely take the time to thank them for following them. I make a point of thanking my children when they complete their chores, when they remember to close the garage door, and when they help themselves rather than asking me to do something for them. They in turn appreciate my telling them thank you because it acts like a positive reinforcement for them to do these acts again. It's verbal praise that adds to their desire to create more of the same. They feel acknowledged and seen for who they are: good people. They shine brighter when we see them in this light. It's another way for us to demonstrate our love.

Appreciation doesn't have to be felt only at the Thanksgiving holiday. You can incorporate it into your ritual prior to eating any meal. When my kids have had a grumpy afternoon and we sit down to eat, I ask them to share one thing they appreciate about another person at the dinner table. It never fails; soon after we begin sharing, there are giggles, smiles and happy faces. The mood shifts, and we are appreciating not only our meal but each other as well.

When you let appreciation into your heart space and really feel into it, your body responds and your spirit soars. It's an expression of love and the more you give, the more you get. Expressing your appreciation is heart-opening. Have you ever noticed when any spiritually evolved individual (such as the Dali Lama) speaks, they are always so thankful, and their presence is full of appreciation? They are emanating this blissful state. They carry this energy with them wherever they go, appreciating everything from the sunlight to a cup of tea. When we appreciate life, we are loving what *is*. When we are loving what is, we are in a high state of being or consciousness: a loving presence. And we are expressing our connection to the Divine.

If you can't appreciate much in your life because you are full of despair, you can still appreciate the landscape. When you look up into the sky, you can appreciate the shape of the clouds, or feel the sun's warmth on your skin. When it's night time, there is nothing like a huge sky full of stars or a glowing full moon. These moments can help us to connect to Mother Nature and appreciate her beauty. In turn, we share the enormous bounty of her life-force energy.

You can greet each day with a cup of appreciation, and I guarantee you will have a great day! I gave up drinking coffee—it's been a year since I have relied on my cup of coffee in the morning to make me feel good. Without the coffee, I have learned to use other means to greet my day. My new ritual begins with the moment my feet hit the floor, and I make it a point to appreciate this day. It has become my starting point for following my bliss and what I'd like to create that day.

APPRECIATION

Here are some suggested thoughts to rouse your appreciation for the new day:

- The warmth of your covers
- The light breaking the dawn of day
- That first sip of coffee/tea
- The potential of a new day full of promise
- The quiet just before the day "officially" starts

End the day with an inventory of everything you appreciated happening that day. Many of us use this time of day to go over worries, review our to-do lists, or remember something that went wrong that day. When, by contrast, you take the time to only reflect on those things for which you feel thankful (the nice weather, the smile or hug you received, the nice meal you ate …), you are instantly filled with good feelings. The best way to have a restful sleep is by ending your day with good feelings and peaceful thoughts. Here are eight questions to initiate a contented state of being:

- What (heart-felt moments) touched me today?
- Who or what inspired me today?
- What made me smile today?
- What's the best thing that happened today?
- What made me laugh today?
- What help did I receive today?
- What act of kindness did I give/receive today?
- What did I learn or accomplish today?

What better way to drift off into sleep than knowing and feeling that *"All is well. Everything is working out in my best interest."*

In this way, not only does appreciation succeed in helping us to keep the wheel of creation going, it also acts as a wonderful conclusion and starting point in our transitions. For example, we have a renewed sense of appreciation for life after a near-death experience. Consider those accidents you have been in or witnessed. It has been said that those near-death experiences can provide the call to, "pump up the volume" on your life—time to turn it up and get creating!

"What the caterpillar calls the end of the world, the master calls a butterfly."
~ Richard Bach

Use Appreciation to Transform Negative Experiences

After re-writing your story in chapter five, hopefully you have a new sense of empowerment. You can feel appreciative of that, especially if you weren't feeling empowered before. When we feel empowered, we feel strong and capable—even free to do things we previously thought impossible. This is something to be appreciative of! You transformed a negative experience into a positive one using your power of appreciation.

Consider a break-up from a relationship. Do you want to carry those feelings into your next one? Probably not, whether it was a friend or a romantic partner, we'd like to be able to feel good about leaving that one and moving forward with the next one. How do we get there? With acceptance and appreciation of what happened. We can feel good about the fun experiences we shared and the affection we were given. Once we feel grateful for the good times we had or those traits that person offered to us, we feel good about moving on. It also provides us with a very good sense of what we can appreciate in our next relationship.

"By appreciation, we make excellence in others our own property."
~Voltaire

I have a close friend, Rachel who came down with breast cancer. It threw her life completely out of order. Suddenly the only thing that mattered most was her health. Daily functions such as going to her job, being a good wife to her husband and a good mom to her children were still important but lost their first priority. Her new life consisted of doctors and chemotherapy appointments, making a will, getting sleep at night, managing not to feel nauseous, and researching which herbal supplements would help her with side effects. Her transition happened over night— the minute she received her diagnosis. The cancer quickly forced her to re-focus all of her attention on herself, whereas prior to this, she had been placing herself last—after her husband's and children's needs had been met. She didn't mind living like that, in fact, she didn't ever know anything different. It's how her mother lived and her mother's mother lived. In other words, it was a generational pattern of self-sacrifice to always put others first. Although truly a gift in disguise, this transition didn't feel easy at all, because she wasn't used to placing her needs above those of others.

The cancer also gave her great clarity about what's truly important—her life. For the first time, she was forced to consider herself and her own needs before anyone else's. It was difficult at first. She struggled with having to make decisions like letting someone else pick up her kids from school because she was too sick from vomiting. She didn't like that she had to stop cooking meals for her family because she was too tired. And she felt like she was letting down her community when she resigned from being president of the PTA because the meetings were too difficult to organize and sit through. In fact, she was angry! Cancer was causing her to make all of these changes she didn't want to make!

Slowly, the blessings unfolded. Yes, she was having to start a new life that involved having cancer, but once she began living it by placing her needs first, her perspective changed. Her life became all about living instead of dying. Living life to the fullest —experiencing each day as her last became her most important blessing. Now, she could see how loving herself transpired into the love she was able to give to her family and friends.

It was Rachel's appreciation that carried her through her transition from being a healthy mother, wife and active community member to someone who was dying. She used to say, "I stay positive, try not to focus on the negative, and be grateful for all the things that I do have." She used her feelings of thankfulness to greet each day as her last. Doing this increased her joy and ability to manage the stress and disappointments along the way. Despite the hardships of failing health, she lived each day feeling appreciative of the experience for living.

Native American Prayer

Aho Mitakuye Oyasin . . . All my relations. I honor you in this circle of life with me today. I am grateful for this opportunity to acknowledge you in this prayer . . .

To the Creator, for the ultimate gift of life, I thank you.

To the mineral nation that has built and maintained my bones and all foundations of life experience, I thank you.

To the plant nation that sustains my organs and body and gives me healing herbs for sickness, I thank you.

To the animal nation that feeds me from your own flesh and offers your loyal companionship in this walk of life, I thank you.

To the human nation that shares my path as a soul upon the sacred wheel of Earthly life, I thank you.

To the Spirit nation that guides me invisibly through the ups and downs of life and for carrying the torch of light through the Ages. I thank you.

To the Four Winds of Change and Growth, I thank you.

You are all my relations, my relatives, without whom I would not live. We are in the circle of life together, co-existing, co-dependent, co-creating our destiny. One, not more important than the other. One nation evolving from the other and yet each dependent upon the one above and the one below. All of us a part of the Great Mystery.

Thank you for this Life.[41]

Aho. Mitakuye Oyasin is a simple yet profound statement. It comes from the Lakota Nation and means *All my relations*. It is spoken during prayer and ceremony to invite and acknowledge all relatives to the moment."[42]

Manifesting With Appreciation

Sometimes transitions can seem long and convoluted, leaving us feeling like we can't see the light at the end of the tunnel. However, having appreciation will offer another point of access to help us manifest our desires into reality. This can be the case when trying to reach our goals. Use your feelings of gratitude to help you stay motivated to eat healthy. Be grateful when you do lose some weight (regardless of the number of pounds). Feel appreciation for when you stopped smoking for two days (regardless of the time passed; you can feel grateful for not smoking for an hour, for goodness' sake). Feel this state of appreciation inside your body. This act will help to serve your intention by keeping your motivation high. Again, it helps to keep that forward motion going. (More about this type of manifesting inside Chapter 11: Setting Intentions.)

When we feel worthy of, excited by, and appreciative of the experiences we are in the process of creating, we literally magnetize, or draw toward us, more of those experiences into our lives. To quicken the process, we need only to focus our attention on the way we will feel once our goal is attained. We can feel into the future and appreciate what is coming.

For example, a few months ago I was helping my client Tammy to begin her weight loss program. She had just made a transition by moving from another state and beginning a new job. She also thought it would be a good time to start a weight-loss program (she was 100 pounds overweight). But in order for her to move forward in losing the weight, she needed to begin with appreciating how she was now. To be more specific, she had to be able to look at herself in the mirror and smile. Was she able to do that? Not right away; it took some time to shift the hatred she felt for her body. Sometimes when the overall picture seems impossible to appreciate, it helps to break it down into smaller pieces. I asked her, "Can you appreciate your eyes?" She replied, "Yes." "Do you like your hair?" "Yes," she said. "How about your face—can you look at your face in the mirror and appreciate that you have a nice-looking face?" Slowly she responded "Yes." Okay, so we had our starting point of feeling appreciation for the way she was at that moment. That first step was important so that she could move forward in losing the weight from a space (state of being) that was full of potential.

I also helped her develop a new perspective about her weight that would allow her to see it as having served her in the past but not relevant in her new life. For instance in the past, the weight served her for self-protection reasons. Having difficult abusive relationships, she could appreciate that her weight had acted to guard her from future potential hurt. Like a safety blanket, she could perceive her extra weight as helping her to prevent further abuse by keeping men and future relationships away. She could then feel thankful that her weight had served her in this beneficial way. It was a new idea to say to her extra weight: "Thank you, you did your job well. And now I am ready to release that kind of help."

You can also use hope to get closer to appreciation. I asked my client Tammy when she was in the middle of despair if she could feel hopeful about losing the weight. She replied yes and that she could even see herself thin again. If in fact, you have experienced appreciation for what you have accomplished in the past, you are more likely to obtain hope again in the present. This serves as your platform to leap into appreciation. Focus your attention on only those things that make you feel good. In this case it was those things she was able to do with her body: make people laugh, attract comments about her beautiful face, and be a deep, sound sleeper. She definitely appreciated these things about her body. Being who she was led the way for good feelings to emerge about her body—a huge feat for overweight women because they are typically so filled with negative thoughts and feelings about their bodies.

Hand Over Heart. Breathe. Meditation: Grateful Heart

Now that you have been reminded of the power of feeling and expressing appreciation, close your eyes and tune into your heart. Take a few minutes there to explore how you're feeling. I'm hoping that your heart feels open and expansive. And that maybe there's a little inspiration in there? Take some more deep breaths, and reflect on those things that have happened in your day so far prior to reading this section. Maybe it's easier to recall a good time you recently had. Let the corners of your mouth curl up until you reach a grin or even a full smile. Feel the love, joy or compassion that your heart is expressing to you. Let it continue to unfold and grow even more with another deep breath . . . and another . . . life is good, wouldn't you say? Now imagine sending your expression of gratitude to another person either via your thoughts or in physical form with words or an email.

Next, write down or communicate to another person what you appreciate about them. If you live with someone, make a list of five things and spread these items around the house. Surprise them by placing one on their pillow and another inside the coffee can, for instance. Be brave and look into their eyes to share what you appreciate about them.

Imagine these people receiving your messages of appreciation and the positive emotion that this provides for them. How does that feel? This is powerful creation here . . . To send appreciation to another person, without a need for anything in return, is an act of love and therefore, an act of creating good karma. It will return to you tenfold.

I remember a very moving exercise I did at a mountain retreat where we formed two circles—an inner and an outer one. The inner circle stayed put while the outer circle moved from person to person. We placed our hand over the other person's heart while looking into their eyes, and sang, *"I honor your heart. Your heart is safe with me. Here in this sacred union, here where our hearts are free."* Once the outer circle completed their round, the inner circle became the outer circle switching the recipient of the love song. I hadn't ever felt anything so amazing before that exercise of appreciation. Everyone was teary-eyed, with hearts opened wide and love flowing all around the room; it was very special.

When we conclude our yoga practice, we bring appreciation to mind by bringing our hands to our hearts to express "Namaste," which means the light (the Divine spark) within me honors/acknowledges/appreciates the light within you. It's an act of bowing in reverence to another. At the end of class, the teacher initiates Namaste as a symbol of gratitude and respect toward his/her students and his/her own teachers, and in return invites the students to connect with their hearts, thereby allowing the truth to flow—the truth that we are all one when we live from the heart.

Part Three will help you employ certain methods and techniques to bring your creation full circle. The spokes on your wheel of creation are moving forward now. Let's keep it going!

<u>Keys to Reflect On:</u>

- Appreciation is aligning yourself with Spirit
- Use appreciation in addition to gratitude to optimize your experience
- Appreciation has the power to uplift your spirits
- Use appreciation to transform negative experiences from your past into positive ones for your present moment
- Incorporate acts of appreciation into your daily living to encourage manifestation and maintain good feeling-states

Part III:
Build Your Bright Future

Chapter 9
Everything Is Energy

"Everything in the Universe has a rhythm; everything dances."
~Maya Angelou

Welcome to Part Three: Building a bright future! In this section of the book, you will learn the "building blocks" of creation to satisfy the desires you have for your new life. It's one thing to learn how to manage your new life and feel good about your past. But do you ever give yourself time to dream about your future?

I realized that I didn't spend much time dreaming. It felt as if I needed courage to do so. Do you dare to dream? It's easy to see how readily we get caught up in our daily lives. Especially if you are a single parent; all of your focus is needed for everything that goes on from day to day. You might not even notice (like I didn't) that you don't dream about your future.

However, what happens if we never stop and plan a vacation for example? What happens if we don't take the time to use our hearts to feel into what kind of life we want for ourselves—whether that be next year or five years from now? We become stagnant, even unmotivated. And yet, dreams can offer us hope, vision, and motivation for our present lives. We need energy to feed our dreams in order to create our future.

In Part Three, first we will examine the underlying principle of all these building blocks: everything is energy. Then I will share what was missing from the popular book and movie, *The Secret,* so that you can achieve results in using the Law of Attraction. Then I will finish up this section of the book with all the subtle yet powerful nuances involved in setting intentions. Finally, using grace as the last spiritual truth, you will realize how all previous truths embodied can shape your new life and let grace be the outcome.

I invite you to place your hand over your heart and breathe for a moment.

One morning while outside in my yard, I was reminded that we can learn from Mother Nature. I was looking at one of my plants, a banana tree (the non-flowering kind), and talking with a friend about the parts of the plant that were dead. We reflected on how the energy of the tree was diffused, because the dead parts had not been cut off yet. It wasn't able to grow and strengthen its core as well as it could have because of this. The tree was still sending energy to the parts that were dead.

How applicable is that to humans? Completely! What have you been sending your energy out to? Are you sending energy to places, people, or things that are dead? What a waste of time and energy! You will know you are doing this if you feel drained, stuck or tired a lot. It's amazing how once we decide to stop giving our energy to these places, people, or things that don't reciprocate, just how much *greater* our energy levels can be. Those "dead parts" that don't benefit us don't need to consume our energy anymore. Your ability to create will benefit from increasing your awareness of the ninth spiritual truth: everything is energy.

Sometimes even after we make the transition, we continue to feed those "old parts" of our past or previous self. It could be an old story you re-tell to the new people you meet in your life about how you were fired from your favorite job. We might use self-talk ("I loved that man."). With each of these actions, we send our energy in that direction. This chapter will help you to realize how your thoughts and emotions create energy and thus your reality. You will see that you have the potential to use this energy to create wonderful interactions with yourself and others. With this new awareness, you increase your ability to build a bright future.

It was one of the first things I noticed after my divorce. I had more energy because I wasn't sending it out to the dead parts in our marriage anymore. I had spent lots of time wondering where my sons' father was or what he was doing. It was a waste of my time and energy. Instead of focusing my energy on him and his whereabouts, I could now focus my energy on a new life, comprised of myself and my kids, pure and simple. With a new abundance of energy, I could begin to make our new tree (family) take root and establish a strong solid core.

Managing our energy will help us to have even more energy during our transition and assist us in creating our future. But first I invite you to consider the fact that there are different kinds of energy that influence us. They are: revitalizing energy, other people's energy and emotional energy. Once you learn about each of these you can use them to fuel the Law of Attraction in the next chapter.

Other People's Energy

It will help you to learn how to discriminate what is your energy and what belongs to others. Other people's energy can sometimes be felt without us knowing. If you are sensitive, you probably walk around like a sponge absorbing other people's feelings and moods. By the end of the day, you could have *grocery store clerk Martha's* bad mood, *teacher Mrs. Smith's* stress, and *your kid's* anxiety all wrapped up in your body. You may wonder why you are feeling so tired at the end of the day… this is why! The energy you collected during the day wasn't even yours to begin with.

The same can be said of our feelings. Often, what we are feeling didn't originate within us. In other words, next time you feel a sudden change in mood, ask yourself, "Is this really mine?" Then take a moment to recall where you have been and who you have been with. As you recall these things you will notice a change or shift in your body, heart and mind. For instance, you might remember that your close friend arrived at your house flaming mad; she vented to you about her awful job. This memory of what happened previously might resonate strongly or trigger something in you. That's when you can say "Ah-ha" and breathe it all out. You realize the anger or edginess you're feeling isn't yours; it's your best friend's and you had taken it on as your own. Just be aware that you can choose to listen and absorb other people's energy— or not. *Once you take back your own energy you will feel good again.*

We forget that we have the choice whether to let others into our space or field of energy. I recommend that we protect ourselves, that we don't walk around like a vulnerable doormat for other people to stomp their feet on. Simply have an awareness of a boundary between yourself and someone else. Keep in mind that you are two separate and different individuals. You can still be a good listener, present and willing to support others while at the same time choosing not to take on their "stuff" as your own.

Hand Over Heart. Breathe. Body Bubble Exercise:

Whenever you have stressful situations or difficult people to be around, imagine yourself encased in a bubble. Compare it to when you were in the womb and you floated safely, protected from outside influences. Consider viewing the membrane of a cell through a microscope. You can see the inside of the cell but other cells cannot permeate the membrane. It's the same idea. All you need is your imagination. Visualize your bubble, you can even use a color. Set the intention that this bubble won't allow other people's energy to get through unless it's in your best interest. State that only those people and situations that are for your highest good will be allowed through. Try it out in public one day and see if it makes a difference in how you feel coming home after that experience. I also recommend using this exercise if you plan to be around people drinking excessively such as in bars or at cocktail parties.

Revitalizing Energy

Revitalizing energy is another way to describe participating in those things that feed your soul. Think about occasions when you have lost track of time. You were doing some activity and you were so immersed that time flew by and before you knew it you were done and it was time to stop—only you didn't feel tired, you felt great and you felt energized! This is how artists feel when they get in "the flow." They get lost in the creation and lose track of time. The experience is enjoyable and fills them up. If you haven't yet found this activity for yourself, consider those times that you have felt unusually happy or joyous, maybe even excited. Your body feels alive and full of potential. You feel empowered and motivated. Possibly you feel an overall sense of peace, calm and serenity. Begin to build an awareness of these activities that have the potential to energize or revitalize you. Notice how you feel when you read about others who inspire you, or when you hear a friend describe to you what they did that was so thrilling to them. If you hear a voice inside say, "I'd like to try that!", that is your signal: listen.

Now that you have gained some self-awareness by tuning into how you feel, you can know this about yourself—you can start taking action. I'd guess that pretty much everyone can feel energized by walks outside or hikes in nature. Maybe you gain energy from lovemaking or receiving a hug from your child. I know a lot of people feel joyous when they are taking photos. Expressions of love both given and received will have the same effect and will feel revitalizing. Music! Music also has this kind of power. Frequently, I will turn on our favorite songs to get my sons up and ready for school in the morning. Soon they are jumping around the house to the beat of the music, dressing without me nagging them to do so, and with an improved mood. Use whatever means to raise your energy level.

Energy Zappers

A friend told me an interesting story the other day about his ex-wife. They were walking back from lunch with their son when a stranger walked up to his son's mother and asked, "Why are you mad at me?" The stranger was a little girl who had *seen* or *felt* this woman's energy and interpreted it as anger. For this woman, the experience could have been an opportunity for her to see how she carries herself in the world: in an angry fashion. This little girl reflected back to her in a most unique, articulate way. Interesting, don't you think? How do you carry your energy when you're out and about town? Typically we don't talk about it with others, but people do pick up on our energy. (Especially young children and animals; they will mirror our energy back to us.) On the flip side, it would be good for us to steer clear of people who carry a lot of negative energy.

People can be "energy zappers." I don't know if any of you sit on boards, but this is a prime place to find an energy zapper, the type of person my father would describe as a "loud mouth."

Another might say, "They like to hear the sound of their own voice." These people are the "pontificators." They get lost in the emotion or drama of the discussion and use the time to "hold the floor." Listening to them might make you tired. Then again it might not—maybe you are the type that would join them in the argument and offer up the "devil's advocate" opinion because you like the energy all that provides. If so, be careful as usually this road leads you nowhere. Tune into your energy after interacting with an energy zapper and most likely you will feel drained.

These are also the same individuals who will walk up and tell you their life story, using you as an audience so they can vent or feed on the emotional intensity they create. The term "drama king" or "drama queen" would also fit them. Have you noticed, however, that if you stay calm and don't engage with them or what they are saying, they will eventually stop talking to you and move on? Of course you could always interrupt the person and excuse yourself to use the restroom or make a phone call. You can feel at liberty to do something about it to avoid feeling zapped.

Other types of energy zappers include certain situations or environments. These include staff or board meetings, for example, or maybe even family get-togethers such as Thanksgiving dinner or family reunions. Not everyone has a family that gets along smoothly, so that means personality conflicts or unresolved issues rising to the surface. *How you handle these situations will determine if they are energy zappers or not. Remember that you always have a choice—the freedom to choose how you'd like to respond. It's all a part of taking charge of your heart, mind and body by remembering that you have the ultimate power to decide your action.*

For some people, the act of multi-tasking can zap their energy. This makes sense, because we are sending our energy in all different directions to accomplish a variety of different tasks at the same time. The problem with multi-tasking is that it scatters our energy in too many places for us to keep fully mindful of them. When we multi-task, it can be difficult to remember things.[43]

Emotional Energy

Like you learned in Chapter Four, emotions are energy in motion, so don't attach yourself to them. When we attach ourselves to the emotion, we *become* the feeling. Then our mind creates a loop according to this proclamation we just fed ourselves. Pretty soon we are running the loop, "I am tired" over and over again while at the same time wondering why we feel so tired. Substitute "tired" for "depressed" and we have another loop or thought pattern that controls us. *Can you see how quickly and easily your thoughts become the energy you emanate?*

Emotional energy is expended when we hold on to our feelings. If you carry around anger, for example, longer than necessary, it will make you feel tired. Similarly, when you hold on to excitement arising from a great idea, you will feel energized as a result. Feelings are meant to pass through you, not attach and cling. When they are good feelings you can use them to increase your energy. Remember (Chapter Two); just as emotional recall can take you out of the present moment, so too can it increase or decrease your energy.

Each time you remember the past prior to your transition (a death, break-up, job loss, etc.), you are calling in the emotional energy of that experience. For instance, each time you remember the words, "I don't love you anymore," they bring in the resonance of how it felt when you heard them. Do you want to experience that emotion all over again? Be mindful of the energy you choose to recall memories with.

You need only to try it in order to know that emotional recall changes your energy. Recall a recent argument with someone and feel into it for a minute or so—or however long it takes you to feel the emotional resonance of the words exchanged; the hurt, or disappointment felt. Don't kid yourself by thinking they were only words, because words are powerful. Each time you remember that experience, it will bring back those emotions in present time, thus making you feel a certain way. Simply decide not to do so anymore. Catch yourself each time and re-direct your thoughts.

There are feelings attached to each word. Words carry energy. If you notice, the feeling will register in your body. For example, when I tell you, "Stop!" your attention is called and that may cause you to feel a certain way such as angry. I might say, "Thank you," and as a result you'd feel good or appreciated. Remember the Ho'oponopono exercise using those key words: thank you, I'm sorry, please forgive me, I love you? Those words were mindfully chosen.

Balance Your Energy

You can keep tabs on your energy by running a constant awareness of how it's being expended. (I invite you to use the pie chart visual aid inside Chapter Three.) Let's say you notice that a lot of your energy went into having lunch with your mother, then more energy went into work, and after you got home the remaining energy went into cooking dinner and helping your kids with homework and getting them to bed. You realize it's no wonder you are so tired at the end of the day! But you can use those times in between activities to fill yourself back up with revitalizing energy. For example, you can listen to your favorite song as you drive home. In between your lunch break and getting back to work, have a brief feel-good conversation with a friend. When you get home from work, have a good long hug with your loved ones or maybe share some love with your pet. These acts of receiving revitalizing energy will balance out those times when you're expending too much energy and are left feeling drained. In the long run you won't feel so tired; you might even have more energy later.

Use exercise or other activities such as yoga or meditation, to release the negative energy you ingest each day. This will help to keep your body clear and balanced.

Hand Over Heart. Breathe. Energetic Waterfall Exercise:

If you know you are a "water sign" (according to astrology) or if you simply love water, you in particular will appreciate this exercise. Did you know you have access to an energetic waterfall each time you take a shower? That's right, the shower head has the potential to turn into a brilliant shaft of white light entering your body from the top of your head, washing away all negativity stored inside your body. Feel the water touch your body and visualize all toxins leaving through the bottom of your feet. Imagine one long stream of water or one long beam of light washing everything away from the top of your head out through the bottom of your feet, down into the drain/earth to be neutralized. When you are done, declare that it is so. Aho![44]

We all have times when we know we are carrying negative energy, so decide: how long will you wait before you do something about it?

Choose the Energy You Digest

Be mindful of your energy as you build your future—know that you have the freedom to choose what you'd like to take into your body, heart and mind. Once you begin living in this fashion, acknowledging that everything is energy, you begin to take more control over what you let into your body, as well as how you'd like to express it. This means being thoughtful of what you decide to put into your body—including television watching. I always tell my teenage son who loves those reality shows to be careful what he watches. Everything we watch, from reality shows to the news, to YouTube videos, is all energy that we are choosing to allow into our bodies. Just like food, we can choose wisely what we ingest. It *does* affect our energy.

When it comes to the news, be aware of what you listen to; bad news most likely will affect your energy (causing you to feel angry or sad). You can take control of what you ingest by turning it off for a day or a week and watch what happens. I have found that the news I need to hear gets to me one way or another—by word of mouth or my Facebook newsfeed.

Food is also a form of energy you can choose to ingest or not. Some say a high fiber; carbohydrate-rich breakfast will boost your energy.[45] There are certain foods that are known to be high in energy (among them broccoli, almonds, kale, spinach, and avocado, to name a few) and certain foods that are low in energy (processed foods; fried foods, junk foods, and foods high in sugar, for example)[46].

All you have to do to know that certain foods are/aren't good for you is to feel into it—listen to your body. See how your body feels after eating a bowl of chips. Then see how it feels after eating a bowl of steamed broccoli. Visit your local farmers markets to get fruits and veggies that are organic (without pesticides or genetically modified organisms/G.M.Os[47]) to receive the highest potency. Food can be medicine. Use chamomile tea or cucumber in your water to calm anxiety. Use protein shakes to renew your energy. Sweet potatoes are good for grounding your energy. Definitely stay away from too much sugar and caffeine—these are stimulants that have the potential to throw your blood sugar levels into a disruptive pattern, making your time feel more like a roller coaster ride than a nice even-keeled day. Try keeping a food or sleep diary to track how restful your sleep is each night. Record everything you ingested each day along with how your body responded.

When choosing your interactions with others, pay attention to the fact that there are givers and takers. I like to look at the give and take energy of the exchange—first of all, *is there one*? Or are you the one who is always giving? Does it take a lot of "work" to be around this person? When you stop to consider it, how much do you work to compensate for what that person is incapable of? Just thinking about it now may make you tired. For example, let's say you have a friend who is usually depressed when you are together. You have been doing your best to ignore this detail by trying to cheer them up or make them feel good, but you haven't noticed much how this person makes *you* feel—or what you get out of the relationship. However, now that you take time to think about it, you realize this person doesn't support you or offer you help when you need it. And when you do ask for help, it's begrudgingly given. It makes you question what you saw in that friendship in the first place. Another word for this is co-dependence; when we lose touch with our own needs and tune into another's before our own, we create an unhealthy mix of interaction that eventually has us sacrificing our own needs altogether and feeling depleted of energy.

Hand Over Heart. Breathe.
Meditation: Energize Your Heart

You can choose to bring in "healthy" or "healing" energy as well. Light a candle to mark this sacred space for extra effect. Begin by tuning into your body and your breath. Let all previous actions and thoughts go. With your feet firmly grounded on the floor and your eyes closed, do your rhythmic breathing. *Inhale to connect with your heart, pause and exhale to ground into your heart* for longer counts of breath, then pause and repeat. Once you get the sense that you are relaxed and aware of your inner life, use your imagination to visualize the color green. (This is the color that resonates energetically with your heart chakra[48].) Trust yourself to choose any color of green that you feel best suits you. (Green is the color of nature.) Now, as you breathe in, do so using that shade of green so that you are filling up your heart space with this

192

color. Visualize anything different from this color leaving your body. You might visualize a black oily substance or a brownish/yellow-like smog. Imagine that as you breathe new life (using the color green) into your heart space, the ugly stuff is pumping itself out. Repeat using your inhales and exhales, and stay with it until there is no more left to pump out. It will be easy to imagine your heart appearing a very pure shade of green. Acknowledge and appreciate this new energy inside your heart. Know you can practice this mediation whenever you choose to - with or without the candle - to purify and energize your heart.

Fill Yourself Up With Energy

Taking control of your body helps you to manage your energy so that when you feel low and want to feel high, you can do something about it. Will you reach for a Coca-Cola (or a Diet Coke)? Will you visit Starbucks? Maybe the chocolate in the kitchen drawer will do the trick. Notice these times when your blood sugar is low and acknowledge this biological shift in your body. But rather than choosing something "bad" for you such as a shot of caffeine, drink some water, eat some raw veggies or make a salad. With the amount of stress I was feeling during my divorce, I took myself to the gym to fill up. When my sons left to go to their father's house, I worked out at the gym to relieve my sadness but also to fill myself back up by feeling my physical strength and endurance. Use bodily movement, do some stretches or yoga postures. Dance or simply jump up and down to fake excitement! This may seem ridiculous, but give it a try, it actually works! Why? Because you are *acting the part*, going back to that old saying "fake it till you make it" with your mind playing the game as dictator and using your body as receiver. A few minutes will pass and before you know it you are actually feeling the change in energy level.

With the new demands our transition brings, such as an increased work load, it would be easy to put this off. There are times when I don't feel like running, but I will force myself anyway. In other words I will get ready, and start moving my legs with the intention of going for a run. Soon enough I am fully engaged in the run and so glad I am doing it. I have never regretted going for a run, because I have filled myself up by being physical. Think about how you have done this in the past—you forced yourself out the door to go do something … did you later regret it? Probably not! Most likely you appreciated that you made the decision because it shifted your energy. When you have energy, you're motivated to create your future.

My nephew, Fin, tells his mommy and daddy when his "love tank" is low. They have a mutual agreement that when it's low they give each other a hug or a kiss. This energy exchange fills them back up again. You can do this for yourself as well. Stay in tune with your needs and realize when your love tank is low or maybe even on empty. Go back to my "feed yourself energy" section for ideas of how to fill yourself back up. You can even consider all the different kinds of "tanks" that need to be kept full in order to function with plenty of energy; not only is there a need for love, but for connection, for nature, for play, for affection, for intellect, for friends, for family, for personal time, for quiet/solace, for physical activity, for order … decide what your needs are and fill them up! This is an act of self-love.

Hand Over Heart. Breathe. How Full is Your Tank? Exercise:

Take a minute here and there throughout your day to check in with yourself and ask, "How is my love tank? What percent is it full?" "How full is my energy tank?" Then do yourself a favor: listen and respond. Do something about it. If you realize you need a hug, ask for one. If you realize you are feeling depleted of energy, slow down and rest. Do this check-in using your hand over your heart to signal that you are listening to your body. Becoming aware of how much energy you have throughout your day will help you to manage it. Just like you learned in Part One of this book, by listening and taking action to honor your body, you are building a loving relationship with yourself. Keep this up and soon you will have so much power within to draw on, that creating something for your future will be easy and effortless.

Intuitive Energy

What is intuitive energy? We all acknowledge the relationship between our senses and perception, right? We use our senses: to know other's moods, to orient our way around the house, to decide what foods to eat, and to help us interpret interactions with others. The same can be said for perception: what we perceive, we believe. These are the two necessary ingredients for using your intuition, pure and simple!

The act of managing your energy will influence your intuition; playing a bigger role in your life and this will benefit you greatly. Learn to use the energy you sense in others and in situations. Having this knowledge and realizing you are first and foremost a spirit living in a physical body will help you manage your energy and reach your highest potential. How do I know? Because I am living proof of it. And so are you … Maybe you just haven't realized it yet.

Hand over heart. Breathe. Take this in: using your intuition is readily accessible to you because you use your senses and perception each and every day! Wow, pretty cool, right?

I found this story to read to my six year old son and loved it so much I wanted to share it here because it explains how our intuition is an energy exchange (based on our senses) with the world around us. Bats are inherently skilled at this! The baby bat's "song" is her intuition/sense. From "Nightsong" by Ari Berk:

> A mother bat comforts her baby bat prior to his first flight out into the night on his own. She says, "There are other ways to see… other ways to help you make your way in the world." "How?" the baby bat replied. "Use your good sense," the mother answers. When he asks her what that is, she explains, "Sense is the song you sing out into the world, and the song the world sings back to you. Sing, and the world will answer. That is how you will see. Now do not go out farther than the pond, not unless your song is sure."

Once you are attuned to (and sense) the energy moving through and around you, there are new opportunities to use your intuition. You begin to realize that when you send energy with intention to others *they will feel it*. It goes both ways—*you will also sense the energy they are sending you.* This part can get tricky (as stated earlier): the ability to discern what is your energy and what is others' will take some practice. That's another reason why it's important to stay connected. However, you can utilize these energy exchanges. Taking even just a few minutes to get quiet and be still is your way of connecting and remembering Spirit: that part of you that is connected to everything, but most importantly, that part of you that can "download" information. This is intuition, the energy you sense and perceive.

The benefit in using your intuition is that you learn to trust yourself more. In doing so, you make better decisions and choices, which in turn leave you feeling happier and more joyful. When you hear your intuitive voice speak to you: listen! For me, it backfires if I don't! Just the other day, I avoided sitting in traffic due to an accident and attended a meeting that ended up giving me exactly the information I needed to hear.

Over the years I have played around with my ability to be intuitive with myself and others. Most recently since I began aligning my truth with my actions, my intuition began to grow at a more rapid pace. I started taking the time to be still and tune in on a more regular basis. When I worked with Susann Taylor Shier, author and speaker, she shared her belief that it's only when we are separated that we are not intuitive. Separation from that universal truth, Spirit—the disconnection—is the only thing that can get in your way.[49] When you know and actively practice that connection with Spirit, there is no turning away from intuition—it becomes a part of you and how you live your life day in and day out. For example, you can use your intuition to make travel plans. During the planning process of my first solo trip to Europe, I focused primarily on those areas I felt drawn to. I decided to trust my intuition. Soon after that, these areas included sacred sites and stone circles and soon after that these areas were narrowed down to Southwest England and Ireland. It was an awesome trip!

Start by intending to use your intuition in your daily life. This potential is everywhere! If you are starting over in a new town, for example, the next time you go to a coffee shop or any public place you are desiring to get familiar with, feel into the energy of the room. Is this a place you'd like to re-visit or steer clear of? When you meet someone for the first time, observe how that person makes you feel inside. Do they make you feel good? You can also tune into the people around you and the conversation they're having. Not to eavesdrop but to sense the topic of their conversation—if it feels heavy then you have just intuited that it's not a conversation you'd like to join or it's not a good time to interrupt them to ask a question. However, if you sense those people are fun and open to having additional company, then you might feel drawn to ask to join them. We all do these things subconsciously when we're at a party or social gathering. Use this skill more and more to create more ease in your life.

Meeting people and spending time at new places is one thing, but you can also use your intuition at work. Peter had started a new job, but was having trouble forming new relationships and establishing a good rapport with his new boss. Once he began using his intuition by sensing the others' energy in the office, he was able to settle in and feel good being there. It's the old "fish out of water" syndrome . . . we're new or a beginner and we feel terribly awkward and vulnerable. However, once we realize that everything is energy, we can tap into what's really going on. Peter tuned into his boss's energy and sensed that she was extremely stressed out — she simply didn't have time to show Peter a smile or ask how he was settling in. In other words, he didn't have to take her lack of friendliness personally. He could intuit her situation was beyond her ability to give him what he desired. He also used his intuition concerning the lunch hour. Peter liked to go out to eat and forget the workplace, so he was looking for a companion to do that with. Soon, after tuning into the energy of his co-workers, he could sense who might be up for that and who would not. By listening to his intuition and acting on it, he was able to develop some good "lunch buddies."

Let's say you're using your intuition but you think you're not getting any good results. Just like anything, using your intuition takes practice. When you learn how to play a new instrument, do you expect not to make any mistakes? Probably not—first, you realize you have made a mistake because the tune doesn't sound right after you played it. Then you try a different method until the tune sounds right. Gradually you build a song, listening note by note. The same is true for using your intuition. With each action taken that ended up not feeling right, you use your feeling or senses to try again until eventually your actions validate your feelings. Gradually you build trust, listening feeling by feeling.

Not only will you learn to trust more, but you will also realize that you are not alone. You will experience Spirit to know and affirm that you are always supported. At the last Inipi sweat lodge ceremony I had the privilege of participating in, we prayed on this truth. That only when we stop and let ourselves be still to listen, can we understand that we are not the only ones doing the work. We are never truly alone: there is so much support for us! We are co-creating our life with Spirit.

I invite you to carve out some time in your schedule to sit regularly alone. Yes, I know that sounds weird. We live in a culture that perceives being alone as "bad" or "lonely." For example, when I google searched for images of "people sitting alone," the images that came up were of people who looked sad or upset. Women were sitting on their beds looking forlornly out the window. Men were sitting with their arm covering their forehead as if to shield themselves from the loneliness. There were very few images of people happily or peacefully sitting alone. However, when I google searched "people meditating" there were plenty of images of peaceful and content people sitting alone. I invite you to ignore those cultural beliefs that being alone is not okay. Rather, I invite you to embrace the time to be alone. Enjoy your company! This is your time to connect to yourself and Spirit.

Living As a Co-Creator

Now that you know you are influenced by the energy around you and that you too have the ability to influence others, you can run free with the fact that you are a Co-Creator with Spirit. Your life is built on each experience of you living as a Co-Creator. You know that your energy has the potential to create and that the infinite energy from which you create is partnered with Spirit. You're aware of the possibilities! You are taking command and working with the energy within and around you. You are now ready to purposefully use this energy with the Law of Attraction, the next chapter in this book.

Keys to Reflect On:

- There are different types of energy—build your awareness
- Begin to discern what is your energy and what is others' energy
- Be proactive: balance your energy; choose the energy you ingest and fill yourself up
- Begin to tap into intuitive energy and use it to create good decisions for yourself
- Expand with the knowledge that you can live as a Co-Creator

Chapter 10
The Law of Attraction
Will Help You Manifest Your Desires

"You attract what you are, not what you want"
~Law of Creation

The Law of Attraction says, "The essence of that which is like unto itself, is drawn." And, "You are a Creator. You create with every thought."[50] The essence of this spiritual truth is the energetic vibration that is inherent in everything. Just like you learned in the last chapter: everything is energy. That means each living thing has a vibration. Once we are aware of this, we can use this knowledge for our benefit. The Law of Attraction is just that: aligning with the energetic vibration you want to have in your life. In this chapter you will learn how embodying the experience you want to have will help you to create it.

It's interesting to note the origins of The Law of Attraction. Historically, the first person to speak about this concept was Thomas Troward (1847-1916) who said, "Thought precedes physical form." This man lived in British-ruled India at the time he wrote the Edinburgh Lectures on Mental Science in 1904 whose content states that your reality can change if you have faith in it. The philosophies he shared are "required reading for anyone wishing to understand and control the power of the mind," a popular online bookstore shares. This New Thought writer pre-dates the next gentleman known also as a New Thought writer who shared wisdom inside The Law of Attraction, Wallace Wattles, who wrote *The Science of Getting Rich* in 1910. (You can get all three of Wattles' revolutionary books together in a book called *The Science of Success.*) Some say these ideas were "stolen" by the authors/directors of *The Secret,* a best-selling self-help book from which a movie was made in 2006 that combined the Laws of Attraction and positive thinking. I am glad this is the case; that there is no copyright because information like this has the potential to make the world a better place. Now, it is practically mainstream because there are so many spiritual teachers currently presenting this information, such as Abraham Hicks, of whom I quote through-out this chapter.

There was criticism about The Law of Attraction after the book and subsequent movie, *The Secret,* came out. Many people listened to *The Secret's* message and expected it to work miracles. They thought they could obtain happiness and material goods by simply wishing it to be so. People learned quickly that "You can't just think your way into getting what you want!" While it is true that positive thinking is helpful, you also have to take action and be aware of the energy in and around you to make it work.

If people aren't familiar with the concept of energy then it can be misunderstood and misinterpreted. Without energy, there is nowhere for the engine to go—we can't *think* the engine to start up and go, it requires energy. For instance, "positivity" is more than just "positive thinking," it contains energy. Positive thinking is purely mental; it's just our minds thinking positive thoughts, whereas positivity *embodies* that energy. I think people felt misled into thinking they could wish and hope using their positive thinking while sitting on the couch to make their dreams come true. Fortunately for you, you now have a good understanding that *everything is energy*—you know how to use it, balance it, and feed yourself with it. This information will come in very handy here in this chapter.

Okay, so now that those clarifications are out of the way, you can begin learning the tenth spiritual truth with a clean slate!

The following information will work if you stay connected to Spirit and act from your heart space. It cannot be used from purely a mental point of view. Therefore, I invite you to practice putting forth action that originates from your heart, action that stems from having your thoughts aligned with your feelings, wherein they are congruent without a doubt. It's that excited, "Yes!" decision you make because every ounce of your body resonates with it. Having this kind of clarity will translate into a very clean vibration—this is the energy you want to send out to the Universe/world. And that is what this spiritual truth is all about: the vibration you are sending out to the Universe.

The Law of Attraction has transformed my life in many ways. I will show you that you too can benefit from using this spiritual truth. I'll use my own personal examples as well as those of clients' to explain in detail how this truth works. And I'll add a few more to keep your interest! You will see step-by-step how to embody and implement this truth.

Use Your Emotions to Create and Align Your Energy Vibration

You learned how to manage your emotions and feelings in Chapter Four. Now you can combine this knowledge with what you have just learned about energy and intuition. You can see that your emotions carry an energetic vibration. Your emotions can also be a source of energy. Now put that information to good use and create some fun experiences for yourself! Using The Law of Attraction, you can use your emotions (the energy of them) to increase those things in life that you would like to have. *The Universe will reflect back to you how you are feeling about it inside your heart.*

When you take charge of the energy/emotion you put out into the world, you can attract that which you would like to have more of. Here is an example of how I began with one feeling, transformed the feeling into something useful and then used the emotion behind it to manifest something I was wanting.

One summer, I began feeling sorry for myself as a single parent with three kids and my inability to provide a great vacation for them. Luckily I caught myself! Thanks to practicing The Law of Attraction, I am always tuned in to how I am using my emotions. *I want to have good things occur in my life so it's important that I feel good in order to produce them.* I could not produce a fun summer vacation for my family if I stayed in that frame of mind feeling sorry for myself. So I challenged my own sorry thinking with the thought, "Who says I can't take them somewhere?" I tuned into what a vacation I could provide them would *feel* like . . . fun! I let my whole body resonate with that feeling. I became excited! Then, I began searching for family-friendly summer vacations. I realized location would be very important so that I could stay within my budget. But nothing felt right, so I discontinued my search and decided to take a break for a while. *The trick is to stay open* even when you need to take a break. You never know what will come your way. By staying open to your original intention or idea, most times new opportunities will find you. But if you stay with your nose to the grindstone building pressure and frustration, those emotions will usually win and your efforts will die, leaving you feeling upset and hopeless. This will surely stop your efforts to apply The Law of Attraction.

Sure enough, during that break I was on Facebook and saw a post by a friend about a place called "Cat Haven" located a few hours from here. I immediately got excited (big emotional clue I'm on the right track.) My sons are in love with the big cats; leopards, jaguars and lions, oh my! Then I noticed that this place was just inside a mountainous region I had been wanting to visit: Kings Canyon National Park, all within a reasonable driving distance. What better way to combine my own interest with my sons' and in the process show them a famous park full of giant redwood trees. I had wanted to see the General Sherman Tree (known as the largest tree on the planet) for years . . . and now it would become a reality thanks to The Law of Attraction.

By focusing my attention on joy and those things I *did* want to happen on that trip, I was able to create the kind of vacation I had originally yearned for and almost missed out on, due to some sorry thinking at the beginning.

The following summer, I used the Law of Attraction to help me take our first camping trip as a single mom. Using the same principles, I created a fun time for our family. I also overcame my own fear that I wasn't capable of making it happen.

Hand Over Heart. Breathe. Manifestation Exercise:

The key to manifesting what you desire lies inside the feeling you hold about it. Take some time right now to let your imagination run free. Imagine what you'd like to have happen without holding back. Once you have completed the picture of what that looks like in your mind and heart, ask yourself, *What feeling does that give me?* This is the root of what will manifest because it's that vibration that you are sending out to the Universe.

For example, if it's a new love partner you are desiring, after you imagine that person at your side and doing all those things you'd like them to do/be, get reflective—how does it make you feel "experiencing" this person in your life? Maybe in addition to feeling loved, you feel supported, comforted, taken care of. This is the very experience/vibration that you want to hold and send out to the Universe for manifestation. There is a time buffer; nothing is instant, the time lapse is there for your protection.

Holding that emotional vibration, embodying it, and engaging in it transforms the vibration into the physical dimension. Focus on the emotional vibration of what you're really wanting to create and make the request—acknowledge that your higher self can and will activate it into your Divine line (the energy coming from Spirit that runs up and down your spine) and hold it for two minutes. Then ask for the reflection to serve your highest good. Since you are meeting an internal need, it will reflect your innermost desire. Our higher selves know how to do this work that will create the blueprint of what we want to embody and be supported by.

The Law of Attraction explains how, when your focus is on joy, all action to be taken and interaction to occur will be byproducts of that joy.[51]

Back to my example of our first family trip as a single mom: Once we arrived at our destination, our room was nice and the swimming pool was our first stop. With plenty of swimming and a pizza dinner, the first night of our vacation made our mission complete. It can only get better from here, right? (Another positive vibrational attitude to have when you are seeking to create your heart's desire: "Does it get any better than this?!" will be answered with "Yes, it most definitely does!" Give this one a try!)

The next hurdle, after finding the hotel in a town I'd never been to was finding our destination, "Cat Haven." Again, I fueled this trip with lots of excitement (positive emotional energy) and *focused my thoughts on expecting the best outcome.* This trip proved to be everything I had hoped it would be for my sons. Despite temperatures of 100 plus degrees, they walked happily and excitedly around the big cats. Having the ability to walk right up to the cage to practically sniff the cheetah was, well, amazing! We also got to meet the owner, who founded Project Cat Haven[52]. I purchased cuddly stuffed animals at a reasonable price for each son and they left happy campers. Later we talked about the cats and remembered their names. A picture of Tango the Cheetah hangs near the bed where my son sleeps.

Many times I was faced with trusting the unknown and having faith in the outcome. Again and again, the outcome affirmed this belief: *have faith and trust; not fear and doubt.* I had not been to any of these places I planned for us to visit on our trip. Each time I focused my attention on the joy this experience would bring. I stayed away from fears of getting lost. I ignored the fearful "what ifs?" and I allowed the intention of this visit to take hold. I had always loved redwood trees. And now we were about to be surrounded by them. I was also introducing them to my sons. This was enough to keep the energetic vibrations high.

The environment cannot be controlled, so learn how to navigate through it by choosing how to respond when things do feel challenging. It became clear that having no prior experience or knowledge of the road we were on would present some anxiety for me. This emotion had the potential to take us off course and away from using the Law of Attraction. We had just finished our walking tour around the General Grant Tree (one of the top five largest trees in the world). The boys got to walk inside a hollowed out giant sequoia, and see one of the last remaining log cabins originally built when logging was allowed there. As my car mounted one of the peaks inside the park and then began the drive down, I couldn't tell how long it would take us to reach our next destination within the park. We had planned to eat lunch there and we all had growling stomachs. Earlier, when I planned this day visit, I found a place inside the valley where we could eat our lunch next to a river and offered kid-friendly food. With three kids complaining they were hungry and bored of our snacks inside the car, I tried to make the best of it by offering them my camera to take pictures as we drove along. Thirty minutes later, it became clear that lunch would not be coming anytime soon as we still had miles to go before even hitting the valley floor. We stopped and got out again—this time my anxiety was heightened. Prior to stopping, the brakes on my car had started to smoke due to the steep grade of the road. We were far from services. But I stayed focused on how beautiful the valley view was and took pictures of the boys. This fed me new energy. It was hot. Really hot. But would it serve me or my kids to freak out and stress? No, it wouldn't, so knowing this I looked for ways to keep the good energy flowing. Another car came along: a camper. After chatting with the couple, I learned they had not driven to the valley floor either, ugh! But the assurance they gave me that my car would be fine, and that it couldn't take much longer to get there helped me to stay positive and get the boys back in the car for more driving.

That felt like a turning point—cave into my fear of having car problems in the heat without any services or people around to help us, or keep going having faith in the unknown and our own capability of handling any situation that could deter us. I decided that meeting that nice couple was a good sign that allowed an opening for this kind of faith. Thus with three unhappy boys, we piled back into the car and completed our trip down the mountain. It really wasn't much longer until we came upon a beautiful river that held their attention and I found our destination for lunch. The restaurant was perfect for kids, with all our favorites: hamburgers, hotdogs and chips. All was well again. We even met a worker who shared his pictures of the bears that lived nearby and his stories of walking up pretty close to them. Second point of contention completed! *(See those challenges you overcome as a major accomplishment and relish in them for a while giving yourself credit for committing to something you wanted and overcoming your fears and doubts.)* We lingered by the river after lunch near a beautiful patch of yellow wildflowers. I watched as the boys skipped rocks atop the water and hopped on the boulders to reach the middle of the river. I also took some beautiful pictures.

Hopefully you are beginning to see that it's not about being perfect or saintly in your ability to not let things get you down. It's about choosing to respond in ways that keep you in a high state of consciousness—of feeling good. This way you can manage to stay within the realm of using The Law of Attraction. *When you remain at that level of "all is well" where having faith, trust and knowledge reigns, you can base your actions on the belief that whatever unfolds will be in your best interest—everyone's best interest.*

My story is intended to help distinguish those moments when what you decide to do with the experience really matters. It's the minute you go into automatic reactionary mode that will take you out of that state of consciousness that "all is well," and send you up into your head. When we get into our heads, we become susceptible to the ego chatter and lose our high energy state of consciousness.

The best example of listening to our ego chatter is getting stuck in traffic, right? Everything could be going along smoothly and you start building expectations to get to your destination as fast as possible. Either you're tired or hungry; those instincts kick into full gear and without knowing it your mood then depends on it. Then bam, the traffic ahead of you stops you cold in your tracks. You have no choice but to slow down because the cars ahead of you have. All of a sudden life is out of your control and maybe some feelings of helplessness creep in. Now you have those insecure feelings of being without control of your life combined with primary instincts: hunger and tiredness. Under this combination of emotion, we usually crumble into a heap of unconscious yearnings:

"I want to get there . . . now!" (An Id impulse; self-centered and demanding that basic needs be met[53])

"This person is in the way of what I want!" (Blaming others)

"*Why* can't they speed up already?" (Anger or Betrayal)

"This is hopeless . . ." (Grief)

All of these emotions combine to cause stress and perhaps some actions we wouldn't otherwise choose under these circumstances. The ego/mind chatter takes away any possibility of using The Law of Attraction.

Transforming Negative Energy

Again, the trick is to rise above it all—transform your negative energy. To stay in the state of consciousness where, as in a state of grace, all is well. The intent is not to ignore these very strong emotions, but to acknowledge them and use them. Then you can still use the Law of Attraction.

For example, when I am able to "rise above it" this is what it looks like when I hit traffic using the previously mentioned emotions:

I will say out loud (expressing self),

"Oh great! Perfect! Now I am going to be late! I should have allowed more time..." (Transforming anger into personal responsibility)

"Why can't they have two roads instead of one leading into this area?!"

(Transforming blame into higher order of organization—seeing the bigger picture, problem solving/analyzing)

Then my thoughts go to, "Oh well, there is nothing I can do about it now." (Transforming grief into letting go/release/surrender)

Finally to action: *"I should make a phone call to let them know I will be late"* (proactive) or I can think up a plan, like with where I will park the car when I get there (solution-focused, multi-tasking) or I can take this time to relax and look out the window, and do some deep breathing.

We can keep our vibration high by taking personal responsibility. Using The Law of Attraction requires you to live this way: taking charge and finding solutions as opposed to remaining stuck with strong emotions and feeling like a victim. *There are always choices you can make.* This may not seem to be the case in the heat of the moment, but that is only because your emotions are clouding your ability to see them. Once you take a deep breath and focus on your breathing, your emotions won't be front and center. This will help you to see that you do have a choice in every situation. You can always break it down to your ability to breathe a little deeper, right? That is a choice you will have in every situation . . . Choose to be in a high, feeling good state to maintain The Law of Attraction.

Feeling Good is Important: It's the Point of Attraction

Feeling-states are very important when using The Law of Attraction. Consider those times when we feel bad and the emotions that are with us at the time. Basically we are swallowed up with a heavy feeling and there is no "I" anymore . . . we are lost in a sea of emotions . . . as if we are drowning and getting dragged down to the bottom of the sea. We have attached our concept of "I" to the emotion, therefore we *are* the emotion. Ask yourself, "In this state of being, do I feel capable of new ideas?" When you are feeling this way, ask yourself, "Can I see myself accomplishing my goals?" Do you even *want* to make plans? The answer is "No," because these emotions and feelings have a negative vibration . . . the energy of these emotions is vibrating low. As learned in previous chapters, if energy is everything and emotions carry energy, then we want to choose our feelings wisely, right? When we remember we have an opportunity to choose our feelings, then we get back to that state of feeling good. When we make a conscious choice to use The Law of Attraction, then we make decisions around keeping our energy high and vibrant. Knowing that we have the ability to create what we want will be hampered if we stay in a negative feeling-state. Remember we can choose another option: to feel good. As stated in previous chapters, simply telling yourself you *want* to feel better can be your next step toward getting there.

One way to do this successfully is to focus on what *is* working in the moment (see exercise in Chapter Eight: Appreciation). You can do this once you have some breathing space and feel a little less weighed down from your strong emotions. The great thing about this choice is that it serves The Law of Attraction so well. It's all about our focus: where we decide to place our attention. Choose: will we focus on the traffic stopping us in our tracks or will we focus on the time we have just been afforded to slow down? Which focus has a positive vibration and which has a negative vibration? Which choice makes you feel good? *This is the crux of using The Law of Attraction—always choose the thoughts and emotions that make you feel good.*

When I ran my first half marathon, there were things that I did on purpose along the way that helped me to finish and meet my desire to not stop and walk. For example, when the path on the hard packed sand of the beach moved into soft sand, away from the beach and onto the street for a loop toward the end of the race, I knew it would be a challenge. So I made a conscious choice to place my thoughts and emotions (focused energy) only on having this work for me rather than against me. I decided that the soft sand was merely a transition from beach to street; a short distance that was doable. (There were no thoughts of "I don't want that soft sand to ruin my pace!" or "I don't want that soft sand to cause me to walk and mess up my goal to keep running"). My focus was "This will work fine." Then, to add another layer of good energy coming my way, when I passed other runners on my way back through this awkward transition, I directed my motivated energy their way so that they could receive a boost (the boost that I needed) to get through it. In doing so, I was able to embody the experience I wanted to have. Then I was awarded a boost of energy myself once I hit the last portion of the race. I put out energy to help others at a time when they needed it and so that is what I received in return: more energy for me to feel motivated to finish the race. And believe me when I say I felt good crossing that finish line! I was high as a kite!

Use Your Focus to Direct The Law of Attraction

When we focus on what is working (as with the traffic example), it will look like this: we have been given more time; our energy shifts, and our hearts open and expand again. When we choose the option that points us in the direction of feeling good again, we can see better as well. Our emotions lift and we achieve clarity. Suddenly we can realize that maybe we had our appointment time wrong in the first place, or maybe we remember something like the fact that we forgot to take dinner out of the freezer to thaw for that night. We can't see or realize things when we feel bad. When we feel bad, all focus and energy revolves around that negativity. We could swim around in circles getting dragged down by anger, sadness, or stress. It's why stress relief is so important; finding/using outlets for stress is essential for taking care of yourself. If we can't get our thoughts to change using our minds, then we can make use of our bodies. Remember Chapter Four, about managing emotions and changing moods? Go outside or go for a run or a walk. Turn on some music and dance. Get your body moving to shift your energy back into a higher feeling-state.

Simply moving can and will shift your negative emotions into positive ones so you're feeling good again. I dare you to turn on some music; force yourself to move to the tune and not begin to feel better. And when I say "move to the tune" that can be as simple as using your finger tips to tap the beat. Force yourself to go for a run, and stay mad . . . will that work? Go for a walk and be sad at the same time . . . will it last? Get up and go outside and interact with your plants (water, tend to) . . . but stay frustrated. Reach down and pet your dog for a few minutes, looking into his eyes, but stay stressed out. You can begin to see how these simple actions of movement can begin to shift your energy back to *feeling good again*. You can't remain in your negative mood when you participate in these bodily movements. Something shifts no matter what. Even if it's just a little, it's still a starting point; a starting point to build upon what is working. In this way, soon we can apply our choices and actions like building blocks; building upon each step toward feeling good by consciously focusing where we place our attention and energy. This helps us to embody the energy we want to create.

When we take charge by choosing where to focus our energy, we can use The Law of Attraction to help us manifest what we want to happen. The Universe will have no other choice but to cooperate and reciprocate in kind. According to Abraham Hicks, "The Law of Attraction says: "That which is like unto itself, is drawn . . . You will begin to recognize the exact correlation between what you have been thinking about and what is actually coming into your experience. Nothing merely shows up in your experience. You attract it, all of it, no exceptions. Giving thought to it is inviting it."[54]

Use Perspective to Keep Your Energy Vibration High

You can also use perspective when you have setbacks. It's easy for us to get so focused on the outcome that we miss the process of getting there. As you have probably heard before, it's the journey that is so rich with opportunities. We have the ability to open up to them by changing our perspective. When we change our perspective from focusing on the negative detail, we can go wider to the bigger picture containing the negative detail. All of sudden we can see clearly that this detail is much smaller than we thought and that we have an ability to navigate away from it by choosing something different to look at. When I was feeling down about some drama at school, my mother would always tell me, "Imagine that you climb up a ladder and look down on yourself and this problem—what would it look like then?" We also had a big hill in the back of our house, so other times she would tell me to go climb the hill and look down on everything so that I could come back home with a new perspective. Expand your awareness by focusing on the bigger picture to see that the setback is really just a pause at the side of the road. You will get back on your path and choose differently next time.

One of the women in my the support group I facilitate, *Women Starting Over*, came to group the other day sharing how she used the Law of Attraction to get her new job. But first she had to overcome her own fears of not getting hired because of her age. She had just turned sixty, and while successful in an earlier career, it had been a while since re-joining the work force. However, with our help, Judy increased her courage to begin her job search. Judy had always been great at letting people see her for who she is. Sure enough, at one of the interviews she was told, "You are exactly the demographic we are looking for and want to attract for our business." Judy didn't get that job but she used that comment to change her perspective about her age being a problem. She allowed this comment to help her embody confidence in herself and her new perspective (that her sixty year old personality can be exactly what they're looking for), and carried it to her next interview where she got the job.

Perspective will always help us to shift our energy into a higher state of consciousness. Whether it's a shift or a transformation, they both serve to help us with The Law of Attraction. When we orient our life (and more specifically our actions) around the concept that we are co-creators in manifesting what we want, we understand the significance of feeling good. We simply cannot create or produce new things for ourselves when we feel bad. This is the basic crux of The Law of Attraction. *In order to manifest and attract those things we want in life, we need to do so from a space of feeling good.*

Placing Focus on What You *Don't* Want

There's a common phrase that describes what is going on with The Law of Attraction that you might not have considered. Have you ever heard anyone, in discussing something bad that happened, say, *"I don't pay it much mind."*? What they are saying (at least mentally), is that they are actively choosing not to invest their energy in negativity. They are choosing not to go there. They have decided not to place their attention and focus on the bad thing that happened. As a result, they are propelled by the force of staying positive and choosing good thoughts. In this action, they are maintaining a high level of vibration and not getting dragged down by negativity. They may even be able to use the experience to help themselves and others.

On the other hand, when you place your focus and attention on what you don't want to happen, well . . . that is what *will* happen because you attracted the vibration you put out—*that which you don't want.* When you see something that you *do not* want to experience and you shout, "No, no, I do not want that!" through your attention to it you invite it into your experience.

There is no such thing as exclusion in this attraction-based world. Your attention to it will be carried in your vibration, and if you hold it in your attention or awareness long enough, The Law of Attraction will bring it into your experience. There is no such thing as "No" in an attraction-based Universe . . ."[55]

A friend told me a story about when she had gone out to a very nice Italian restaurant with her folks. They had made their reservation so they were prepared to have a very nice meal without any problems. (Of course, things happen that are outside of our control.) The restaurant was short one waiter because he had to take his son to the hospital. So my friend and her parents had to wait for their food for a while, which turned into a long while which really tested the patience of her father. My friend explained that the minute her father heard they were short on help, his fears/doubts sent him straight into thinking "I don't want to have to wait long for my food!" It was all he could think about. Despite the birthday gifts they exchanged and the conversation to be had, her father was filled with "Don't make me wait!" What the Universe heard was, "Make him wait!" because there is no such thing as "no" according to The Law of Attraction.

His energy attracted what he didn't want. You might be familiar with the saying, *"What you resist will persist."* This has been referred to as the Law of Humility which uses the same principle as The Law of Attraction: using your energy, focus and attention are key. What you place your attention on will manifest more of the same. Had my friend's father focused his attention and energy on his family sitting before him, (helping to shift his perception), the long wait would have been more bearable, less of a bother and probably shorter!

It's when you go out into the world and interact with others that The Law of Attraction gets trickier to use, because of the simple fact that you cannot control others' actions. But when you begin to practice using your focused energy around others like this, you will see results. And it's fun! It's really fun when you get evidence of The Law of Attraction at work.

Hand Over Heart. Breathe. Journal Exercise: Abundance

Ask yourself: which energy are you holding most of the time: scarcity or abundance? If you are looking at life as scarce then that is what you will get, whereas if you view life as abundant and rich, that is what you will receive. Scarcity-energy is having the feeling that there will not be enough to go around for everyone—that if you take, then you could be causing someone else to be without. Scarcity-energy is also feeling like you have to compete with others to get what you want. In other words, someone must lose in order for you to get what you want. On the other hand, abundance-energy is feeling like there is plenty to go around for everyone. There is always enough. You are free to choose what you want because there will still be enough for others. You don't worry about not having enough one day. And you don't fear losing it once you have it either. Write down your thoughts about this and any previous experience that comes to mind. Gaining this awareness allows you to catch yourself thinking this way. If necessary, use your awareness to then shift your focus.

The Law of Attraction is about maintaining a good feeling-state, keeping a clear focus and calling attention/placing your focus on those things you'd like to create. The feelings and thoughts you embody and carry around with you during the day will be what you get in return. It goes beyond being able to buy that brand new car or bigger house. The Law of Attraction is a state of being in the world. In order to create change you need to *be open* to change. Using my half marathon example, in order to meet my expectations, I needed to be/embody my expectations (follow through). Using the example of my family trip to the mountains, in order to have a happy experience, I needed to *be* the happy experience.

Remembering that you are a spirit or soul living in a body to Co-Create your reality is key. When something in life happens to take you off course, you can use this principle to re-focus and steer yourself back toward attracting what you want. Navigating through hurdles and maintaining your focus of attraction is what matters. In the next chapter, you will see how using The Law of Attraction combines well with *setting intentions*.

Keys to Reflect On:

- You attract what you are—so manage your energy
- Use your emotions to create and align your energy vibration
- Maintain a good feeling-state because that is what will be reflected back to you
- Feeling good is important; it's the point of attraction
- Pay attention to where you place your focus, or those things you don't want will manifest too!

Chapter 11
Setting Intentions
Will Help Create Your Reality

"We are Divine enough to ask and we are important enough to receive."
~Wayne Dyer

The Law of Attraction works in conjunction with your intentions. When you make conscious choices both in heart and mind you begin to create what you want. I would identify Dr. Wayne Dyer as the "Father of Intentions" due to his vast experience in writing and speaking on this subject. Dr Dyer says, "Our intention creates our reality."[56] I agree with this, which is why I consider it to be the eleventh spiritual truth for creating your bright future.

Dr. Dyer is an internationally renowned author and speaker in the field of self-development. He holds a doctorate in educational counseling from Wayne State University and was an associate professor at St. John's University in New York. Just recently, I learned that he actually was afforded the good fortune of having Abraham Maslow as a mentor. That's impressive to me, as Maslow is one of the forerunner theorists of the humanistic psychological perspective and movement. Maslow is the theorist behind "self-actualization" and the "hierarchy of needs." These psychological concepts have stood the test of time and most of us use them unknowingly every day. The basic assumption of the humanistic approach is that we have an innate desire for personal growth, and this is the crux for setting intentions. Use your innate potential for personal growth to create what you want.

A Chumash medicine man once told me a story to illustrate the importance of deliberate intent. A pelican captured a fish and was struggling to eat it while many seagulls gathered around him. Each seagull was trying to steal the fish out of his reach. While the fish flipped and flopped around him, the pelican became anxious. It wasn't until he was able to focus all of his energy without becoming distracted by the other seagulls that he was able to master getting the fish into his mouth to swallow. At first he couldn't accomplish this task because his energy was diffused. However once he focused all of his energy, he had deliberate intent which allowed him to capture the fish.

I describe intention as *the energy* that drives those things we would like to do or have. You're probably familiar with the phrase many people use in everyday life when asked to do something: "I intend to!" When we intend to do something we are really saying that our thoughts are energetically supporting us. There is no outcome yet. However, our good thoughts are what drive us. As you have learned, thoughts are energy.

Intention can also be a type of knowingness. If we know something to be true without a doubt, there is no other option. By extension, there is no possibility of negative thinking to interrupt the process of creation. So expect the best outcome. When we expect it, we believe it whole-heartedly; we *know* it to be true. For example, when we put water into an ice tray to form ice, we *know* it will become ice, and as long as our freezer is working as it should, it does. We know that when we order a pepperoni pizza we will get a pepperoni pizza. We expect that when the water boils, we can brew a tasty hot cup of tea. It's this kind of knowing that is required in the energetic field of setting our intentions.

Intentions Are Different Than Goals

Intentions are different than goals. Here is why. *Goals project your desired outcome and expectations into the future, whereas intentions allow you to begin living how you want now.* It may help to use the principle from the book, *The Power of Now.* Recall that all creation is possible in the moment to which you bring your conscious awareness[57]. When you set an intention you set in motion your energy, focus and attention and apply it to the present moment. With intentions, the focus is the energy you give to your desire with each moment of every day. There is no waiting to enjoy the outcome because you can begin to feel the changes happening now, in present time. The outcome is no longer the focus, and the process of getting there is more important. For example, in my yoga class, I am told during poses to "Lead with your heart" and before I begin, to "Set an intention for your practice." These statements start the energy flowing in the direction where I want my desire to go.

It's certainly possible to combine your goals with the driving force of your energy/intention. For example, in getting this book completed, I wrote the first forty-six pages on and off for a couple of years and then let it sit. It wasn't until I meditated on what my next step needed to be, that I realized I needed to continue writing and feel the effects of completing the book. My energy perked up again and allowed me to finish. So I set an intention—a very powerful intention—to finish writing the book in 90 days. But I didn't do so blindly or carelessly. I used what I learned about intentions *and* goals. To make a strong goal I used the SMART Goals technique: 1. Make a declarative powerful *statement*. 2. Be sure that it is *measurable*. 3. Be sure that it's *achievable* and realistic. 4. Have it be *relevant; relatable* to the bigger picture you want. 5. Make it *time-based* using a check-in system to *track* your success/progress. [58]

Hand Over Heart. Breathe. Use the SMART Goals Technique:

First, relax your body and tune into your breath. Use your breath to connect with your heart. With your inhale, connect to your heart and with your exhale, ground your focus there. After a few minutes, or when you feel ready, feel into your heart to ask what it desires. If it's a new year and you'd like the upcoming year to be a certain way . . . if your heart desires a new love interest . . . or if your heart desires a job change, make note of this with your mind. Now with your eyes open, take out a piece of paper and write down your heart's desire. Then follow the five steps outlined above. Write it out until the words leap out at you with enthusiasm and clarity. Be concise and precise with your statements. Avoid writing more than one or two sentences as this dilutes the statement. There is more strength in simplicity.

For example:

S—*Statement:* I am writing my book in 90 days!

M—I am *measuring* my goal by writing almost every day for an hour and a half = which translates to a couple of pages a day. I will know it's complete once I reach 90 days.

A—I know this is *achievable* because I enjoy writing and I feel very motivated. I also hired a writing coach to help keep me motivated by checking in with me each day.

R—Writing this book *relates* to my purpose in life—helping others through inspiration or empowerment—and it helps transform my experience into something positive and meaningful.

T—I am keeping a *time table* to keep *track* of my progress by talking to my writing coach each day.

It's important to set up the goal so that it includes all five principles. What I like about the fifth criteria of setting goals according to this method, is that it does bring your desire into the present moment—the action of checking in to see how your goal is progressing helps to bring the goal into the present moment.

Another difference between goals and intentions is that goal-setting usually only measures your progress weekly, whereas an intention is lived every day. How so? You can monitor your intention by how you create your energy each day. When you step out of bed and into a new day, you choose thoughts, and connect to your heart. Your actions will then align with your intention. You breathe it. Your intention becomes *who you are now versus who you could be* once you have reached your goal.

Let's look at the example of writing my book in 90 days. The coach I hired told me, "As long as you keep the book alive, you will be okay." In other words, on those days when I couldn't find the time to write, I didn't have to lose motivation. I found that on the days I was too busy to actually write, I could keep the book alive by *thinking* about it. My thinking about it kept the energy flowing. I also "acted the part as an author" in how I viewed myself and in how I related to others. For example, during Christmas time I was around family "24/7" for four days without much opportunity to write. I still had my intention to write every day so instead of writing during those busy times, I talked about the book. Due to the fact that I was "acting the part as an author" with my energy, I was embodying that sense and that perception. I

220

was putting that energy out there for others to sense and feel in return. Due to that vibration, I was sending out *I am an author,* they asked me about my book—not just once or twice, but many times. And in the act of sharing what the book was about, I got to also share the juicy content with them and my excitement about the project. These actions helped to keep the book alive during those days I couldn't write. It worked too, because the minute I had free time again, I readily got back into the flow of getting the content out on paper. The first day back from vacation, I wrote a couple of pages; the next day, four pages; within a week I was done writing the book! The greatest part of this outcome was that I accomplished writing the first draft of the book in 30 days rather than 90!

Intentions embody your focused energy, so set them up right. Use your deep knowing of what your intention feels like: get in touch with that truth.

Embody the Intention You'd Like to See
Come to Fruition *by Living It*

I'll go into greater detail, still using my book as an example. *I started living the book every day.* (Does this remind you of the Law of Attraction?) Due to the fact that my energy (thoughts, emotions and actions) were in alignment with writing this book, the content for the book started to appear left and right. Whether I heard something when I flipped on the TV, overheard a conversation at the park, or listened to something my sons said, the content was being presented to me all the time. When this kind of thing happens it's synchronicity because I am staying connected and living my intention. Webster's dictionary describes synchronicity as "the experience of two or more events as meaningfully related, whereas they are unlikely to be causally related." The subject sees it as a meaningful coincidence, although the events need not be exactly simultaneous in time. Staying connected and living my intention brings me joy and peace in the moment and allows for a magical experience as all the pieces come together. Rather than spend my time and energy worrying about how the pieces will fit together in the future that a goal describes, I can place my trust in the deep sense that I now have: my book is getting done . . . now, with my intention.

It's Scientific and Biological

In allowing yourself to feel into your intention in the present moment, you are actually forming a new *blueprint* in your brain.[59] Another favorite teacher is Dr. Bruce Lipton who wrote a revolutionary book *The Biology of Belief* in which he actually connected science with thought patterns. He suggests that our thoughts have the potential to impact our genes and DNA. His extraordinary work is debatable but still has far-reaching potential to help people evolve into their best selves. Just think of the possibilities if we took charge of our own DNA. What if those traits and behavioral patterns we thought we were stuck with because we were born with them don't send us to our destiny anymore? He suggests the possibility that each cell in our body is receptive to change. Right up to the cells on those thighs you anguish about every day (grin). His work explains that all of those hateful messages we send to those body parts we wish were thinner, better looking, or better functioning have an impact; those cells are listening to us and acting accordingly.

So if your intention is to lose weight, think twice the next time you send your body parts hateful energy with your thoughts. Choose instead to send them love and admiration for the true miracle that your body is. Stop a minute here and consider how miraculous your body really is . . . Consider what it's able to accomplish for you on a daily basis. Reflect on all its organs. The mere fact that your heart beats, that your liver acts like a wastewater treatment plant, that your muscles can remember movements, or that your wounds can heal all by themselves, it's truly amazing work! Yes, we are not just a body—we are a spirit in a body first and foremost, but when we live this life in cooperation with our bodies, life becomes a coordinated dance. With *all of you* at the helm, captain of the ship or pilot at the command center, you can become totally self-sufficient. Be cognizant of all that it takes and do this dance with full recognition. Life is amazing. This will bring joy into your intention to lose weight.

The Energy Behind Words is Powerful

Words carry an energetic resonance with them. I touched on this in Part One of the book, but here you will feel into them and begin to use words that motivate and have a greater capacity for creating and manifesting. Use them when setting your intentions. Use them in your communication with others. When I work with clients, I tell them to stop using words that project them into the future such as, "I want" or "I will" and replace them with phrases that immediately put them in the present moment such as, "I am" or "I am willing." (See my SMART goal for example.) The words "I am" in particular carry a very high vibration that will start the energy flowing faster now as opposed to later. When we live in the present moment with our intention, the manifestation process can begin.

One simple way to live your intention using powerful words is to use one for your password when you need to create one. If you do online banking, visit social networking websites like Facebook or Twitter, and/or use email, for example, you will have a password for each account. Use a word that reminds you of your intention. Use a word that makes you feel powerful. It's a quick way to remind yourself of your intention and align yourself with that energy.

I also ask clients to stop using words that project them into the past for instance when using the "T"—(time table and tracking progress section), of the SMART Goals technique. Some clients tend to use the past when making intentions for what they want in the present/future. They will say, "I was so tired that I didn't go to my Zumba class." However, it's the clean slate we're after—bring all language and conversation into the present moment. Yesterday's problem about not getting to the gym doesn't matter, nor does last week's binge on ice cream. Bring all attention and focus to the present moment and eliminate all conversation about the past. For example, "I have enough energy to go the gym on five days out of seven." This will align with the concepts from chapter two; the present moment, wherein all creation is possible in the present moment. This is important when using the Law of Attraction as well, because if you use words/language in past tense then you will get—nowhere, whereas if you use present tense language, Spirit can then reflect back to you what you are.

The energy of now is present, the energy of past is not.

The most important thing is that the present moment affords you with all that is possible! You are completely free in this very second in time. So you get to begin your intention with a completely clean slate right now, thus making you full of potential, right?! That's exciting! Use language of the present moment to bring life into your words and intention.

I invite you to place your hand over your heart and breathe. When you feel into words such as, *"I am"* versus *"I want,"* what differences do you notice? Does one phrase project you into the future and separate you from yourself, while the other keeps you connected and feeling whole? Say aloud each statement separately. Take a minute or two to let yourself resonate, percolate and feel into it. Again, notice the difference between the two.

Now tell me how you feel. Did you notice the shift in your capacity to feel empowered?

Journal Exercise: "I Am"

Right now, I invite you to come up with a desire, large or small, and write it down here, with as few words as possible; make it simple.

Now play around with the words to optimize the potential of the statement and to bring it into this present moment. Use words that carry an emotional resonance—this is what makes words powerful.

For example: I want to lose 20 pounds: "I am losing 20 pounds!"

"I want to get out of debt" transformed into: "I am getting out of debt!"

Can you see how immediately you begin living your intention using these words? There is action in the "I am" statements. They hold energy.

Now go further with it and add more powerful words such as; "I know I can do it!" "I trust that I can Co-Create with Spirit for this to transpire." "I have faith in my ability to . . ." "I can't wait to . . ." "I can already feel the results!" "I sense it happening now!"

If you used the SMART Goals technique in the previous exercise, go back and change the wording to incorporate present tense, "I am or I have" instead of future tense, "I will or I want." You can also make your statements read as if they have already happened. This is very powerful because it will increase your positive emotions. For example, "I will lose weight, or I want to lose weight" versus, "I have started losing weight, or I AM losing weight."

"Emotion is a powerful motivator of future behavior"
~ Don Childe

Embody Your Intention

I attended a workshop put on by the one and only Dee Wallace (the actress who played the mom in the movie "E.T.")[60] She now has her own acting studio/school and is a leader in the self-help movement. I really admire the way she created this workshop using different language/words to empower the attendees. She used the word "playshop" intentionally so that attendees would feel relaxed and could have fun.

She took the word "work" out of "workshop," knowing that it's difficult to create changes when we feel like we have to work for it. She decided that by playing we could incorporate these teachings and learn easier and faster. Next she offered her own heart, by standing at the door and giving each one of us a hug as we entered the room. How heart-felt is that?! This was her very first "playshop" and she was highly aware of how she was intending (intentional word use!) to create it, moment by moment. Dee is all about the *"I am"* statement[61] as she embodies it, models it for others and teaches it. It was extraordinary to listen to her speak and experience her creation as we followed a hands-on approach to learning and then playing—the playing part is what served to integrate what we had just learned. She had fabulous exercises that included dancing in line, singing and role playing. We practiced these concepts using our *"I am"* presence so that by the end of the day we embodied as much as we possibly could. It was an unforgettable event and a wonderful example of how to embody your intention.

State Your Preference

What is your preference? Are you capable of stating it? Are you willing to ask for it? If there was something presented to you (without anyone asking), could you tell them what you would prefer? Stating your preference is an opportunity to express your desire. It's one thing to talk about what you desire or what you want. It's another to put it into words—and yet another thing to request it of someone else. Are you *able* to do this? If not now, then are you capable? *Everyone is capable*—it's getting to that point of feeling like you can, that moves you from feeling unable to capable. How do you get there? Practice! I invite you to begin practicing stating your preference to friends, family and strangers.

Stating your preference will build confidence in your ability to manifest it. When we feel that who and what we are is enough, then we are comfortable in our own skin. When we feel like we can never ask for too much, then we are strong in our convictions. When we state our preference, we are expressing our value—that which we believe we deserve. Try it out the next time you are asked to choose. Simply say, "My preference is ..." and experience how good that feels. It's a declaration of self—you're declaring who you are and that your desires are worth knowing and having. This will set your intention into forward movement.

Believe

You have heard people say over and over again "You have to believe in yourself" in order to get what you want to happen. Well, that is what you are creating here—a strong belief in yourself. Using a playful, light-hearted loving approach, you invite and allow all possibilities to begin entering your life to make it happen. Nothing will come to fruition if you get stuck on repeating "I have to believe in myself!" without positive energy behind it, will it? To me, it feels heavy and full of effort. Again, manifesting and creating cannot spring forward easily out of seriousness and effort. Know that you are, trust that you are (just as you do the fact that water placed into trays for the freezer will turn into ice), and place your faith in that you simply are... These are much different energetic statements than, "I want to believe in myself" and, "I don't want this . . ." or, "Believe believe...!" *BE what you are—live it now and embody it so that you can simply say and declare "I am" . . . this is how you manifest!*

Use the Law of Attraction

"You attract what you *are*, not what you want." As I said in the last chapter, frequently the message of the movie/book, *The Secret* gets misconstrued as suggesting that you can simply wish for what you want (like a new car) in order to receive it. But as you have learned, when you go deeper with the Law of Attraction and the energy behind it, this is an oversimplification of the actual message. Attracting what we want takes the form of a mirror. The energy of the Universe and Spirit responds to the energy that you are putting out, so your thoughts, actions, heart, spirit, soul . . . all of these things make up who and what you are about *inside.* "Be what you are" means beyond what you do for a living or that you are a wife or a daughter, etc. The vibration of energy you give off must be in alignment with what you want in order to acquire more of it. As you learned in the last chapter, the Law of Attraction works with your energy. So if it's new friendships you'd like to acquire, hold the energy of friendship inside your heart (for example, feelings of support, kindness, fun, loyalty). Express these qualities to yourself to attract them in friends that you want. This will propel your intention into manifestation.

Allow

"Your task is not to seek for love, but merely to seek and find all the barriers within yourself that you have built against it."
~ Rumi

This is such a profound statement, isn't it?! How do we allow our intentions to come true? We remove the blocks in our awareness. In other words, if it's losing weight we'd like to accomplish, then allow it to happen by releasing your insecurities (such as fear of success or failure). How do we do this? Bring those fears to light and push back on them with a high level of trust. The opposite of fear is faith and trust. "I trust that when I lose weight everything will fall into place for my highest good." Or "I trust that I will lose weight to the best of my ability no matter what happens and that I will feel satisfied with the outcome." Use your focus on the present moment to allow intentions to flow. You can interrupt the flow of your intention by focusing on the past or the future, but not when you experience the now. When you allow things to happen you are not forcing the outcome. It's a space of being open. Just like you are open to reading a new book, you feel the excitement and intrigue. There is no fear of not finishing it or fear of completing it. It just *is*. I think this is where the popular saying comes into play, "It is what it is." Acceptance allows everything to happen, and your trust and faith that perfect order will ensue is what's needed; allow it to happen.

To further illustrate how allowing your intentions to work helps the process become a reality, I'll re-tell my experience running my first half marathon. I had been running for only about four months. My friend and I were running four times a week, usually four miles. It felt great and made me feel powerful. About a month prior to the marathon, we decided we could enter the half marathon here in town, a 12.5 mile race. To prepare, we increased our run to six miles twice a week. However, we didn't commit or register for the race because my friend got injured. It wasn't until days before the event that I decided to just go for it anyhow, on my own. Okay, I knew I had to have a pretty solid intention to make this happen with only six miles of running on pavement (the race was on the beach), half of what was required of me to complete!

I knew I needed to allow this experience to unfold to the best to my ability. I set the intention that I would complete the race without stopping—this was number one. To this I added my intent to keep a slower pace—around an eleven-minute mile. Along the way, my fears crept in of course, "What if I can't make it?" Then another barrier presented itself: Because I started later in the pack, I was at the end of the crowd, therefore there weren't many people around while I ran. (I tend to do better when I feel supported by the presence of others.) How did I not let these things get to me? My motivation began to sink. To prevent these barriers from getting the worst of me, I focused all of my attention on my intention. My thoughts focused only on the present moment, I drew strength from the uplifting music I had with me, and I kept my energy up with a lot of positive self-talk/affirmations. Pretty soon I found myself sprinting for the finish line (two and a half hours later).

SETTING INTENTIONS

Let Go of *How*

It's only too easy to get caught up in, "But *how* will my intentions come true??" We want to know and understand how things happen; it's our nature, right? I know that my day flows much better and I *feel* better when I can let go of *how* everything will get done by just intending that certain things will. When you are in this space of conscious awareness, spiritually connected to your spirit/heart and mind, things become effortless.

The key I have to always keep in mind is to let go of the struggle of *how it will all take place.* One way to do this is to fall back on one of *The Four Agreements* by Don Miguel Ruiz, so that I can rest assured—"Always do your best." This brings me comfort, because there are times when I can't get it all done according to what is expected, but if I am truly doing the best that I can, then it's easier to let it go. No beating myself up required! Less stress to make it happen, and faith in the orchestration of all creation: *thy will be done.* Sure it's a tall order at times! But the more we practice these concepts the easier times we have. (And I say "we" on purpose because when I am stressed, my sons are stressed.) *So it all begins with me.* Sometimes, there are days that are full of activity and I wonder, "How will I get a specific task done?" When I practice these principles, it's as if time magically appears for me and I am invited to sit down and write. I am aware and present, so I notice when time opens up. Trust, know, allow . . . *Letting go of how it will be done* is a wonderful concept to live by.

David Hawkins, a philosopher and founding member of the Federation of American Scientists and, claims to have had a number of profound spiritual experiences since the age of three, said, "All of the great teachers throughout time say, 'Let go of your attachment to the linear, to the definition of things, and as you do that, you begin to experience the nonlinear aspects.' [They then] become the greater reality, and your own consciousness advances as a consequence. The linear is limited to this world." When we let go of how, we allow for "other forces" to take place. Our ability to Co-Create is increased. What are "non-linear" aspects? These include things like your imagination, sensing your energy and that of others around you, or feeling your faith and trust inside your heart.

Hand Over Heart. Breathe. Journal Exercise: Receiving

When you *do* receive what you want, how are you with *having* that experience? Let's say that new love interest did come knocking on your door, would you open it and let it in? Or would you hesitate, question it or back away? Sometimes we put great energy into creating what we want without much thought to what happens once we receive it! But this is part of the package. Are you ready to receive what you want? Can you see it happening? What would that experience be like?

My friend Katrina's husband bought her a Porsche. It was a 72' 911 with a targa top and almost falling apart but she loved it. She told me she was having a hard time receiving it—this was her dream car—and now she was behind the wheel! How could she rationalize that? Well, she couldn't. She had to come to terms with receiving and begin to experience the joy of having what she had wanted. It wasn't that difficult for her. Sure, it felt strange and a little overwhelming for her at first. She had some insecurity about deserving it. But gradually after she allowed those emotions to come and go, she let herself have fun driving it. She learned to receive the car and love it whole-heartedly. It was one of her first "dreams do come true" moments. If you let yourself open up to receiving, your heart expands—and the people on the giving end get to receive your gratitude and joy. Now that's a complete circle!

In her book, *Stroke of Insight,* Jill Bolt Taylor said, "What if we are all capable of downloading God? *That the only thing stopping us is our own inability to receive it?* What if that is all God wants—to provide downloads for us to receive, and it's up to us to learn how to receive it—that love?" I invite you to consider Marianne Williamson's *Course in Miracles* and what she teaches about love— the energy of love is the highest form of energy[62], so what more is there to aspire to? It also makes it clear why loving ourselves is so important! If we can't love ourselves then we can't receive love, true? When we don't love ourselves, we partake in many destructive actions that end up hampering our ability to receive love because we're ignoring that connection. When we are separated from this connection, we fail to remember what's in our heart's best interest.

It can be helpful to take some time to wonder about this with yourself. Take out your journal and ask yourself, "What is my capacity to receive what I want? Is there anything that would block me from having it? Would I let another person ruin it for me? Would I give it away?" Take a few minutes right now to visualize yourself receiving your intention. Once you feel relaxed and easy with your visualization, breathe. Imagine yourself having what you want. Can you involve all of your senses (colors, scents, feelings, sound)? Does it feel natural or awkward? Are you able to embrace it or are you hesitant? Do you see yourself grimace or with a smile on your face? Is there any part of you that screams, "Wait! I'm not ready!" (That used to be one of my reactions.) Write down your blocks and hesitations. Now that they are known, you can work with them.

They say we can be our own worst enemy. Well here we are. Rumi wrote, *"Your worst enemy cannot harm you as much as your own unguarded thoughts."*

Take this into consideration, so you can get out of your own way. Stay open and ready to receive.

"All the powers in the universe are already ours. It is we who have put our hands before our eyes and cry that it is dark." ~Swami Vivekananda

Use Your Imagination

It's been said that without imagination, nothing could be realized into existence. When you consider everything around you and begin to notice, each "something" began as someone's idea. It's one of the reasons I love TED.com, an online presentation forum based on this very concept; that all creation begins with an idea originating from your imagination. Do you think Einstein invented the link between mass and energy ($E = mc^2$) without his imagination?

"An idea can be created out of nothing except an inspired imagination. An idea weighs nothing. It can be transferred across the world at the speed of light for virtually zero cost. And yet an idea, when received by a prepared mind, can have extraordinary impact. It can reshape that mind's view of the world. It can dramatically alter the behavior of the mind's owner. It can cause the mind to pass on the idea to others."[63]

To me, that concept is very powerful and full of potential, but we cannot be in a space of imagination unless we are allowing it to happen. Consider those times when your imagination is at its best:

- Are you making a huge effort to get this done?
- Are you forcing it to happen?
- Are you doing some "hard thinking" when you use your imagination?

The answer to these questions is *No*, because imagination simply won't happen when you are in that state of being described above. Imagination comes when we allow it to be so. Now consider those times when you felt light and playful . . . maybe you were playing with your children or maybe you were doing teamwork using a brainstorming session at work. These are times when it's easy to invite your imagination. You can structure these times as well, using meditation or visualizations. These are methods that will help you facilitate your imagination in very productive ways.

Hand Over Heart. Breathe. Visualize Your Intention:

Take some time away from everything to pause and go within. Turn off the phone, close the door and ignore everything else but yourself for a few minutes. Give this to yourself because you are worth it. Tune into your breath and begin to breathe in for four counts slowly, using your stomach as opposed to your chest. Watch your stomach expand as you inhale and then pause briefly before exhaling to a count longer than six—try it until you are out of air - then inhale again for a count of four and exhale for a count of six. (Don't get too wrapped up in the number of counts- the point is to manipulate your breath so that you begin to relax- there is no right or wrong way of doing this.) Next, after you have gone a few rounds breathing deeply, center yourself in your heart space—simply bring your attention there, to your heart. Now see yourself having your heart's desire. It's done and you've accomplished it. *Engage all senses. See* yourself happy, elated, excited and let your body *feel* these emotions—take it all in and let yourself have these feelings right now. *See* who is there with you to celebrate. *See* where you are—*see* your surroundings, what colors are present, where are you? Take in the scenery. *See* the smiles on others' faces ... on your own face. *Feel* the satisfaction that you have done this for yourself. *Feel* the pride. *See* the looks on those faces around you and feel their love. *Feel* the love you have for yourself. You did it and it feels good. You have arrived! Stay with this as long as you see fit—feeling these emotions and seeing yourself there, having accomplished this goal. Imagine how you get up the next morning after having your heart's desire complete —how you go to bed at night—notice any differences between before this happened, and now. When you are ready, bring yourself out of this visualization by bringing attention to your feet on the ground, then the room you are in and breathe a deep sigh remembering you can have this. Remember that you have this knowledge of yourself—it's easily accessible now because you have just created a new memory for yourself!

The more times you repeat or recall this experience/visualization, the stronger the memory gets. The stronger the memory gets, the stronger your intention becomes. And the stronger your intention becomes the faster it will manifest into existence.

> *"Mental image pictures are as powerful as the amount of energy you put into them. A picture with none of your energy has no effect on you. A picture with a little bit of your energy has a little effect over you. A picture, however, that you put a whole lot of your energy into it will have a whole lot of effect over you. So, it's not the picture, it's how much of your energy you put into it."*[64] ~Michael Tamura

I heard a story about an astronaut the other day. He was flying solo in space for his NASA job, enjoying his views of the earth... when suddenly he heard a tapping sound. It was so loud that it was terribly annoying to him. What made it worse was that he couldn't figure out where it was coming from. Hours went by with this sound constantly aggravating him . . . and then days . . . he feared he would go "mad!" He had nowhere to go and his mission in space wouldn't be complete for another 23 days. He knew he had to do something. He thought, "What would happen if I fell in love with the sound?" *So one day he decided to set an intention—he would learn to love the sound.* He imagined falling in love with the sound and soon the tapping sound was transformed into a symphony of beautiful music. The aggravating tapping sound had disappeared. He sailed blissfully around space for the remainder of his mission in love with the sound he imagined in his mind to be beautiful music. The reason this mental image worked for him was due to his ability to put so much positive energy into his imagination—his energy made this mental image multi-dimensional to the point where even sound was influenced. We all have this capacity to use our imaginations to help live out our intentions.

What would happen if we spent more of our time using our imagination? Would we be able to create more for ourselves? Could we fulfill our dreams more readily?

One of the women in the support group I facilitate, *Women Starting Over*, is working with the intention to feel fresh and new. Her husband passed away last year, and she'd like to continue her process of moving on in her life. She's using her house to symbolize this transformation by re-decorating each room. By the time she is done, she'd like to have a house where she can feel fresh and new when she walks through each room. With her imagination, she can decide what feels good to her—colors, furniture, and design. Using her heart connection, she can feel into her decisions to change things around. [And knowing that her late husband would want her to be happy and not guilty for doing so], she can empower herself to make this change. She could choose instead to keep all of this desire inside her head—like a dream that someday might come true. However, if she loves herself enough, she will begin living out this intention each day by completing a task that aligns with this intention.

In creating or manifesting change there is really one question for everything comes down to one simple truth: self-love—you cannot create anything new if you don't love yourself enough to *do* it. Will you love yourself enough?

I hope I have given you enough perspectives, truths, examples, exercises and practice in connecting with yourself . . . **hand over heart. Breathe** . . . now say, "I love myself enough to
_____." And yes, please fill in the blank to set your intention.

Keys to Reflect On:

- Upon arriving at clarity, set your intention to begin the process of manifesting
- Use the Law of Attraction
- Embody your intention
- Use the power of words and the present moment
- Be open to receive and allow your intention into fruition
- Use your imagination/visualize your intention

Chapter 12
Grace is the Outcome of All That You Create

"Grace has been defined as the outward expression of the inward harmony of the soul."
~Alan Cohen

his last chapter will help you to realize whether you have embodied all previous spiritual truths thus far. It's my hope that you are practicing and truly benefiting from them now; that you are feeling more capable and free; that you have the ability to manage your present, forgive and let go of the past and feel motivated to create a bright future for yourself. How do you live life this way without falling back on old habits? Or feeling a victim to life's drama, or giving into feelings of despair? You keep doing the work so that your result is a state of grace. Grace is that mysterious quality we often wish for. In this last chapter, you will learn how practicing these truths can help you to acquire grace. That with grace, your life can take on a magical quality where it seems to flow effortlessly. This is the best part!

Carolyn Myss says that you can, "recognize grace in your life by describing some of the countless ways we experience it—both internally as a sudden insightful voice, and externally as synchronicity in the world."[65] Synchronicity certainly feels like grace, serving to affirm we are "on the right track." The concept of synchronicity was first described by Carl Jung, as a grouping of meaningful events seeming coincidental yet profoundly affecting our consciousness. He said, "Synchronicity is an ever present reality for those who have eyes to see."

There are all kinds of interesting ways to define grace. There is the Christian context: "Let us give thanks for God's grace," in which the word is used to exemplify bounty and goodness. A woman may be described as having grace by the way she walks into a room with poise and elegance—the Queen of England might come to mind—just as a ballerina is judged by the way she carries and moves her body. It is also used to characterize a way of behaving with dignity, or with courage in the face of crisis. When we think of people who embody this kind of grace, we might conjure up a historical image of Jackie Kennedy Onassis and how she dealt with her husband's death in front of our nation. Maybe you relate more to certain African Americans from our dark (American) history, who, in the face of slavery and racism, maintained their dignity and held their heads high.

All of the above are commonly accepted uses of the word grace; however, I am going to use it to describe an energy that you can both sense and feel directly from Spirit. Grace enters our lives to affirm our connection with Spirit, to confirm we are co-creating our reality. Almost like synchronicity, we experience meaningful connections with things outside ourselves. In a state of grace, our lives easily click into place: we find "our calling" and all the doors open for us seemingly without effort; less dramatically, we open up a book randomly landing on a page whose message is exactly what we need to read.

I'm also going to use the word grace to describe a quality we have that illuminates within our hearts. It's the inner beauty people recognize and feel attracted to. We feel it when we sense our connection to Spirit, and we radiate it outwards to others when we feel filled up with love. Both types of experiences of grace have a magical, wondrous quality about them. And what's inspiring is, ordinary people like us can have these moments of grace.

How do you feel or sense grace? I will de-mystify the experience by providing examples of how you can invite more grace into your life. There are certain things we can keep in mind to facilitate grace, including: having faith and trust in ourselves and Spirit; surrendering, non-attachment to outcomes or having a neutral state of being; using karma; sensing; and knowing; "I know that I know." Let's look at each concept and how they foster grace.

Faith and Trust

Musicians work hard on learning a new piece of music. They practice every day. They make mistakes then learn from them, moving forward from where they left off. They continue with their quest to master the piece. With each day, the process is less frustrating and more enjoyable. They can hear their improvements and feel good about their progress. At some point they have let go of all thinking (worry, fear and doubt) and place their faith and trust in their ability to create. The result seems like magic because now when they perform the piece it's effortless and pure fun.

Now that you have learned how to manifest your future using Gratitude, the Law of Attraction and Setting Intentions, you can relax in knowing that "it's happening!" You've turned over several new leaves, and now you can have faith and trust. These two words offer so much comfort, especially in the face of fear. They also provide us with some relief! If we feel like we've done the best we could, we've worked hard, that we had the best intentions . . . then we can have faith and trust that whatever the outcome, it will be in everyone's best interest or highest good. Grace can then slip into our lives. We can feel it when things go our way . . . when our confidence fills our heart, it's a beautiful thing! Feeling grace fills us with a profound sense of faith and trust, whether it's mastering a new song to play on our piano without looking at the sheet music, or being the only one to observe two dolphins synchronize their jumps to form a heart. All of our cares and worries wash away. Whenever I experience grace I immediately want to drop to my knees and thank Spirit, for hearing me, for acknowledging me and for having faith and trust in me.

However you experience moments of grace, take them as your own to affirm that you Co-Create your reality. As we show faith and trust in our ability to create, so too are we able to receive creation straight from Spirit. I invite you to have faith and trust in yourself and in your journey. Believe that all your work places you in exactly the place you need to be. Can you believe that where you are right now is divinely perfect? If it hasn't happened yet, is it possible that you are on the cusp of a giant breakthrough? Just like a baby bird leaving its nest, are you ready to fly and have grace support you?

Surrender

"The glory of the universe flows through me!"
~ Denise Linn

"Grace is as real and tangible as sparkling sand on the beach," teaches Caroline Myss. Myss's audio book, *Channeling Grace,* describes what it means to live in the spirit of true surrender. When we surrender we let go and have acceptance for whatever happens.

At this point, if you've done the work you can surrender everything to Spirit. There is nothing as fulfilling as when you realize that all the work you've done on yourself has made your life harmonious and all the pieces fall into place. This is when you experience that beautiful sigh; that "Ah-hah" moment in which you discover grace has entered into your experience *because* you have surrendered.

For me this experience usually happens after letting go of an ongoing question that had been bothering me. Recently it was whether to self-publish this book or not. Once I surrendered, I received my answer, perfectly provided with enough detail for me to know for sure that this is what I was looking for. My whole body resonated with the answer; it rang true. I also began to feel inspired and excited once I received my answer—another clue that I had received what I needed. When answers like these arrive with such good timing, without any effort, you can call it grace.

When we surrender, we can get into the flow. There is a Native American saying, "It's best to ride the horse in the direction the horse is going." According to Native American legend, horses symbolize our personal power. So it's easy to visualize this saying and see how our own will can actually stop the flow. We *will* our lives to go in this certain direction or we fight what comes easy to us. However, *when we let go of trying to control outcomes, grace can then enter our experience.* "Will is to grace as the horse is to the rider," Saint Augustine said.

Often when, many people are out of work and looking for jobs, putting an enormous amount of effort into their search. I've had friends tell me how they were totally serious, charging with all their effort and energy each day but to no avail, only to have it come together once they surrendered their struggle. Letting go of the energy that put them in a negative frame of mind helped to open a window for grace to enter in. All of a sudden places that they frequented often with their children like the preschool or the gym had job openings for them. These places had been staring them in the face. It wasn't until they surrendered that grace could slip in to provide clarity and offer a solution.

Surrendering to something is not simply giving up; surrendering is letting go of all expectations and attachments to the outcome. It's letting go of any negativity or negative beliefs. It's letting go of control. This basic premise is included in this prayer and saying that many religious people use: "Let go and let God," or:

> God grant me the serenity
> to accept the things I cannot change,
> courage to change the things I can,
> and wisdom to know the difference.

This prayer is used in various twelve step programs, such as Alcoholics Anonymous. It doesn't necessarily share my belief that we Co-Create our reality. However, letting go is letting go—no matter what your belief is. This prayer can act like a mantra when you need it.

Use what you have learned thus far to feel into surrender, whether it be: prayer, affirmations, meditation, or experience. It will help you to get into that state of flow, so grace can enter and magic/miracles can happen.

Non-Attachment

I heard a great story today. I was in the bead shop finishing up a necklace I had made when I asked for the shop owner's help to complete the necklace with the clasp. I was in a hurry and didn't want to blow it by tying the clasp on wrong. Sensing my anxiety, she told me about a man who taught pottery classes. Once the students had completed a project, she said, he would ask them to pick out their very best piece, the one they were most proud of. Then he would direct them to take it outside and smash it to pieces. "Do not get attached to what you create," he told them. "You can always start again. Art is not perfection." His lesson for his students taught them that the value of creation was far greater than the outcome.

One of the biggest pieces in manifesting anything new is not having an attachment to the outcome. "What? That's impossible!" you might be thinking. Let me try to explain. Going back to the concept that everything is energy, consider the feel and type of energy you have when you *do* attach to something . . . consider those feelings when you want something so badly it feels like you will die without it . . . remember those times when fear crept into your wanting and made you feel like if you didn't get what you wanted then you would be hugely disappointed. Your fear of *not* getting what you wanted interrupted the flow of energy to getting what you *did* want. What happens too, is that your energy gets so attached to the object of desire that it actually ends up "choking" the desire—not allowing space for the energy to flow. You end up stopping the very thing you want to happen. That's attachment to the outcome. Grace can't slip in to help us when we feel desperate or needy for control.

Now consider what a *neutral* state of consciousness feels like. Recall those times when you "silently" told yourself you wanted something but life went on, and you didn't think about it much— your desire stayed strong, but you didn't attach yourself to it. Having a neutral attitude means you can "take it or leave it" and you won't feel crushed if the outcome is poor. Sure you might feel disappointed, but it won't be crippling disappointment that will send you into a deep depression for days or weeks. When you *live* life with a neutral attitude you maintain your center. What do I mean by that? Remember your heart space and how everything is always infinitely good there? Remember how centered you feel when you enter life with your heart in mind? You feel connected, content and satisfied with whatever happens. Why? Because you know that space—you know your heart intimately as your, *I am* love presence—that you are a spark of the Divine . . . so how can you go wrong?

"By choosing to stop fueling judgments, expectations, competition, and effort, and your emotional reactions that run them, you start growing your neutrality back."[66]
~ Michael J Tamura

You *can* go wrong by having expectations, judgments and feelings of competition with others. These will take you out of your heart space and out of a neutral attitude where life is good and you feel centered in your knowing *I am* love presence. These types of emotions and actions will separate you from *all that is*—the place where you can accept non-attachment. Sure, you will feel challenged to remain in this space or presence when around certain members of your family or certain people at work, for example. But that is also your opportunity to get better at staying connected to your heart space/neutral attitude.

Another way to look at challenging times is that you're getting stronger within. Why? Because with all of the crisis and unrest going on in the world today, your heart *is* the only place that will feel strong. It *is* the only place that you can depend on for stability. In growing your heart space presence, you will be a stronger person who can withstand all outside elements. What's the added benefit of that? You get to be a person whose beauty shows from the inside because you have grace flowing within. That sense that you are connected with grace will create a strong sense of stability.

We can't feel grace in our interactions with others if we are too attached to the experience. You have almost certainly heard the expression, "no strings attached." How many times have you received a gift, a favor, or money and yet could feel that strings were definitely attached? "Strings" are actually chords of energy running from you to the other person, filled with expectations for you to *do* something for them in return, whether that be payment, doing them a favor, or giving them something. In other words, what you have just received is conditional, based on expectations, judgments or attachments to an outcome. There is no neutrality or unconditional love involved. You will notice too, that you can *feel* the strings attached after that person gives you something. It's not until that energy becomes an even exchange that all is well, homeostasis returns . . . and that state of neutrality is present again.

Rather, we strive for synergy with others to occur where solutions that work for everyone's highest good is the intent. When we stay open to all possibilities using faith and trust, surrender and the present moment, it becomes easier not to get attached in our social interactions. This allows us to know and sense grace—that energy does exist and play a role in an easy effortless outcome. I invite you to let go of trying to control the outcome. If your interactions have a grace and flow to them, you will feel like "paying it forward" using random acts of kindness or other feel-good methods. It's this type of interaction that makes you feel inspired. We can feel grace when our interactions with others have the space and freedom to flow without our effort to control them.

You will also have the ability to manifest what you want more quickly and easily with a neutral state of consciousness. Why? Because with fewer attachments, expectations and judgments your energy gets clearer. Your energy becomes a clear channel that is unencumbered by junk. Going back to the fact that everything is energy—imagine yourself as a beam of light that starts at the top of your head (this is your crown chakra) . . . there are at least seven channels for energy to flow through you (chakras)[67] . . . that are influenced by your ability to stay neutral. The crown chakra (above your head) is your download gate, so to speak. So if you're not open (if you're bogged down with junk), your channel for receiving from Spirit will be clogged up or spotty. The cleaner your energy is, the higher your energy can vibrate and attract those things into your download gate that you want. Grace can then flow through you.

Use Karma

Grace is more likely to come to fruition if you use the law of "karma" which refers to the law of cause and effect, where all actions have reactions and ethical consequences that become available. You have probably heard of using the "Golden Rule," which carries the same message: treat others according to how you'd like to be treated. "What goes around comes around," or "As you sow, so shall you reap," are similar expressions of karma. If you want more good friends, then you must be a good friend to the ones you have now. Practice giving unconditionally. By practicing the law of karma you remain in a state of giving and receiving. It keeps the point of creation going. And when the flow of energy is in a constant interactive state, grace can then enter into our lives. There are several ways to build a karma bank.

I invite you to practice "random acts of kindness"—it's a way to build your karma bank while helping another to succeed or feel good. These acts can be as simple as holding open a door for a stranger, giving a smile, or filling up the parking meter for the next person. Some other examples are: sharing your wealth in some shape or form (donations or charity work); volunteering for a cause; helping to build your community using city boards/committees/non-profits; sharing beautiful pictures and quotes with people you care about; wishing a stranger a nice day; picking up garbage on the street; praising someone's efforts to start something new; helping a stray animal; visiting your local animal shelter to adopt pets; baking cookies for a neighbor; and extending your willingness to take a photo or provide directions for a tourist . . . I'm sure you could add on to this list for yourself making it easy for you to sense grace. Your actions intending to produce good karma will result in a chain of grace/events that could bring you a better fate. "What you put in you get back." These are acts of unconditional love that will facilitate grace.

"It is in giving that you receive. As you sow abundantly, you reap abundantly. This is the Divine Law." ~ Grand Master Choa Kok Sui

I have noticed that whenever I am in need of help from others, it's offered to me right then and there. And I don't even have to ask. I believe it's due to the constant flow of energy I maintain giving to others. Whenever I have left my wallet behind, had car trouble, lost keys, needed directions . . . people have been right there ready and willing to help me. I believe this is grace. As a result I can rest assured that I am supported (grace) whenever I need help (grace)— how wonderful is that?

Sensing

Can you sense when grace is present? In Chapter Nine, you learned about energy in all its various forms. If you cannot sense energy, then you probably won't sense grace unless it hits you in the face (smile). Which, of course, can happen—for instance, when you feel desperate to find a parking space and one magically opens up right before your eyes. Otherwise, using our intuition is one way to sense when grace is present.

The perfect example for this section of the book arrived just the other day. I printed out this chapter and took it with me to the water's edge. There is a lovely bay where I live. I had been feeling a little stumped, so to get clear I went to Mother Nature. I found my spot beside the water where the land before me expanded into a wide vista of estuary and mountains. I sat down and felt the sun warm my face. Soon I was making edits and back in the flow of what this chapter's essence is about. To confirm my progress I was greeted by geese flying overhead. I watched their "V" formation and listened to them honk. Two of them flew low and landed in front of me. I sensed that the timing of their arrival was significant for me. I felt graced by their presence. When I got home, I looked up the meaning of the goose in a book I have on animal totems. It was so rewarding to read that according to American Indian legend, the goose aids communication, in particular, writers having creative blocks. Thank you geese, what a gift!

Once you are attuned (and sense) the energy moving through you and around you, there are new opportunities to feel grace. You begin to realize that when you send energy with intention to others *they will feel it*. So it goes both ways—*you will also sense the energy they are sending to you*. You can utilize these energy exchanges. Taking even just a few minutes to get quiet and be still is your way of connecting and remembering Spirit—that part of you that is connected to everything but most importantly, that part of you that can "download" information. This is intuition: the energy you sense and perceive that will allow more grace. You cannot force these magical moments to happen. But you can decide to listen and to see.

The other day I was sitting with a client and noticed a Blue Heron land atop a pine tree nearby. Immediately I thought that was unusual and rather special. We do have Blue Herons in the area, but to see one land atop a pine tree was different from what I was used to. Usually I see them near the water or estuary. I listened. I looked up its message in Ted Andrews' book, *Animal Speak*. It was perfect for my client. The message was to follow your heart and stop listening to what others say you should do. Use your innate ability to Co-Create your circumstances by using your self-determination and your own unique wisdom. She resonated with that message and reflected how lately it seems like everyone is telling her what to do and which path to take. Receiving this kind of grace from the Blue Heron helped confirm this next step was necessary for her to move forward.

Hand Over Heart. Breathe.
Fine Tuning Your Antenna Exercise:

Find a nice place outside where you can sit and be still. You might want to consider how much privacy you'd like to have, so choosing a place that isn't crowded or too busy would be best. Ideally, you are in a place where you can be surrounded by nature. Once you are there, quiet your mind and listen to the sounds produced around you. Maybe there are dogs barking in the distance, maybe there is a cool wind . . . See how many different sounds you can tune into and just focus on listening for a while. Now notice any wildlife or birds in the air. Watch them fly, listen to their songs, observe their movements. Experience appreciation for the way a tall thin tree holds its core against a strong wind, or for the way a slow moving stream of water moves a leaf. Let yourself experience these acts of nature as if you were a part of it. Maybe a butterfly enters the space where you are sitting—what if it were giving you a message? Are you open to sense it? "Thank you for seeing the beauty around you. I hope you continue to do so for it will bring you more peace and joy." Maybe a raven flies up to the tree you are sitting next to. Connect to the raven—listen and watch. How does he make you feel? This was your last hand over heart meditation or exercise. I hope it was sweet!

By tuning in and heightening your abilities to sense with all that you are, you become a part of your environment, and nature becomes a living part of you. You get to experience what interconnectedness feels like.

Knowing

It's a very secure feeling to know deep down inside ourselves that what we believe is true. Our experience is our experience. Trusting that absolute truth is key. When you can stay in the space of knowing, life becomes so rich! So interesting and joyful! You attract all kinds of wonderful experiences and synchronicities and in turn feel extremely grateful and full of love. "Wonder" becomes a fun space to be in, and the world around you takes on a new light showing you the beauty that exists. There are times when I will stop and marvel at a leaf all curled up just waiting for that moment to unravel into a bigger, gorgeous, fully spread-out leaf.

Louise Hay is the "queen of affirmations," in my opinion. She affirms daily, "Patience, commitment, grace and purpose will guide me today and always." That process of unfolding . . . blooming . . . to meet our potential. It is amazing!

Inspired Morning
By Karen Croley

Morning light beams
upon freshly coated petals
damp from dew.

Ruby red
indigo blue
iris purple
and buttercup yellow.

Iridescent glow emits
and adds to the brand new day.
Hope and birth
ring forth
while tiny fairies dance away.

Sunlight graces and ignites
the passions from within
What do you want this day to be?
What magic do you intend?

I had the good fortune of meeting Dr. Jean Houston and loved her book, *The Wizard of Us,* which uses Dorothy's story from *The Wizard of Oz.* There are so many words of wisdom inside Dorothy's story and Dr. Houston does an amazing job applying them to our everyday lives. She reveals the psychological underpinnings of Dorothy's transformation from fear of the unknown (what was beyond the rainbow) to returning home as a fully empowered, mature woman who realized, "that if I ever go looking for my heart's desire again, I won't look any further than my own backyard. Because if it isn't there, I never really had lost it to begin with." Like you, inside Dorothy's journey she learned how to: face adversity, stay true to her heart, live in the moment, expand her heart, find courage/inner strength, embrace magic, (the sacred potential that is within each of us). She returned home with a deepened sense of who she was and appreciated all of the different aspects. Dr. Houston concludes, "She is ready and able to co-create a beautiful new world."[68] And so are you . . .

It's my greatest hope that in reading all previous 12 spiritual truths and with all of the practice you've done using the exercises, you are more in harmony with your heart and soul. That starting over now doesn't just feel do-able, but exciting and juicy. You have built the spokes of creation. Not that this work is ever done; transitions are journeys without a specific ending. Just like you can never find the end of a rainbow because its colors seemingly blend into the landscape. So too, does your process of starting over. Knowing that journeys take twists and turns, please feel free to review chapters as you see fit.

What I do know for sure is that life gets so much easier this way! My clients have found that once they are connected to their hearts, that foundation helps them through all types of transition. When you know and actively practice that connection with Spirit there is no turning away from grace—it becomes a part of you and how you live your life day in and day out.

I encourage you to practice these truths, set aside time to connect to your heart regularly, and feel into the energy around and within you. My prayer for you: Continue to open, expand and grow. Bloom into your highest potential. Feel the grace that surrounds you and supports you. Trust that you are supported at all times. Thrive!

Namaste ~ (The light within me honors the light within you.)

Notes/Resources

Introduction

[1]Wiki

[2] Kornfield, J. (1993). *A Path with Heart: A Guide through the Perils and Promises of Spiritual Life*. Bantam.

[3] Winfrey, O. (2014, June 9), John Mackey interview (Video file). http://www.oprah.com/own-super-soul-sunday/Oprah-and-Whole-Foods-John-Mackey-The-Conscious-CEO-Video

Chapter One: Your Heart

[4] McCraty, R., Atkinson., M., and Tomasino., D. (2001). "Science of the heart" HeartMath Research Center, Institute of HeartMath, Publication No. 01-001. Boulder Creek, Ca.

[5] Ibid.

[6] Ibid.

[7](2008).The Power of Emotion, Heart Math Org.

[8] Houston, J. (2012).*The Wizard of Us; Transformational Lessons from Oz*, Atria Books/Beyond Words.

[9]See symptoms of depression at http://apa.org

[10] Cope, S., (2000). *Yoga and the Quest for the True Self*, Bantam Press.

[11]"DiaphragmaticBreathing" http://my.clevelandclinic.org/disorders/chronic_obstructive_pul monary_disease_copd/hic_diaphragmatic_breathing.aspx

[12] Ibid.

[13]Dossey, L., (2009).*The Power of Premonitions: How Knowing the Future Can Shape Our Lives*. Dutton/Penguin.

Chapter Two: Present Moment

[14]Tolle, E., (2004). *The Power of Now: A Guide to Spiritual Enlightenment;* 1st edition. New World Library.
[15]Tolle, E., (2004). *The Power of Now,* New World Library. pg 27.
[16] Kabat-Zinn, J., (2005). *Wherever You Go, There You Are; Mindfulness Meditation in Everyday Life.* Hyperion.

[17] Dyer, W., (2005). *The Power of Intention: Learning to Co-Create Your World Your Way.* Hay House.

Chapter Three: I AM Love

[18]DeAngelis, B., (1994). *Real Moments: Discover the Secret for True Happiness.* Delacorte

[19]Keen, S. (1992). *Fire in the Belly: On Being a Man*, Bantam Press.
[20]http://noetic.org/noetic/issue-fifteen-october/psychology-of-the-future/
[21]Gauman, C., (2011), *Opus Lux, How To Create Your Own Light.* OpusLux DNAScan Seminars.
[22]Tolle, E., (2003). *Stillness Speaks,* New World Library.
[23]Tamura, M., (2007). *You Are the Answer,* Llewellyn Publications.
[24] Saint Germain & Ballard, (1999). *The "I Am" Discourses.* Saint Germain Press.

Chapter Four: Managing Emotions

[25] Taylor-Bolte, J. (2009), Stroke of Insight; A Brain Scientist's Personal Journey. Plume.

[26] Tamura, M., (2007). *You Are the Answer, Discovering and Fulfilling Your Soul's Purpose.* Llewellyn Publications.
[27] Chardin, T. P., (2008). *The Phenomenon of Man*, Harper Perennial Modern Classics.
[28] Http://meetup.com

Chapter Five: Perspective

[29] Nobel Prize. (2007). "Al Gore — Nobel Lecture." Retrieved from
http://www.nobelprize.org/nobel_prizes/peace/laureates/2007/gore-lecture_en.html

[30] Winfrey, O. (2012, December 9), Elie Wiesel interview (Video file). Retrieved from Super Soul Sunday website:
http://www.oprah.com/own-tv-guide-magazines-top-25-best-oprah-show-moments/Moment-10-Webisode-Oprah-on-Elie-Wiesel-Video

[31] Myss, C. (2003). *Sacred Contracts*, Harmony.

Chapter Six: Letting Go

[32] Hahn, T. N., (1992). *Peace is Every Step*, Bantam Press.

Chapter Seven: Forgiveness

[33] Carlin, J. (2013, August). Nelson Mandela's Legacy. The Cairo Review of Global Affairs. Retrieved from
http://www.aucegypt.edu/gapp/cairoreview/pages/articledetails.aspx?aid=69

[34] Meditation on Twin Hearts, Master Stephen Cho.
http://pranichealing.com/meditation

[35] Farndale, Nigel. "Hillary Clinton Interview" The Telegraph, (June 18, 2003) Retrieved from
http://www.telegraph.co.uk/culture/3596846/Ive-forgiven-him-now.html

[36] Vitale & Len, (2008). *Zero Limits*. Wiley Press.

[37] Tolle, E., (2004). *The Power of Now: A Guide to Spiritual Enlightenment*. New World Library; 1ST edition. p. 27.

Chapter Eight: Appreciation

[38] Hicks, J. & E., (2006). *The Law of Attraction; The Basic Teachings of Abraham,* Hay House.

[39]Roberts, O. (2011). The Huffington Post, Retrieved from http://www.huffingtonpost.com/ocean—robbins/having—gratitude—_b_1073105.html

[40] Ibid.

[41] 2011 Wolfwalker Collection. The Wolfwalker Collection P.O.Box 2586 • Taos, NM. 87571

[42] Ibid.

Chapter Nine: Energy

[43] Clark, J. (2010). *Huffpost Healthy Living.* Retrieved from http://www.huffingtonpost.com/josh—clark/multitasking—how—does— mul_b_552673 l mul_b_552673 l

[44] "Aho" is Lakhota and has been borrowed into many other North American languages as a result of the abundant use of the word at pow-wows in the 20th century. "Aho" means "Yes, I agree." It is used in prayers in somewhat the same way that "amen" is used ("amen" means "I agree"), but it is not used exclusively in prayers. It can be used in any situation where a discussion is being conducted.

[45] http://www.webmd.com/diet/fiber-health-benefits-11/fatigue-fighters-six-quick-ways-boost-energy

[46]http://www.health.com/health/gallery/0,,20723540_last,00.html

[47] http://www.nongmoproject.org/learn-more/

[48] Heart Chakra: Your heart chakra is an energy center located in your chest around your heart. It facilitates the energy around your ability to love. http://www.mindbodygreen.com/0-91/The-7-Chakras-for-Beginners.html

[49] Shier, Taylor Susann, (2011), *Soul Reunion; The Return Home From Separation.* Velvet Springs Press.

[50] Hicks, J. & E., (2006). *The Law of Attraction; The Basic Teachings of Abraham.* Hay House.

[51] Ibid.

[52] https://www.cathaven.com

Chapter Ten: Manifesting Your Desires

[53] This is the Id at work, the subconscious part of our personality, as defined by Sigmund Freud - whose job it is to fulfill our basic urges, needs and desires. In this case, it is demanding we take care of our hunger and fatigue.

[54] Hicks, J. & E., (2006). *The Law of Attraction; The Basic Teachings of Abraham.* Hay House.

Chapter 11: Setting Intentions

[55] Ibid.
[56] Dyer, W. (2005). *The Power of Intention.* Hay House.

[57] Meyer, P., (2003). *Attitude is Everything.* Meyer Resource Group.

[58] Ibid.

[59] Lipton, B. (n.d.). *Controlling Your Genetic Blueprint with Bruce Lipton, Ph.D.* See more at: http://www.newdimensions.org/program-archive/controlling-your-genetic-blueprint-with-bruce-lipton-ph-d/#sthash.XYnzC4sE.dpuf [Audio podcast]. Retrieved from New

Dimensions website: http://www.newdimensions.org/program-archive/controlling-your-genetic-blueprint-with-bruce-lipton-ph-d/

[60] Wallace, D., (2010). "I love me play shop" retrieve at https://www.youtube.com/watch?v=Z4q4GUDX9_c

[61] Wallace, D., (2010). *Conscious Creation*. Toto Enterprises, Inc.

[62] Williamson, M., (2008), *Course in Miracles*, 3 Combined edition. Foundation for Inner Peace.

[63] http://ted.com

Chapter 12: Grace

[64] Tamura, M. (2012) *"Psychic Practices to Heal Yourself When You've Been Slimed, Whacked or Bullied"*

[65] Myss, C. (2008). *Channeling Grace; Invoking The Power of the Divine*. Sounds True Audio.

[66] Tamura, Michael, J. (2007), *You are the Answer*, Llewellyn Publications. p. 118.

www.ingramcontent.com/pod-product-compliance
Lightning Source LLC
Chambersburg PA
CBHW031830090426
42741CB00005B/186

* 9 7 8 0 6 9 2 2 1 6 5 3 8 *